# Ketogenic Diet, Meal Prep, Intermittent Fasting, Fat Bombs

(4 Book Box Set)

Mark Evans

© Copyright 2018 by Mark Evans - All rights reserved.

The following Book is reproduced below with the goal of providing information that is as accurate and as reliable as possible. Regardless, purchasing this Book can be seen as consent to the fact that both the publisher and the author of this book are in no way experts on the topics discussed within, and that any recommendations or suggestions made herein are for entertainment purposes only. Professionals should be consulted as needed before undertaking any of the action endorsed herein.

This declaration is deemed fair and valid by both the American Bar Association and the Committee of Publishers Association and is legally binding throughout the United States.

Furthermore, the transmission, duplication or reproduction of any of the following work, including precise information, will be considered an illegal act, irrespective whether it is done electronically or in print. The legality extends to creating a secondary or tertiary copy of the work or a recorded copy and is only allowed with express written consent of the Publisher. All additional rights are reserved.

The information in the following pages is broadly considered to be a truthful and accurate account of facts, and as such any inattention, use or misuse of the information in question by the reader will render any resulting actions solely under their purview. There are no scenarios in which the publisher or the original author of this work can be in any fashion deemed liable for any hardship or damages that may befall them after undertaking information described herein.

Additionally, the information found on the following pages is intended for informational purposes only and should thus be considered, universal. As befitting its nature, the information presented is without assurance regarding its continued validity or interim quality. Trademarks that mentioned are done without written consent and can in no way be considered an endorsement from the trademark holder.

# Table of Contents

# Ketogenic Diet

FOREWORD ................................................................................................ 12
Chapter One: What is the ketogenic diet? ........................................ 13
Chapter Two: The trouble with carbs. ............................................... 15
Chapter Three: What are the benefits of a ketogenic diet? ............ 19
Chapter Four: What conditions may make ketosis hard, impossible, or unhealthy? ........................................................................................... 24
Chapter Five: Starting a ketogenic diet. ............................................ 27
Chapter Six: Tips and tricks for handling carb cravings. ............... 31
Chapter Seven: Adapting a ketogenic diet for maintenance. ........ 34
Chapter Eight: Weight maintenance on a ketogenic diet. .............. 45
Chapter Nine: How to know you are in ketosis. .............................. 48
Chapter Ten: Ketogenic recipes. ......................................................... 51
   High Fat Meals ................................................................................... 52
      Pork And Plums. .......................................................................... 53
      Meatloaf with Mushrooms, Traditional Version. .................... 54
      Chicken and Sprout Bake. .......................................................... 55
      Coconut Milk Ice Cream. ........................................................... 56
      Cheese Dip. ................................................................................... 57
      Avocado Eggs. ............................................................................. 58
      Low Carb Cassoulet. ................................................................... 59
   High Fibre Meals ................................................................................ 60
      Vegetable Wraps. ......................................................................... 61
      Coleslaw. ....................................................................................... 62
      Collard Greens and Bacon. ........................................................ 63
      Sprouts and Ham. ....................................................................... 64
      Broccoli Soup. .............................................................................. 65
      Lamb Spinach Rogan Josh. ....................................................... 66
      Veggie Stew. ................................................................................. 67
      Onion and Kale Salad. ................................................................ 68
   Protein Boosters. ................................................................................ 69
      Bacon Balsamic Beans. ............................................................... 70
      Simple Egg Omelette. ................................................................. 71
      Shredded Crispy Chicken. ......................................................... 72

- Slow Cooker Chicken Salad Topper..................................................73
- Chicken with Tomato Mediterranean Sauce........................................74
- Osso Bucco – Bone Soup...................................................................75
- Thai Chicken Curry For Slow Cooker. ...................................................76
- Chili Orange Shrimp............................................................................77
- Alternatives to Carbs................................................................................. 78
  - Root vegetable mash ........................................................................79
  - Root vegetable chips.........................................................................80
  - Vegetable breads...............................................................................81
  - Berries ..............................................................................................82
  - Artificial sweeteners .........................................................................83
- Seasoning Your Food.................................................................................. 84
- Eating Keto Out and About ........................................................................ 87
- Chapter Eleven: Ketogenic diet FAQs. ........................................................ 90
- Conclusion.................................................................................................. 92

# Meal Prep

Introduction ..................................................................................................94
Chapter 1 – The Basics and Benefits of Low Carb Keto Meal Prepping........95
    How to Meal Prep the Right Way ..............................................................96
    Common Mistakes in Meal Prepping .......................................................97
Chapter 2 – 30-Day Low Carb Keto Meal Plan ..........................................99
Chapter 3 – Keto Meal Prep Breakfast Recipes ........................................130
    Recipe #1: Savory Cheddar Pancakes ...................................................130
    Recipe #2: Chia Cinnamon Vanilla Granola .........................................132
    Recipe #3: Cheese and Sausage in Portobello Breakfast Burgers ..........134
    Recipe #4: Cheesy Keto Quiche .............................................................136
    Recipe #5: Blueberry Breakfast Scones.................................................138
    Recipe #6: Cinnamon Coconut Porridge...............................................140
    Recipe #7: Easy Scotch Eggs ..................................................................142
    Recipe #8: Easy Breakfast Tacos ............................................................144
    Recipe #9: Bacon and Ricotta Breakfast Muffins ..................................146
    Recipe #10: Keto Mini Waffles ...............................................................148
    Recipe #11: Creamy Herbed Baked Eggs ...............................................150
    Recipe #12: Keto Bread ..........................................................................152
Chapter 4 – Keto Meal Prep Lunch Recipes ............................................. 154
    Recipe #1: Savory Beef Balls with Asian Style Dip .................................154
    Recipe #2: Chicken Curry with Oil-Roasted Peanuts............................ 156
    Recipe #3: Baked Parmesan Chicken Nuggets in Mozzarella Marinara Sauce...................................................................................... 158
    Recipe #4: Zucchini Beef Lasagna .........................................................160
    Recipe #5: Chicken Bell Pepper Kebabs................................................162
    Recipe #6: Easy Grilled Shrimp with Avocado, Tomato and Onion Salad .......................................................................................................164
    Recipe #7: Mediterranean Style Tuna Salad .........................................166
    Recipe #8: Creamy Cauli Mac 'n' Cheese ..............................................168
    Recipe #9: Balsamic Herbed Pork Tenderloin.......................................170
    Recipe #10: Keto Squash-getti with Herbed Meatballs ........................ 172
    Recipe #11: Sardine and Garden Salad..................................................174
    Recipe #12: Herbed Parmesan Chicken Fingers....................................176
    Recipe #13: Ham, Onion and Green Bean Salad ...................................178
    Recipe #14: Cheesy Avocado Beef Patties .............................................180
    Recipe #15: Cheesy Sausage, Mushroom and Spaghetti Squash Casserole .................................................................................................182
Chapter 5 – Keto Meal Prep Dinner Recipes............................................184

- Recipe #1: Deviled Eggs with Chopped Bacon ..................................... 184
- Recipe #2: Keto Caesar Salad ............................................................... 186
- Recipe #3: Fried Cheesy Avocado Wedges ......................................... 188
- Recipe #4: Simple Beef Chili ................................................................. 190
- Recipe #5: Low Carb Hearty Pot Roast ............................................... 192
- Recipe #6: Miso Beef and Tender Zucchini ........................................ 194
- Recipe #7: Roasted Garlic Butter Cod with Bok Choy ..................... 196
- Recipe #8: Creamy Chicken Soup ........................................................ 198
- Recipe #9: Ginger Sesame Halibut ...................................................... 200
- Recipe #10: Hearty Beef and Mushroom Stew ................................... 201
- Recipe #11: Goat Cheese and Smoked Onion Pizza .......................... 203
- Recipe #12: Savory Butternut Squash Soup ...................................... 205

Chapter 6 – Keto Meal Prep Snack Recipes ............................................ 207
- Recipe #1: Avocado, Cream Cheese and Cucumber Bites ................ 207
- Recipe #2: Ham 'n' Cheese Puffs ......................................................... 209
- Recipe #3: Walnut Parmesan Bites ...................................................... 211
- Recipe #4: Cream Cheese Bacon Stuffed Jalapenos .......................... 212
- Recipe #5: Low Carb Guacamole ......................................................... 214
- Recipe #6: Smoked Salmon and Dill Spread ..................................... 216
- Recipe #7: Coco Lime Fat Bombs ........................................................ 217
- Recipe #8: Coco Lemon Fat Bombs .................................................... 218
- Recipe #9: Choco Peanut Fat Bombs .................................................. 219
- Recipe #10: Almond Olive and Herb Tapenade ................................ 220
- Recipe #11: Chocolate Coated Bacon .................................................. 222
- Recipe #12: Portobello Mushrooms Stuffed with Ricotta Cheese and Spinach ................................................................................................. 224
- Recipe #13: Cinnamon Butter .............................................................. 226
- Recipe #14: Roasted Eggplant Spread ................................................ 227
- Recipe #15: Cauli Cheddar Bites ......................................................... 229
- Recipe #16: Bacon Mozzarella Sticks .................................................. 231

Chapter 7 – Keto Meal Prep Smoothie Recipes ..................................... 232
- Recipe #1: Creamy Matcha Green Tea Smoothie .............................. 232
- Recipe #2: Peanut Butter Choco Smoothie ........................................ 234
- Recipe #3: Super Berry Almond Smoothie ........................................ 235
- Recipe #4: Strawberries and Cream Smoothie .................................. 236
- Recipe #5: Pumpkin Spice Smoothie .................................................. 237
- Recipe #6: Zesty Green Smoothie ....................................................... 238
- Recipe #7: Chia Seeds and Crisp Greens Smoothie .......................... 239
- Recipe #8: Buttered Coffee Smoothie ................................................. 240
- Recipe #9: Smooth Vanilla Smoothie .................................................. 241
- Recipe #10: Avocado Coco Smoothie ................................................. 242

Chapter 8 – Keto Meal Prep Dessert Recipes ................................................ 243
    Recipe #1: Keto Choco Brownies ............................................................ 243
    Recipe #2: No Bake Coconut Macaroons .................................................. 245
    Recipe #3: Raspberry Cream Cheese Pops ............................................... 246
    Recipe #4: Coco Peanut Butter Bites ....................................................... 248
    Recipe #5: Cocoa Nibbles with Cream Cheese ......................................... 249
    Recipe #6: Creamy Vanilla Pudding ........................................................ 251
    Recipe #7: Lemon Poppy Seed Cupcakes ................................................ 253
Conclusion .................................................................................................... 255

# Intermittent Fasting

Introduction ..................................................................................... 257
Part I – Everything You Need to Know About Intermittent Fasting .......... 258
Chapter 1: The Practice of Fasting ................................................. 259
Chapter 2: Intermittent Fasting ...................................................... 263
Chapter 3: Benefits of Intermittent Fasting ................................... 270
Chapter 4: Intermittent Fasting – Key to a Healthy Weight Loss and Muscle Growth ............................................................................... 275
Chapter 5: Types of Intermittent Fasting ....................................... 281
Part II – Comprehensive Guide to Intermittent Fasting ...................... 294
Chapter 6: Taking the Action .......................................................... 295
Chapter 7: The Beginner's Protocol ............................................... 300
Chapter 8: The Complementary Guide .......................................... 307
Part III – Supplemental Section ......................................................... 312
Chapter 9: Fasting Foods and Liquids ........................................... 313
Chapter 10: Recipes for the Hungry .............................................. 319
Conclusion........................................................................................ 327
   60 Best, Delicious Fat Bomb Recipes You Absolutely Have to Try! ....... 329
      Cocoa Almond Delight Fat Bombs ......................................... 341
      Toffee and Peanut Butter Fat Bombs ..................................... 342
      Creamy Almond Fat Bombs ................................................... 343
      Chocolatey Coconut Fat Bombs ............................................ 344
      Very Mocha Fat Bombs .......................................................... 345
      Creamy White Bombs ............................................................ 346
      Dark Choco Truffles ............................................................... 347
      Lemon Squares Keto Bombs ................................................. 349
      Vanilla and Nutmeg Keto Treats ........................................... 350
      Spiced Pumpkin Fat Bombs .................................................. 351
      Choco Coconut Flakes Fat Bombs ........................................ 352
      Peanut Butter Keto Bombs .................................................... 353
      Spiced Cheesy Keto Treats .................................................... 354
      Coco-Vanilla Bombs .............................................................. 355
      Baked Cheesy Jell-O Flat Bomb Cookies .............................. 356
      Minty Layered Fat Bombs ..................................................... 358
      Cheesy Bacon Bombs ............................................................ 359
      No-Bake Red Cheesecake Bombs ......................................... 360
      Mediterranean-Inspired Fat Bombs ....................................... 361
      Lemon Keto Bombs ............................................................... 362
      Double Chocolate Keto Bombs ............................................. 363
      Guacamole Healthy Treats .................................................... 365
      Pecan and Bacon Keto Treats ............................................... 367

- Coco-Choco Candy Cups ............................................................. 368
- Egg-Free Mini Lemony Tarts ....................................................... 370
- Choco Candies with Coconut ...................................................... 372
- Yummy Keto Rolo ....................................................................... 374
- Frozen Cocoa Bombs ................................................................. 376
- Fudgy White Choco Bombs ........................................................ 377
- Spiced Keto Candies .................................................................. 378
- Low-Carb Chocolate Bars .......................................................... 379
- Double Chocolate Truffles ......................................................... 380
- Cheesy Almond Keto Bombs ..................................................... 382
- Coconut and Berries Fat Bombs ................................................ 387
- Chocolatey Strawberry Swirl Bombs ......................................... 388
- Blackberries and Cheese Fat Bombs ........................................ 390
- Blueberry and Cheese Fat Bombs ............................................. 391
- Raspberry and Choco Treats ..................................................... 392
- Low-Carb Strawberry Cheesecake Delights ............................. 394

Chapter 4 – Low-Carb Fat Bomb Recipes with Nuts .................... 395
- Chewy Bombs with Macadamia ................................................ 398
- Walnut Keto Delights ................................................................. 399
- Orange and Nuts Low-Carb Delights ........................................ 400
- Choco-Macadamia Treats ......................................................... 401
- Pumpkin Treats with Pecans ..................................................... 402
- Nutty Choco Treats .................................................................... 403
- Macadamia Coconut Bombs ..................................................... 404
- Pecan Treats with Stuffing ......................................................... 405
- Choco Walnut Delight Bombs ................................................... 406
- Spiced Pistachio Fast Bombs .................................................... 407

Chapter 5 - Ketogenic Specific Fat Bomb Recipes ....................... 408
- Basic Fat Bomb Recipe ............................................................. 412
- Walnut Keto Treats .................................................................... 413
- Lemon-Flavored Cheesecake Bombs ...................................... 414
- Breakfast Truffles ...................................................................... 415
- Energy-Boosting Bulletproof Bombs ........................................ 416
- Coco Butter Bombs with Nutmeg .............................................. 417
- Nutty Vanilla Truffles ................................................................. 418
- Spicy Keto Bombs ..................................................................... 419
- Vanilla-Macadamia Healthy Bombs .......................................... 420
- Cheesy Raspberry Keto Bombs ................................................ 421
- Healthy Macha Bombs .............................................................. 422
- Chewy Keto Treats .................................................................... 424

Conclusion ....................................................................................... 425
Thank you! ....................................................................................... 426

# Ketogenic Diet

The Complete Step by Step Guide for Beginners to Living the Keto Lifestyle – Lose Weight, Burn Fat, and Increase Energy

# FOREWORD

In our quest for the best results, humans have done a lot of crazy things with the way we eat. We have starved ourselves living off cabbage soup to be thin, and pumped ourselves full of proteins we barely use so we can gain muscle. We drink cranberries for a UTI and eat blueberries to prevent cancer. It seems that food really is medicine, and that different foods, in different combinations, work in different ways to make us better, fitter, healthier, happier people.

No one diet is perfect for everyone in every situation, of course. But everyone has a lot to learn from every way of eating, and every way of eating has benefits that other ways of eating do not provide. Enter the ketogenic diet.

The ketogenic diet is a diet that your average dieter has more experience with than they might think. Why? Because ketosis is what happens every time we lose fat, no matter what we are eating. We literally can't use our body fat properly without turning it into ketones. What the ketogenic diet does, is it bypasses the middle-man. Rather than fight against constant cravings, hunger, gut imbalances, and malnutrition, a ketogenic diet lets us enter and stay in ketosis for the benefit of our health.

Following this book you will learn what a ketogenic diet is, how ketosis works, in what ways a ketogenic diet may benefit you, and how to follow a ketogenic diet properly and safely, both with short term and long term goals in mind.

This isn't another diet book to make you lose two pounds that you will put back on in a week. This is a fundamental source of knowledge that will change the way you see food forever.

# Chapter One: What is the ketogenic diet?

To understand a ketogenic diet we first need to understand ketosis. You may have been taught in school that our bodies need glucose to fuel our muscles and brains, and some of you may have been taught that there is no substitute for glucose. However this is not correct.

The reality is that we only have two sources of glucose: the carbohydrates in the foods we eat and a limited supply reserved in our muscles and liver. As long as we keep eating, and do not spend much time without food, we can run entirely on glucose. However if we go too long between meals or burn up our glucose stores, such as through endurance exercise, our glucose runs out. If it were true that we only run on glucose, at this point we would die. However we do not.

This is because our body has two main energy sources: glucose, and ketones. Glucose, as we have mentioned, is pure sugar derived from carbohydrates in our diet. But our bodies are very vulnerable to sugar, so we can't store a lot of it. And we all know what we actually store: fat. We turn excess sugar, fats, and sometimes even proteins into our own body fat cells for storage, because these are fairly safe. Obesity may harm our bodies, but if we carried enough sugar in pure glucose form to be obese, we'd have died long ago. So fat is the safer option. But we can't actually burn fat on its own, or convert it back to glucose. So we have a mechanism that we can use to turn fat back into reliable energy.

This process is called ketosis, and the energy we create from it is called ketones. When we do not have enough glucose to run our bodies we will take fat cells and protein cells and combine them to form an energy source that we can use instead of glucose. This happens whether we are eating a lot of food and just no carbs, like with the Inuit populations before Westernization, or whether we are not eating and are burning our own fat and muscle to make ketones. This energy source is just as good for our brains and muscles as glucose is.

Following a modern diet we often rely very heavily on glucose, using ketones only as a back up energy source. This is because carbohydrates are quick, easy energy. As soon as we eat something with carbs in it, the enzymes in our mouths digest it down and we absorb sugars through our stomach lining. So naturally, we have a strong appetite for carbs. Meanwhile, fats are slow and hard to digest, so unless we combine them with sugars we will always choose a carby food over a fatty one. But this reliance is not natural. If we look at humans in wild type environments, such as survivalists or tribal people, they burn carbs when they are eating carby foods, but can go days or even weeks eating no carbs at all. When they kill an animal, or find a coconut tree, they will binge on proteins and fats, and when there is no food they will use up their glucose and start burning their body fat. Our bodies were designed to do this, not because it's pleasant, but because it's the way we evolved.

Like I said, in the modern world we only ever enter ketosis if we miss a meal and are active. Skipping breakfast is a form of ketosis. Doing a fasted workout is a form of ketosis. So our experiences of ketosis are feeling hungry and uncomfortable all the time. However if we begin to follow a ketogenic diet, we can enter and stay in ketosis without restricting our calories, the size of our meals, or our micronutrient intakes. This is a completely different experience that, in the long run, has a completely different effect on our bodies from starvation.

# Chapter Two: The trouble with carbs.

Carbs are our fuel source of choice, and there are two very bad reasons for that. The first reason dates back to the 1970s. In the 1970s the government wanted to release dietary guidelines, in part to control the amount of diet-related problems that were arising from a culture of drinking, smoking, and eating junk food. They worked out that the combination of sugars and fats was common in the diets of people with the worst health problems. They decided that fats were the culprit, based on serious misunderstandings about how dietary fat works, and fat was basically demonized by the big diet gurus and press from then until today. Meanwhile, sugar was alternately portrayed as neutral or a good thing, and we were advised to eat 45-65% of our calories, and a minimum of 130g, in carbohydrates.

The second reason dates back further: to our evolutionary biology. Now, many of us assume that the things we like, the things we are instinctively drawn towards, are inherently good for us. But this is a mistake in the way we understand instincts. Why is it that even though greens and exercise are good for us, great for us, in fact, we rarely if ever crave them? It's because greens and exercise are easy to get. In the wild we didn't have to work for them. And why is it that, even though we barely need a gram of salt a day, we crave it? Because salt was rare. Our body still thinks we need to top up on things that were rare millions of years ago, even if they are common now! In the past binging on carbs was fine because we might not get any more for weeks. But now we never go through that period of carb starvation where we use up our glucose and run on ketones. We just keep eating more and more carbs. And this comes with some nasty side-effects.

High carbohydrate diets, like the current Western one, are actually very harmful to our bodies on a basic level. For starters, high carbohydrate diets send our insulin into rollercoaster mode. When we eat carbs, especially fast release ones, our blood sugars go up. The faster release the carbs, the faster our blood sugars spike. And the more carbs, the higher our blood sugars spike. High blood sugar is toxic to our bodies, so we release insulin. Insulin moves glucose from our blood into cells, so it can be burned as energy. And when we run out of cells that need energy? Insulin moves glucose to our muscles and liver, where it is suspended in water and stored. And when we run out of storage space for our glucose? Insulin turns it into fat. This is why severe diabetes is such a crippling condition for sufferers. It is also why a high carbohydrate diet is so bad for us in the long run.

When our insulin drives our blood sugar down, it often goes too far, creating hunger. This is what is known as the "sugar crash" after binging on candy. It is also why we feel hungry minutes to hours after eating fast food, and why many people feel more energized before breakfast than an hour after it. This process makes us feel hungry all the time when we eat a high carb diet, resulting in a habit of snacking, fizzy drinks, and caffeine to keep us going. And, as constant hunger is very difficult to live with, we may also find that we start putting on weight, unable to continually feel like we're starving. This cycle therefore also harms our appetite hormones, reducing sensitivity to them and making our hunger more intense and our satiety quieter. The cycle can furthermore impact our sex hormones, digestion speed, immune system, etc, causing general wear down and fatigue.

Secondarily, high carbohydrate diets also feed a yeast that grows in our body. Candida Albicans is normally harmless in the amounts we find it naturally, but, like all life forms, if you feed it, it grows and breeds. This starts in our guts, where it starts feeding off the sugar and simple starches we are eating. This lets it grow, which is sped up if we are not eating enough fibre to feed our healthy bacteria. As our healthy bacteria dies off there is less to stop the progress of candida through our guts. When candida has colonized our gut, something interesting happens. We begin to crave carbs more intensely, even though eating more carbs will only make our candida problem worse. It is thought that perhaps, much like some fungi can control the nervous systems of insects and persuade them to help the fungus reproduce, our candida infection sends messages to our nervous system demanding more carbs. It basically pesters us into feeding it.

If we give in and feed our candida, it will keep on growing. As it takes over our gut, we may find we digest other foods poorly, and that our gut transit is too long or too short, resulting in constipation or diarrhoea, cramping, lethargy, and a compromise of our immune systems. The candida can eventually make its way out of our digestive tract, causing genital infections, UTIs, skin damage, dandruff, mouth ulcers, etc.

Thirdly, most of the highest carbohydrate foods are at best empty calories and at worst allergenic or inflammatory. Gluten and other proteins found in grains are common allergens and also cause irritation in many people. Potatoes are members of the nightshade family. Fruits cause diarrhoea and reflux in many people. And all these foods are low in other nutrients, especially compared to low carbohydrate plants.

So how come is it that there are very healthy populations out there subsisting on carbs? Well, the way they eat carbs is completely different to the way we do. For example, the Japanese eat a lot of rice, but they eat a lot of chilled rice, which has less available carbs, and more of something called resistant starches. Resistant starches are not easily digested by our bodies and feed our good gut bacteria. In Europe many people eat wheat, but sourdough breads are more popular in the places where age of death is at its highest. Until recently we only ate sourdough breads, as quick-rise baking powder breads were not a thing. It is thought that the fermentation of sourdough breads breaks down many of the proteins that irritate us in grains. No nation on this planet eats as much high carb, high glycemic index, low nutrition food as America or Americanized countries such as the UK.

There is much to be said about the advantages of consuming higher fibre contents, resistant starches, and fermented products. If they are so good for us, why should we not just start eating a Japanese diet, or swap our breads for sourdough? Quite simply: we can do that later on, if we want to, and if it suits our bodies, but first, we need to undo all this damage. And another high-carb diet, no matter what name you stick on it, will not reverse all the harm that has been done.

# Chapter Three: What are the benefits of a ketogenic diet?

Believe it or not, all weight loss diets are ketogenic diets. This is because to lose weight we must digest our own fat to lose it. And the only way to do that is by eating little enough that we run out of glucose and start making ketones instead. This is why it is so important to keep your protein levels up and work out when you're on a serious weight loss diet: as you lose weight, you will need plenty of protein to mix with your fat for ketones. If you don't eat it, then it will be taken from your muscles.

The difference between the average weight loss diet and a ketogenic diet is that the average weight loss diet usually lets you eat many carbs. It might even be a high carb diet. This, however, interferes with weight loss, comfort, insulin levels, and appetite. Why? We need to be in ketosis to burn our fat. There is no other way of digesting it down and getting rid of it. So every time we eat carbs, we are refilling our glucose. This has many effects, but two of them directly stop us losing weight. The first one is, it takes us out of ketosis. We have glucose, so our body will not use our fat to make ketones. And every minute we're out of ketosis is a minute we're not losing weight.

The second effect is it makes us hungry. We can't just start digesting ketones instantly. First we burn our blood glucose. Then our body starts burning the stored glucose, in the form of glycogens, from our muscles and liver. And only when we start to run out of glucose do we start making extra ketones. But in that middle step, when we have low blood glucose and low ketones, we get very hungry. This is our body saying "making ketones is hard, if there is any sugar, can we eat that please?" So we feel very, very hungry. This is why most people quit their diets.

On a ketogenic diet, we do not have these problems. We are already burning ketones, all the time, so there is no swap. We never refill our glucose, we just go from burning our lunch ketones to burning our body fat. We never have that hunger phase either, as we are already burning ketones and, like with all discomfort, when our body is given no sign there are carbs around it will turn off that aching hunger for sugars. Therefore, on a ketogenic diet, especially a low calorie one, we are burning fat all the time and experiencing less hunger than on a conventional diet, letting us lose weight with ease.

Many ketogenic diets are geared towards weight loss, but the reality is that they can be followed for a whole host of reasons. And all these reasons relate quite closely to fixing the damage done by a high carb diet. This damage was not done overnight, so, much the same way you don't fix a broken leg by going jogging, you can't fix this damage by adopting a healthy diet full of carbs. You need to separate yourself from them to get the best effects.

First of all, a ketogenic diet can protect against diabetes, and can even be used to treat diabetes. A high carb diet is continually spiking your blood sugar, which continually raises your insulin, which puts a great tax on your pancreas. This can result in diabetes or even pancreatic failure over time. If you are pre-diabetic, a long term ketogenic diet can help you reverse the damage done by a high carb diet. And if you are already diabetic, a ketogenic diet has no glucose, so there is no risk of blood sugar highs or lows, just a steady supply of energy. Of course always consult with your doctor before making dietary changes, but also make sure your doctor knows what a ketogenic diet is, and consider talking to a nutritionist or another specialist instead.

A ketogenic diet can correct appetite problems. Most of our appetite problems come either from rapidly cycling blood sugars and insulin, or from appetite hormones that have been badly damaged by a life of constant eating. The mantra "eat little and often" can be very harmful to many people, resulting in a slow wear down of the metabolism and an inability to differentiate hunger cues. Quite simply, if you eat little and often, your body expects it, so you crave it. And your mind expects it, so when you want a glass of water you instinctively reach for a chocolate bar instead. A ketogenic diet relies on eating infrequently, letting you get familiar with your hunger, suppress it, and slowly learn to identify thirst, micronutrient cravings, or plain old boredom. This could be the end of a lifetime of constant snacking.

A ketogenic diet is your best chance of fighting off a serious thrush infection. As has been mentioned, candida not only grows out of control when we feed it, but if the infection gets big enough we can start feeling unnatural cravings as it hijacks our immune systems. Candida is at its loudest and strongest when we give it carbs. Like any life form, if it has energy it grows more, and this seems to make it more able to control our appetite. At first, when it is starved, it will send signals which will make us hungrier. But in short order it will stop being so pronounced. The longer it is starved, the more of it will die, until eventually the infection will be gone.

A ketogenic diet can help with hormonal imbalances, both light and severe. A high carb diet, with its constant highs and lows of blood sugar and insulin, sends stress signals to our bodies. And when we are stressed, our hormones change. We make more testosterone, which then turns to estrogen when it has done its job. We lose a lot of the hormones that help us build muscle and stay happy, like progesterone and serotonin. Our whole body goes into survival mode. Taking away those spikes and drops in blood sugar will take away the stress, giving our hormones a chance to go back to normal. But there is more. Our hormones run on one thing above all others: fat. Without enough dietary cholesterol and healthy saturated fats we cannot make hormones. So if we have a hormone imbalance, even if the thing that caused it goes away, we can't fix it without making more hormones. Eating more fat will help us make more hormones.

A ketogenic diet allows your gut to reset and regrow. Even if you did not have a serious candida infection, if your diet was too high in carbs you will probably have an unbalanced gut. Your good bacteria will be much reduced, and yeasts and dangerous bacteria will be there in high amounts. The high fibre, low carb plants you eat on a ketogenic diet, combined with plenty of protein and fats, will help scrub your gut clean, and provide it with food for your good bacteria.

A ketogenic diet is a great way of boosting your nutrient intake. A lot of our staples are high carb and low everything else. White bread, white pasta, white rice, bland cereals, and potatoes. They have a lot of carbs, a bit of fibre, and maybe one or two nutrients they are high in. Cutting them out forces us to fill up our plates with leafy greens and low carb root vegetables. Just compare the nutritional values of pumpkin against potatoes, or of salad greens against pasta. Your vitamin and mineral intake will be huge. Even better if you have a taste for fish and offal, as seafood and organ meats are very high in micronutrients too.

A ketogenic diet can finally work as an elimination diet. If you suspect you have a food allergy or intolerance, an elimination diet is a great way of testing that. By eating largely protein and fats, you have got rid of most potential allergens. If you have a food allergy or intolerance you will start feeling better after a week of cutting certain foods out. Then, if you try and reintroduce them, you will find your symptoms return. This is a great way of finding out about any food issues you may have and correcting them, even if you do not follow this diet in the long term.

# Chapter Four: What conditions may make ketosis hard, impossible, or unhealthy?

Of course, it isn't all good news. Some health conditions can interfere with following a ketogenic diet. If you suffer these, or any other serious health condition, talk to your doctor before adopting a ketogenic diet. Like all health changes, a new, strict diet can interfere with conditions and medications in ways that are beyond the scope of this book. So always be cautious, always investigate, and always talk to a medical professional if you have any doubts. That said, here are some common conditions that are known to interact badly with a ketogenic diet:

Gall bladder disorders make it virtually impossible to digest fats normally. If your gallbladder has been removed then successfully following a ketogenic diet is impossible. Without the necessary bile that the gallbladder makes, we cannot properly digest the fat we eat. There is a slight, constant leak of bile from the liver to the gut, which is more than enough for most people on a diet with a standard amount of fat. However on a ketogenic diet it may not be enough, and can lead to diarrhoea.

Pancreatitis varies from person to person. Depending on your type of pancreatitis, you may find that you are incredibly well suited to a ketogenic diet, or incredibly poorly suited to one. The pancreas is full of cells that make insulin, as well as the enzymes we use to digest fat and protein. The human pancreas does not have a specific map, so when a part of it fails or necrotizes, you cannot know for sure which cells are left. The only way is testing. If you find it hard to process carbs, or suffer diabetes, then a ketogenic diet is great for you. If you find it hard to process protein, and/or carbs, then you will need to restrict your protein intake, or take an enzyme supplement, but nothing else. But if you find it at all hard to digest fats, a ketogenic diet is not suitable for you.

Kidney conditions mean that processing excessive protein puts us at risk of kidney failure. Although high protein intake is not a requirement of a ketogenic diet, it can be easy to overeat protein when you are trying to keep your fat levels up. If you have a kidney condition you would do well to split your fats and proteins, so you can control how much protein you eat. This can make the diet much harder, though.

Pregnancy and breastfeeding use an enormous amount of calories, including a large amount of glucose. Although women suffering even from starvation have been found to carry children and breastfeed them fairly normally, there are many side effects. It is not known how many of these side effects are due to other nutrients lacking, as there is not much research into the effects of low glucose in pregnant and breastfeeding women. Therefore, we can't recommend following this type of diet if you are pregnant or breastfeeding.

Illness and old age can really take a toll on your body. If you have followed a low carb or ketogenic diet for a long time, there is no harm in continuing to follow them if you are ill, or as you age. This is because your body is adapted. However, if you are currently ill and not eating a low carb diet, you need to wait until you are better before starting a ketogenic diet. If you are over the age of fifty, or you have a chronic illness, consider slowly transitioning onto a ketogenic diet by cutting your carb intake down over the course of a few weeks. Reducing it by 5-10 grams a day is the fastest you should go, to protect yourself from the stressful effects of suddenly swapping from glucose to ketones.

# Chapter Five: Starting a ketogenic diet.

Starting out on any new diet can be hard, but a ketogenic diet can be one of the hardest to start. This is because it is a sudden change to a completely different way of eating. Carbs are everywhere and we are programmed to eat as many as we can, so most of us have not had a carb-free day in our entire lives. For this reason, regardless of whether we are starting by reducing our carbs, or going cold turkey, the first few days need to be as easy as possible.

Make sure that you have got rid of all your high carb foods. Some people may do this by eating them all over a week leading up to the first day. Others may throw or give the food away to remove temptation. Either way, you need it gone before you start your diet, to remove all the foods that are likely to make you give up. For this reason it is a good idea to ask other people to keep their carby foods away as well, to prepare your own meals, and to refuse invitations to eat out for a while.

Make sure you have all the foods you will want to eat at home. Check out our recipes nearer the end of the book for an idea of what you will want to have. But the priority is a lot of leafy greens, low carb root vegetables, healthy fats, and lean proteins. If you can, try making meals in advance and freezing them in individual tuppers. And make sure to get some low carb, high fat, high protein snacks, like peanut butter, beef jerky, or boiled eggs. That way you can always have something quick to eat when you need it.

When starting out on a ketogenic diet, you will want to begin with foods you already like. Liver, kale, and almond butter are wonderful additions to a ketogenic diet, but eating things you don't like is not the best way to start a long-term diet. Instead, look through the recipe lists for recipes with foods you love, so that you can truly enjoy your diet.

Next, you will want to start on a morning, when you are not going to work. Stress makes us crave carbs more, and eating carbs is what starts the hunger cycle in the first place. So if we start with an empty stomach, running on ketones from the previous night, and we are going to have a relaxed day or two, we will be able to stick it out through the first few days. This massively improves our chances of success, as the first days are the hardest.

When you start a ketogenic diet, you will find many side effects. Most of them are harmless and just part of your body recovering from a lifetime on a high carb diet. Carb cravings are the most common symptom. We have already discussed why these happen, so it is important to remain calm and try and push through. In the next chapter we will offer some solutions for these hunger pangs, but remember that they are at their worst for only a few days, and after that they will be gone.

Indigestion can occur when you first start a ketogenic diet. This is due to a common mistake people make, assuming that this diet is low in all plants. That is not true. On this diet you will eat large amounts of high fibre, low carb plant foods, fatty fruits like avocado, and nuts and seeds. If you do not eat enough fibre you will find that your meals cause reflux, indigestion, and gut cramping. If you are eating plenty of plants but still suffering reflux, indigestion, and gut cramping, consider eliminating dairy from your diet. Sometimes following a ketogenic diet can make an underlying cow milk protein allergy come to the surface. You always would have had this allergy, but it would have been masked by other aspects of your diet.

Finally, if you suffer stomach cramps, diarrhoea, or oily, black stools, then you are eating too much fat. How is it possible to eat too much fat on a low carb, high fat diet? The same way it is possible to pour too much water into a glass. When we are following a ketogenic diet we are using fat as fuel. But we can only absorb so much fat in one go, and burn so much fat. When we eat more fat than we can absorb, our bodies just let it pass through us. This is largely harmless, but has the side effect of damaging our gut bacteria, one of the exact things we are trying to fix with out diet. So if you notice these side effects, start reducing your fat intake until your stools return to normal.

Besides these symptoms, you should also experience a whole host of beneficial symptoms. Some of the most beneficial symptoms, like an improvement in metabolism, and weight loss, will take longer to happen. But others happen within days. You will find your appetite begins to come under your control. As your insulin spikes and crashes disappear, your body gets used to having a steady supply of energy. This means that rather than feeling hungry every single time your blood sugar drops, and snacking between meals, you are eating a healthy meal and going straight through to the next one without feeling hungry.

You will find that yeast infections and skin conditions improve, or even disappear entirely. This is because your candida is not being fed, so it has nothing to grow from. Candida causes many types of yeast infection, and several types of skin problem, being the root cause of most cases of dandruff, for starters. It also makes other conditions, like eczema, worse, by irritating the skin and growing under and around dead skin cells.

You will find your moods are more even. That "hangry" feeling you get when your blood sugar drops is not normal. It is your body responding to a lack of glucose, trying to get you to eat carbs. At first you may feel the carb-hungry anger more intensely than usual, but after a couple of days your body gets used to not having those constant spikes and crashes in blood sugar. No energy crashes means no cravings, means no eating carbs, means no spikes, means no more crashes. It is vitally important to fight this cycle and restore order, even if you have no intention of following a ketogenic diet for life.

# Chapter Six: Tips and tricks for handling carb cravings.

Carb cravings are one of the hardest parts of cutting your carb intake right back. We have already discussed why our bodies resist going low carb so aggressively, but that is of little comfort to someone who is going through the cravings themselves. Instead, here are some helpful ways of coping with the carb cravings until they naturally pass.

1: Sweeteners.
Although artificial sweeteners are hardly a health tonic, they can make for a very useful tool when controlling our carb cravings. Consider natural forms of sweeteners first, but most of them have a small amount of carbs, so if you will be using a lot, choose artificial ones.

Some people advise against using sweeteners, claiming that they will prolong the psychological addiction to carbs. However, although this is slightly true, it isn't the point. The physical addiction to carbs is far more intense than any psychological addiction, and if we go long enough without too many carbs, that addiction will break. After we have defeated the physical aspect of our addiction we can then consider cutting out sweeteners and fighting the psychological aspect. But until then, sweeteners are very useful.

2: Eat more protein.
Sometimes when we crave carbs we are just plain hungry. After so long eating too many carbs, all day every day, with every meal, our stomach rumbles and carbs are the first thing we try to get to eat. This means that we need to retrain our appetite signals to crave different foods, not just sugars and

starches. And the first step to that is eating more protein. Eating protein fills our stomachs and triggers the release of hormones that make us feel satisfied. So if we need calories, protein should help.

3: Fill up on greens.
The annoying part of carb cravings, though, is that because they are so misdirected, they could be a craving for any vital nutrient. If eating protein doesn't satisfy you, then it might be that you need vitamins and minerals. A large green salad, or a low carb stir-fry or soup, will fill your stomach with fibre, and add vital nutrients to your diet. This can take longer to have an effect, so be patient. If it works and you feel better, increase your daily greens intake until you no longer feel cravings.

4: Drink some water.
And if protein and greens both fail, you might actually just be thirsty. This is an incredibly common problem for people who do not drink many fluids, or for people who only drink sweetened beverages. When you rarely drink clean, simple water, your body doesn't know how to ask for it. Instead, it will fire up your appetite signals as soon as you get dehydrated. Get a glass of water and drink it quickly. Then get a second glass and sip it over half an hour. This rehydration might make your cravings go away.

5: Go for a walk.
Finally, if nothing hits the spot for your cravings, try and distract yourself. Mental activity can be hard in the middle of carb cravings, and idle distractions like watching television don't really take anything away from it. Instead, try and get moving. A walk around the block, or through some fields, can really take your mind away from cravings. And exercise, at

least whilst you're doing it, will help you fight hunger. Just make sure to have a healthy meal ready for when you are done exercising.

6: Meditate.
Mindfulness is a great way of fighting cravings. You know, on a conscious level, that your cravings for carbs are not a vital need, that your body is misleading you, and that the cravings will go away. But your body, your primitive self, does not know that. It is thought that meditation is a way of communicating with your body and cooperating with each other. Some Buddhist monks can sit on solid ice blocks bare naked, or even slow their heart rates right down, without suffering harm, just by meditating and focusing on their bodies. Even if you have never meditated a day in your life, you may find it beneficial to give it a go.

# Chapter Seven: Adapting a ketogenic diet for maintenance.

If you're looking at the ketogenic diet as a short term weight loss solution, simply taking on board the essentials and avoiding carbs is more than enough. However if you are chasing all-round health, you will need to be more careful with your diet.

All restrictive diets can be risky in that we are used to getting our nutrients from specific places. When we remove one or more of those foods, we can end up becoming deficient in vital nutrients. For instance, many of us get most of our dietary fibre from grains and legumes. If we cut out grains and legumes but do not eat enough nuts, seeds, and greens to increase our fibre intake, we may become deficient. Or we may get all our vitamin C from sweet fruits, so unless we start eating dark green vegetables and nonsweet fruit daily, we could accidentally run out of vitamin C.

Likewise, we are used to only eating a small amount of certain nutrients, but when we change our diet we may eat too many of them. For instance, ketogenic diets are not supposed to be very high protein, and some people are vulnerable to excess protein in their diets. And yet, when we try and increase our fat intake to promote ketosis, sometimes we will eat far, far more protein than we need. Or take vitamin A. Too much of it is poisonous, but if we decide to eat loads of liver pate, because we aren't keen on other types of offal, we could give ourselves vitamin A poisoning.

Therefore, if we are considering following a ketogenic diet long term, we need to be much more careful about the balance than if we were eating it for a week or three. We need to give careful thought to everything that enters our mouths, and ensure we eat a variety of natural, whole foods. In essence, although we are changing our macronutrient balance, by cutting carbs right down and increasing fat intake, we don't want our micronutrients to change at all, or if they do change we want to change them for the better.

There are four keys to following a ketogenic diet successfully and healthily in the long term:

1: Choosing healthy fats.

2: Eating a varied diet full of micronutrients.

3: Not neglecting fibre intake.

4: Following the 80/20 rule.

If these key factors are not approached properly, we risk losing too much weight, gaining weight, provoking inflammation, or causing malnutrition. But if we adopt all four keys to a good, healthy ketogenic diet, we will be fitter and healthier than ever before. Over the next chapters we will explore what each of those points means, and how it applies to our own personal circumstances and specific dietary needs.

Choosing healthy fats is a very important step. Many of us have been made to think of fats as unhealthy due to a misunderstanding which happened in the 1970s. When the government issued health warnings against fat, and in particular animal fats, there were hardly any cases of young people with heart disease, strokes, cancer, or obesity. These concerns had been rising very, very slightly for decades, but were still very rare. And soon after that, these health problems began to spike. Following the recommendation to eat less fat did not work. In the 90s our health issues began to taper off as we realized that olive oil is not bad for us. And now we are exploring animal fats as healthy again, beginning with the omega oils in fish, complex saturated fat in cheese, and cholesterol in eggs.

So why the sudden turn around? Well, obviously in the 70s we were wrong. The biggest factors damaging our health in those days were alcohol consumption and sugar consumption, which were both at levels never seen in any people since the aristocracy in the 1700s. We have already seen what simple sugars can do to our bodies when we eat too much of them, and how they can lead to inflammation, obesity, diabetes, etc. But the element of alcohol made things far, far worse.

Alcohol is a form of calories that is very difficult to access, as the liver needs to break it down to access the sugars. The liver has a limited amount of toxic products it can break down in a day, and just a few units of alcohol can take up all of that allowance. What does this mean in real terms? It means that when we drink, we are giving our livers too much to do, and then they start to fall behind on the rest of their work. Being drunk and having a hangover are signs that your liver is failing to do its job, signs that your body is overwhelmed with toxins.

If we overwhelm our livers and flood our bodies with toxins, our immune system needs to fight twice as hard to keep us fit and healthy. So now, until our liver is better, our immune system is working overtime as well. And when our immune system works overtime, we suffer inflammation, are at an increased risk of cancer, gain weight both in water and fat, and generally find our health declining.

Finally, alcohol consumption leads to decreased inhibitions, which in most people leads to increased food consumption, and being more likely to eat foods which we know are bad for us. Or, in other words, when we're drunk we're most likely to order a large burger meal or a kebab. We want greasy, carby, processed foods and we want it immediately. Not only do we eat worse things, but we eat things with more calories, which will naturally result in weight gain, increasing our risks of heart disease, diabetes, and strokes.

By ignoring how many simple carbs people were eating and taking the focus away from alcohol, the governmental guidelines had inadvertently promoted, not stopped, the rising health problems we were facing.

That's not to say they were entirely wrong. The fats people were eating had increased, of course, but not as part of a conscious decision, rather as vegetable oils began to form part of our processed food options. Vegetable oils are very much a misnomer, as they aren't made of vegetables, but seeds, and most commonly canola seed. There are major problems with these oils, but two stand out above all others: the quantity, and the processing. There is no way that any point in our existence we would have managed to eat four or five tablespoons of seed oil a day. That would have meant eating 50 grams of seeds every day, which would have taken most of our day to collect and press. Other fats were abundant, but these were rare. And furthermore, vegetable oils are highly processed. When fats are heated too much and hydrogenated they become oxidation-causing toxins. And almost every vegetable oil is highly processed. We will discuss the exceptions shortly.

Dietary cholesterol, which had been blamed for raised blood cholesterol, turned out to not increase your cholesterol in the long term. In the short term the cholesterol in egg yolks raises your blood cholesterol, the same way a bite of fruit raises your blood sugar. It's temporary, because what's in your stomach needs to get out. But that doesn't mean it's going to stay up. In fact, in the long term it actively reduces total blood cholesterol, triglycerides, and bad cholesterol, whilst increasing good cholesterol. The more cholesterol you eat from eggs, natural meats, and dairy, the better your blood cholesterol will get.

Saturated fat was then blamed for high cholesterol, in part thanks to a very cherry picked piece of research called The China Study, which sought to uphold the animal fat myth, so as to promote a vegetarian diet for social and political reasons. The China Study looked into traditional diets around the world, and reported that people who traditionally ate more animal fat were less healthy. How did they reach this conclusion? By removing information from countries where animal fat intake was high and health was also high. Or, the short form: vegan activists were happy that we were not eating much animal fat, and didn't want us to see that animal fat is perfectly healthy. Shockingly, it took a while before other major researchers found out about the fraud, and in that time it became such popular knowledge that it is still mentioned by activist documentaries and health gurus today. But as a fact, it has more in common with old wives tales than science. Real data shows natural saturated fat is just another healthy source of calories for the human body.

Some health food advocates would say that this means we must eat animal fats, and not plant fats, but the distinctions of quality must be made. Not all plant fats are bad for us, only the processed ones are. In fact, fats from fatty fruits and nuts are things we would have had good access to twice a year at least. This is because fatty fruit trees, like avocado and olive trees, and nut trees like walnut and brazil trees, fruit prolifically twice a year, giving us fairly easy-to access fats from their fruit. We would also have had regular access to whole seeds in the fruits we were eating. We would not have eaten much in the way of seeds, but they would have not been wasted. We would also have nibbled on some herb and grass seeds, but only in very small amounts. Pumpkin, apricot, and flax seed are all examples of seeds which we may have eaten up to a tablespoon a day of. These fats are not only natural, but are whole, unprocessed, and full of vital vitamins and minerals which will nourish our bodies. And if you want to choose an oil derived from vegetable fats, look at olive oil for cold uses and coconut oil for high temperature cooking. Olive oil is one of the healthiest plant fats around, but denatures quickly when heated. And coconut oil is a healthy plant-based saturated fat which resists high temperatures well.

Likewise, not all animal fats are good for us, only the unprocessed ones are. In the wild, healthy animals go through periods of gaining fat and periods of burning it. This means their body fat will cycle and be fairly low in toxins. They also exercise and eat natural diets. Cows eat grass and herbs; chickens eat insects and leaves and the odd bit of seed; pigs eat greens, roots, insects, and carrion, etc. You may have noticed how none of those animals naturally eat corn or wheat, two of the biggest food sources for conventionally reared farm animals. This unnatural diet, paired with their lack of exercise and being on a permanent fat gain diet will change the composition of the animal's fat. This fat is richer, but also lower in healthy Omega 3s and cholesterol, and higher in toxins. If we want to get enough good fats, we must eat fat from animals which have led healthy lives.

We must also give serious thought to our Omega 3 to Omega 6 *ratio*. For most people, the biggest concern is reducing their intake of Omega 6 and eating more Omega 3. This is because their diets are high in processed fats, both animal and seed-based, which gives them an excess of Omega 6. Having too much Omega 6 can be oxidizing to the body, and we need Omega 3 to balance it out. But Omega 3 is only found in large quantities in a few rare seeds, fish, and naturally raised animals. So the average person has a poor ratio. But it is possible to have a poor ratio in the opposite direction, especially when you are aiming to eat healthy. If you focus too heavily on animal products and neglect plant fats, you could end up with too much Omega 3 and too little Omega 6, a state that, based on laboratory studies of people taking high doses of Omega 3 supplements, is also oxidizing.

But the problem of not eating enough vegetables goes beyond just Omega ratios. Many people use low carb diets as an excuse to stop eating vegetables all together, which is a big mistake which will cost you your health in the long term. This is where the other two rules for a healthy long-term ketogenic diet become relevant. It is perfectly possible to lose weight in a safe and controlled manner by living off healthy, natural muscle meats and eggs for a week or two. But it is not possible to stay healthy on that diet for a long time, because it is lacking in two things: micronutrients, and dietary fibre.

Micronutrients are the word we use to refer to vitamins, minerals, and antioxidants, which may be vitamins or minerals, but may also be other types of compound. Whereas the macronutrients, fat, carbohydrates, protein, and alcohol, provide building blocks for our bodies and fuel, micronutrients help our cells to stay healthy by reversing cell ageing, reducing oxidation, and protecting cell walls. This can result in health benefits ranging from nice skin to a reduced risk of cancer. For these reasons, we need to eat a wide range of micronutrients every single day. And muscle meat is very low in most micronutrients, especially vitamins and antioxidants. To get vitamins and antioxidants, you have five choices: organ meats, berries, leafy greens, nonsweet fruits, and/or roots.

Organ meats, or offal, are exactly what the name suggests: the organs of animals. Unlike muscle meats, that have a few minerals and little else, organ meats are rich in vitamins and minerals. This is because organs are where micronutrients are used and stored, so when we eat them we are getting a super concentrated dose. There are many organ meats to choose from, and the fewer plants you eat, the more varied your selection of organs must become. Liver, kidneys, tongue, sweetbreads, and bone marrow from many animals are widely available. You also eat organs every time you eat whole fish or shellfish. The two main problems with getting your micronutrients exclusively from offal are its low vitamin C content and high vitamin A content. It can be difficult to maintain this balance without using plants.

Berries are great for us, but on a ketogenic diet you want to minimize the carbs and maximize the micronutrients in them. The berries highest in micronutrients are actually bitter or sour, and have a dusty appearance to their skin. This group includes blueberries, goji berries, black grapes, raspberries, mulberries, and elderberries. These berries have high concentrations of both vitamin C and antioxidants, with a very low carb content. This means that you only need to eat a handful a day to improve your health without leaving ketosis.

Leafy greens like kale, spinach, cabbage, and swiss chard are a wonderful food for their micronutrient content too. Choose dark, bitter, or sour greens above mild ones, as mild ones have fewer antioxidants. If you are not sure about eating berries, either due to their taste or their potential carb content, then leafy greens are a great place to start. One caveat is that you must cook your leafy greens very well to access all the nutrients in them, as these nutrients are encased in cellulose, a plant fibre that our stomach cannot digest. By cooking it we encourage it to release the nutrients we need.

Nonsweet fruits is the term we give to fruits that do not have a high sugar or starch content. Nonsweet fruits include ones like tomatoes, lemons, or squash, but also fatty fruits, like avocados. Remember that fatty fruits may have a high carb content in theory, but most of these carbs are fibre, and that the digestible carbs per 100g are under 5g. Nonsweet fruits carry all the micronutrient benefits of sweet fruit with none of the carb loads, so try and eat a variety of brightly coloured nonsweet fruit every day, preferably raw.

Low carbohydrate root and bulb vegetables, like jicama, onions, garlic, carrots, ginger, turnips, radishes, swede, and celeriac, are packed with amazing nutrients and usually incredibly low in carbs. These parts of the plant are designed to store nutrients, so they are very much like eating offal in that regard. However they are also very good to eat raw, unlike leafy greens, and filling and varied in their uses. These plants also make excellent substitutes for carbohydrate foods like potatoes and pasta.

The last four of these five foods are also very important for their fibre content. Fibre is a sort of carbohydrate which we cannot digest on our own. This means that it will not be turned into glucose in our blood and will not push us out of ketosis. Instead, it feeds the bacteria in our guts. And when our good gut bacteria get fed, we reap the rewards. First of all, a large population of good gut bacteria will cleanse our colon. They encourage peristalsis and make up the bulk of our feces, pushing out invasive bacteria and excess candida yeasts. This will keep our guts fit and healthy.

These gut bacteria also produce waste of their own. When our gut bacteria digest fibre, they produce short chain fatty acids, a type of fat, as you may have guessed from the name. These fats are excellent fuel for our bodies, and happen to be what a lot of larger herbivores, like gorillas, live off. Although we could never live off greens like our cousin the gorilla, we still get plenty of energy from the short chain fatty acids that our gut bacteria release after digesting fibre.

A high fibre intake also regulates the speed of our gut transit. If our gut is moving too fast, the added bulk slows it right down, improving water absorption and encouraging our bodies to absorb as many nutrients and short chain fatty acids as they can. All this leads to better hydration and better health. But if our gut is moving too slow, the fibre adds bulk, moving things along, and irritates the lining of the gut, encouraging lubrication and peristalsis. In short, fibre makes our guts work more efficiently. It is not for nothing that a high fibre intake reduces our chances of bowel cancer.

In summary, therefore, when we are looking at a ketogenic diet for maintaining our weight and health, we must ensure that we eat enough healthy, balanced fats, and plenty of low carb plants, to ensure that we get the right stuff to avoid malnutrition. Although we can in theory live off meat alone, it cannot just be muscle meat, and it will be very hard to balance the right amounts and types of offal to ensure we are getting enough of every micronutrient. Instead, it is far simpler to make sure that we eat berries, nonsweet fruits, leafy greens, root vegetables, and bulb vegetables every day.

# Chapter Eight: Weight maintenance on a ketogenic diet.

Finally, we need to consider our calories, as well as the 80/20 principle. No matter what some people may tell you, it is actually perfectly possible to gain weight on a ketogenic diet. As long as you eat too many calories, you can gain weight. The Inuit, for example, ate a ketogenic diet and still did not look like lean bodybuilders. And this is as it should be. *All* animals can gain weight on their natural diets, because having some extra fat is what makes an animal safe during times of famine. If we could not get fat on a ketogenic diet, this would be a sign that the diet is not suitable for us, and that we must stop eating this way. So, once again: if you eat too much on a ketogenic diet, you will get fat.

Conversely, the sort of ketogenic diet you followed at first, where you lost weight, is not ideal in the long term for weight maintenance. This is because the calorie content is typically low, and the protein content is typically high. Why is this? Because ketones are made by combining fats and proteins. So when we want to burn our body fat, we must eat a reduced amount of calories, to make sure our bodies burn our fat and not the fat in our stomachs. And we must eat plenty of protein, to make sure our bodies use the protein in our stomachs, and not the protein in our muscles. Eating a low calorie, moderate fat, zero carb, high protein version of a ketogenic diet encourages us to use our body fat and keep hold of our muscle. But we don't need to do this in the long term.

In the long term, we want our nutrition to come from the food we are eating, to preserve our muscles and basic, healthy layer of fat. This means we must eat a higher fat content and a lower protein content. There is no magical formula for this. Just look at what you are eating and swap a bit of protein for more fat, and keep doing this until your weight becomes stable. At this time you can also swap from zero carb onto a low carb diet, for the reasons mentioned in the previous chapter. Again, there is no specific formula. Just increase your carbs until you exit ketosis (keto sticks will help you here) and then reduce your carbs until you enter it again. This will give you an idea of the maximum amount of carbs you can eat whilst still staying in ketosis.

Finally, we have the 80/20 principle. The 80/20 principle is inspired by the knowledge that a diet which is too restrictive is ultimately unsustainable. It's actually based on human psychology: the idea is that if you are allowed to eat no amount of Food X, then as soon as you eat it you will feel guilt, and to protect yourself your brain will reimagine the event, telling you it is acceptable to eat Food X, which leads to falling off the wagon and overindulging. On the other hand, if you are allowed to eat Food X, but only if it is under 20% of your diet, then you can indulge a little, and have the odd moment of weakness, without feeling guilt and without wanting to throw your whole diet out the window.

With many other diets this principle is applied on a daily basis. For example on a juicing diet you may decide 80% of your calories, volume of food, or meals, should be juice, but 20% can be whatever you want. Or on a low fat diet you could say 8/10 meals must be totally low fat, but 2/10 can be higher fat. This flexibility is not designed to be exploited. You will still aim for 100% healthy food. But that 20% forgiveness allowance improves your ability to stick at your diet. So the 80/20 principle naturally also benefits people following a ketogenic diet.

However we cannot apply the principle to a ketogenic diet on a daily, or meal-by-meal basis. Why? Because if one day we eat a huge high carb meal, we're out of ketosis. If we have carbs as 20% of our plate every meal, we're out of ketosis. If carby foods make up 20% of our calories, we're out of ketosis. If every day we give ourselves an 80/20 split, we will not be in ketosis any more. So how can we apply the principle and be kind to ourselves without being out of ketosis? We must do it on a monthly basis.

20% of the average 30 days in a month is 6 days. This means that from the start to the end of the month, you have 6 days where you can be out of ketosis. This, like with any other diet, is not mandatory. The goal is to be in ketosis 100% of the time. But this principle means that if you slip up, or go out for a meal, or really fancy a slice of cake, there are 6 days a month you can just do as you please. You may be tempted to assign the days in advance, or have them all in a row. Don't. This six day allowance is a rainy day fund: to be used when there is no other option. Also, don't try and roll over days from the previous month. If one month you are in ketosis every day: great! But the next month you just have 6 days where you could be out of ketosis. The days do not roll over and do not "need to be used up". Treat your body with kindness, not like a system to be cheated.

# Chapter Nine: How to know you are in ketosis.

The key to getting and staying in ketosis is to ensure that your blood sugar stays low enough that your body needs to make ketones to make up the shortfall. And the way we do this is by restricting carbs. So how few carbs do we need to eat to get in ketosis and stay there? I'm glad you asked, because the answer actually depends on you, as an individual.

Our blood sugar rises because of the glycemic load of our food. Glycemic load is a calculation that measures the amount of carbs, how fast they enter our blood stream, which then calculates how much sugar will be in our blood and for how long. When we eat foods with fast release carbs, our blood sugar spikes and crashes. When we eat foods with a lot of carbs, our blood sugar stays up for longer. When we eat foods with both, our blood sugar spikes and stays up. The more often our blood sugar spikes, and the longer it stays spiked for, the more likely we are to leave ketosis. This means that you could eat a boiled sweet and stay in ketosis because it is small, or eat a potato and stay in ketosis because the carbs release slowly. But sweet potato casserole will definitely push you out of ketosis. How much your blood sugar rises in reaction to different carbs varies from person to person.

Not all carbs are created equal, though. Dietary fibre is often listed as a carb, but it is radically different from the starches and sugars that give us a blood sugar spike. Dietary fibre is not digested and goes on to feed our gut. Another type of carb is resistant starch. When starch is lightly cooked and cooled, like sushi rice, for example, it becomes resistant to digestion.

It will not raise our blood sugar by much, but it will feed our gut bacteria and promote good health. This is why we need to be careful when carb counting. If we count fibre, then one day we could be fine, and the next we could leave ketosis. Why? The first day we had 50g of fibre and 10g of starch, and the second we had 60g of starch. We need to discount dietary fibre, and bear in mind that only half of resistant starches will become glucose. This is called calculating 'net carbs', and is an important part of healthy ketosis. However always count sugars and processed starches fully.

And finally, your body can make glucose from protein, via a process called advanced glycation. Up to 200g of glucose a day can be made from extra proteins in our diet. If we are not eating enough protein and our body truly needs more glucose, it will digest our muscles. But if we eat far too much protein we are encouraging our body to make glucose instead of ketones. You need to find the healthy middle ground where you are having enough for health and growth, but not so much that you leave ketosis. This is why many people on ketogenic maintenance diets eat low protein as well as low carb.

All this, combined with your body's own personal insulin response, will affect how your body enters ketosis. As a general rule of thumb, a diet with no more than 65g of net carbs a day will make most people enter ketosis. But everyone enters ketosis at different points, some sooner, others later.

There are a few ways of telling you are in ketosis. The first and simplest is a urine test called a keto stick. When we produce abundant ketones, some are secreted in our urine. You will be able to measure the ketones in your urine using a keto stick, and this will tell you how in ketosis you are.

Another way of telling is to see whether you are enjoying the benefits of ketosis yet. When you start experiencing health benefits after a few weeks, you are definitely in ketosis. There is no faking good health. The only issue is that not everyone experiences health benefits from ketosis, as we have already discussed. So you may not be in ketosis, or it might just not be working for you.

A slightly less reliable way is to use a blood glucose monitor and check your blood sugar immediately before, immediately after, and an hour after eating. If your blood sugar goes up a little with a meal, but drops fast and is very low an hour later, then that meal probably did not affect ketosis. It might have affected your ketosis, but it's just unlikely. But if your blood sugar goes up and stays up, then you are at risk of leaving ketosis.

As you are an individual, you may find you enter ketosis on a relatively high amount of carbs, even of sugars, such as 60-100g a day. Or you may find you need to cut your carbs back to 20g a day to stay in ketosis. Bear in mind that your body's reactions aren't permanent either. The longer you are in ketosis, the better your body will get at extracting carbs. You may find that you need to reduce your carbohydrate intake a few weeks into your ketogenic diet, or you will leave ketosis. This is normal and nothing to worry about. Just keep checking and reducing your carbs until you are certain you are in ketosis again.

# Chapter Ten: Ketogenic recipes.

Now we are getting to the section where we understand the theory, more or less, but we need to get into the good habits that come with it. This means developing a meal plan and sticking to it for at least thirty days, which is how long it takes for a human being to form a new habit. Fortunately, a ketogenic diet has the edge over many other diets when it comes to meal plans. Many other diets are very prescriptive about what you can eat, how much, and when. But with a ketogenic diet, as long as you stay in ketosis you are doing it right. All you need is a variety of recipes and meal ideas to allow you to construct your own meal plan as you like. Who cares if you have steak stir fry for breakfast and eggs and bacon for lunch? Eat what you like, so long as it keeps you in ketosis.

# High Fat Meals

A core component to staying healthy on a ketogenic diet is eating plenty of healthy fats. But nobody likes chowing down on great lumps of plain fat. Not even carnivorous animals do that: they will eat proteins and collagen and blood and organs in between. This is because fat is slow to digest. So our high fat meals must be balanced with protein and fibre to make sure they are filling. As fibre has no calories, technically, and protein only has four per gram, our best daily intake will have a 1:1:1 ratio. That's to say, one gram of fat to one gram of protein to one gram of fibre.

These meals form half the base of your diet. A high fat meal has over 15g of fat and will make up most of your calories. Have 1-2 high fat meals every day.

## Pork And Plums.

Pork is a great source of fat as it is one of the fattiest meats around. The plums here will push your carb amounts up a bit, but they will also help digest the fat.

Serves 8. Prep time: 5 minutes. Cooking: stew for 4 hours.

Ingredients:
- 1kg of pork belly
- 4 plums, chopped
- 1 cup bouillon
- 1 tablespoon allspice
- 1 tablespoon cinnamon

Directions:
- Make slices in the skin of the pork so the flavour of the plums soaks through. Rub with allspice and cinnamon.
- Mix remaining ingredients into a sauce.
- Place pork in pot. Stew for four hours.

Nutritional values per serving: KCAL: 316; Fibre: 20g; C 10g; P 24g; F 20g.

# Meatloaf with Mushrooms, Traditional Version.

Meatloaf can be a great meal on a low carb diet. You just need to swap the breadcrumbs for something tasty and low carb, like simple mushrooms.

Serves 6. Prep time: 10 minutes. Cooking: 5 hours on low heat in oven.

Ingredients:
- 1kg minced beef
- 200g diced shiitake mushrooms
- ½ diced onion
- 2 eggs
- 2 tablespoons tomato sauce
- ¼ cup minced garlic
- 2 teaspoons mustard
- 1 teaspoon Italian herbs
- salt and pepper

Directions:
1. Combine beef, mushrooms, eggs, onion, garlic, herbs, and salt and pepper.
2. Form a loaf and place into a large casserole dish.
3. Mix tomato, mustard, and salt and pepper.
4. Spread tomato mix over the loaf.
5. Bake at 135C for 5 hours.

Nutritional values per serving: KCAL: 275; Fibre: 5g; C 5g; P 30g; F 15g.

# Chicken and Sprout Bake.

Chicken thighs and pure cream raise the fat content of this tasty dish.

Serves 6. Prep time: 15 minutes. Cooking: 4 hours in oven.

Ingredients:
- 500g brussels sprouts, halved
- 500g chopped boneless chicken legs or thighs
- 500g mushrooms
- 1 diced onion
- 1.5 cups milk or substitute
- 1 cup cream
- salt and pepper

Directions:
1. Mix the milk, cream, and seasoning.
2. Put all ingredients in oven tray.
3. Cook at 130C for 4h.

Nutritional values per serving: KCAL: 450; Fibre: 10g; C 2g; P 35g; F 30g.

# Coconut Milk Ice Cream.

Ice cream is a huge favourite in most households. With coconut cream and sweeteners, this one is all taste and low carb.

Serves 5. Prep time 5min. Cook time: none.

Ingredients:

- 2 cans coconut milk
- 7 tablespoons cocoa powder
- 7 tablespoons powdered sweetener

Directions:

1. Drain the water from the coconut milk cans and reserve only the fats from the top.
2. Mix in the cocoa and the sweetener.
3. Put in a container and place in the quick freeze section of the freezer.

Nutritional values per serving: KCAL 330; Fibre 0g; C 5g; P 10g; F 30g.

## Cheese Dip.

You need a great cheese dip if you want to eat a low carb diet. This will help deliver those veggies to even the most finicky palate.

Serves 10. Prep time 20min. Cook time: bain marie or low heat pan for 30 minutes.

Ingredients:

- 450g mixed cheese
- 2 cups milk
- smoked paprika
- black pepper and salt
- chives

Directions:

1. Warm the milk on the stove until small bubbles appear. Turn down so it doesn't boil, but retains heat.
2. Grate the cheese into it. Stir continually.
3. Add the spices and keep stirring.
4. When all mixed, take off the heat and allow to cool. When barely warm, chop some chives into it.

Nutritional values per serving: KCAL 242; Fibre 1g; C 6g; P 5g; F 22g.

## Avocado Eggs.

Avocado is an amazing source of healthy fats, as are egg yolks. So why not combine them into one tasty meal?

Serves 5. Prep time 10min. Cook time: pan frying for 35min.

Ingredients:
- 2 avocados
- 5 eggs
- 100g cheese
- lemon and lime juice
- chopped red and yellow peppers
- oil
- salt and pepper

Directions:
1. Mix the eggs with some salt and pepper and fry in the oil, stirring until scrambled and golden.
2. Meanwhile chop the avocado and toss with lemon and lime, salt and pepper, cubes of cheese, and chopped bell peppers.
3. When the eggs are done, add the avocado mix and stir well.

Nutritional values per serving: KCAL 290; Fibre 4g; C 2g; P 12g; F 26g.

## Low Carb Cassoulet.

The traditional cassoulet is much higher carb, but this one focuses on fatty pork again.

Serves 10. Prep time 15min. Cooking time: stewed on low for 5 hours.

Ingredients:

- 100% pork sausages, 10
- 97% pork chorizo 10
- 100% pork frankfurters 10
- 5 red and green bell peppers
- 2 onions
- 2 carrots
- 3 celery stems
- salt and pepper

Directions:

1. Chop everything roughly and add to a pot. Barely cover with boiling water.
2. Keep simmering, with lid on, for 5 hours.

Nutritional values per serving: KCAL 394; Fibre 12; C 9g; P 22g; F 30g.

## High Fibre Meals

When following a ketogenic diet we need to make sure we are feeding our gut bacteria. Although resistant starches and fermented foods are great additions to our diets, the fact is that the best thing for our guts is to feed them plenty of fibre. A high fibre meal is any where calories are very low and roughage is very high. Salads, smoothies, and stews can all be high fibre meals on a ketogenic diet.

High fibre meals form the other half the base of your diet. A high fibre meal has over 10g of fibre and will make up most of your plate. Have 1-2 high fibre meals every day.

# Vegetable Wraps.

These veggie wraps, paired with the right dip, are a delight and a great way of adding fibre.

Serves 4. Prep time 15 minutes. Cooking: none.

Ingredients:
- 1 head of romaine lettuce
- 2 carrots
- 1 cucumber
- 1 red onion
- 1 celery stalk
- dressing of choice

Directions:
1. Finely slice the carrots, cucumber, red onion, and celery into sticks of vegetable.
2. Divide between 12 lettuce leaves.
3. Roll up lettuce leaves and serve.

Nutritional values per serving, without dressing: KCAL: 20; Fibre: 15g; C 5g; P 0g; F 0g.

## Coleslaw.

Coleslaw is a traditional recipe. Add more mayo for a high fat ketogenic meal, or just use a little for a fibrous meal.

Serves 6. Prep time 15 minutes. Cooking: none.

Ingredients:
- 1 head of cabbage or 1kh of various cabbages
- 2 carrots
- 1 onion
- mayonnaise or equivalent dressing

Directions:
1. Shred the vegetables.
2. Mix them into the dressing.

Nutritional values per serving: KCAL: 92; Fibre: 13g; C 2g; P 3g; F 8g.

## Collard Greens and Bacon.

Collard greens are an ever popular Southern food, and also high in fibre.

Serves 5. Prep time: 10 minutes. Cooking: pan fry 15 minutes.

Ingredients:
- 500g collard greens, chopped
- 1 onion, chopped
- bay leaf
- 3 tablespoons balsamic vinegar
- 1 tablespoon oil
- 1 tablespoon minced garlic
- 2 cups vegetable stock

Directions:
1. Put the onions and oil in the slow cooker on high for five minutes.
2. Add all the other ingredients.
3. Cook on low for 6 hours.

Nutritional values per serving: KCAL: 82; Fibre: 15g; C 2g; P 5g; F 2g.

## Sprouts and Ham.

Not everyone likes sprouts, but they are great for us, and baking them in bacon can really help the flavour.

Serves 6. Prep time: 10 minutes. Cooking: 1 hour baked.

Ingredients:
- 1.5kg brussels sprouts
- ¼ cup diced ham
- 2 tablespoons lemon juice
- 3 minced garlic cloves
- salt and pepper

Directions:
1. Mix all ingredients together.
2. Bake in the oven on high, around 190C, for 1 hour.

Nutritional values per serving: KCAL: 58; Fibre: 12; C 5g; P 9g; F 2g.

# Broccoli Soup.

This soup packs in fibre and taste and can be left simmering in the slow cooker as you go to work.

Serves 6. Prep time: 5 minutes. Cooking: 8 hours on low in slow cooker.

Ingredients:
- 1kg broccoli, chopped
- 2 cups chopped onion
- 4 cups vegetable stock
- 1 cup water
- 150g fresh cilantro
- 2 tablespoons lime juice
- 3 bay leaves
- herb mix
- salt and pepper

Directions:
1. Mix all ingredients in slow cooker.
2. Cook on low heat setting for 8 hours.
3. Take out and blend.
4. Serve with sour cream.

Nutritional values per serving: KCAL: 94; Fibre: 34g; C 2g; P 17g; F 2g.

## Lamb Spinach Rogan Josh.

This meal has it all: protein, fat, and fibre!

Serves 6. Prep time: 15 minutes. Cooking: 4 hours on a low boil.

Ingredients:
- 1.5kg diced lamb
- 2 sliced red onions
- 1 cup Greek yoghurt
- 2 tablespoons ghee
- Rogan Josh curry paste
- salt and pepper

Directions:
1. Mix all ingredients together in a pot.
2. Add a little water and simmer for 4 hours.

Nutritional values per serving: KCAL: 450; Fibre: 14g; C 4g; P 38g; F 28g.

## Veggie Stew.

A veggie stew is the fastest way to increase your fibre intake today.

Serves 6. Prep time: 30 minutes. Cooking: 2 hour light boil.

Ingredients:
- 1 cup broth
- 2 large red onions
- 2 cups carrots
- 3 cups pumpkin
- 8 garlic cloves
- paprika
- herbes de provence
- salt and pepper

Directions:
1. Roughly dice the vegetables into similarly sized pieces.
2. Put all ingredients in the pot.
3. Boil lightly for 2 hours.

Nutritional values per serving: KCAL: 80; Fibre: 20g; C 11g; P 3g; F 4g.

# Onion and Kale Salad.

This salad is not as sweet as an onion and orange salad, but by playing with the spiciness you get plenty of flavour.

Serves 5. Prep time:10 minutes. Cooking: none.

Ingredients:
- 2 large sweet onions
- 1 red onion
- 1 large head of kale
- 1 cup lamb's lettuce
- 1 cup rocket

Directions:
1. Chop onions finely.
2. Tear salad leaves.
3. Toss.

Nutritional values per serving: KCAL: 29; Fibre 16g; C 4g; P 1g; F 1g.

## Protein Boosters

Sometimes we can end up eating too little protein when we focus too strongly on fats. If you realize your protein levels are too low and you are starting to lose muscle, you need to add extra sources of protein on at every meal. It varies from person to person, but the most protein we can absorb in one go is around forty grams. So don't eat a huge pile of protein once a day, or overdo it. Instead, add protein dense foods to every meal so that you get an extra 10 grams of protein every meal time.

A protein booster is any meal which adds over 12g of protein. These meals are small and often low in calories, but add an essential amount of protein for when your intake is low. These meals are more supplemental than everyday.

## Bacon Balsamic Beans.

Green beans and oodles of bacon make for a great protein boost.

Serves 8. Prep time: 5 minutes. Cooking: 20 minutes pan frying.

Ingredients:
- 1kg green beans
- 500g bacon
- 100g minced shallots
- ¼ cup balsamic vinegar
- lard

Directions:
1. Mix all ingredients together in the pan.
2. Cook for 20 minutes.

Nutritional values per serving: KCAL: 192; Fibre: 10g; C 10g; P 18g; F 8g.

# Simple Egg Omelette.

Omelettes are the quickest and easiest way to add protein.

Serves 6. Prep time: 10 minutes. Cooking: pan fry for 10 minutes.

Ingredients:
- 10 eggs
- 100g fresh spinach
- 100g cherry tomatoes
- 50g cup mushrooms
- 50g shredded cheese
- Chopped fresh chives
- Pinch of salt and pepper

Directions:
1. Heat some oil in your pan as you prep.
2. Roughly chop all the vegetables ready for mixing.
3. Whisk together the eggs, salt, and pepper.
4. Stir in the vegetables.
5. Pour into the pan and cook 5 minutes.
6. Make sure your omelet is almost completely solid. Flip. Add the chives.
7. When it is firm, remove, dice, and serve.

Nutritional values per serving: KCAL: 150; Fibre: 5g; C 3g; P 13g; F 3.5g.

## Shredded Crispy Chicken.

Use chicken breasts for a pure protein experience.

Serves 8. Prep time: 15 minutes. Cooking: 8 hours on low.

Ingredients:
- 1kg boneless chicken thighs
- ½ cup orange juice
- ½ cup beer
- juice of one lime
- juice of one lemon
- 1 tablespoon olive oil
- Mexican meat seasoning

Directions:
1. Rub the chicken with the seasoning mix.
2. Put in a pot. Pour beer and juices on top.
3. Cook for 8 hours on a low, simmering heat.
4. Remove and shred.
5. Fry in pan with a dash of olive oil to crisp it a bit.

Nutritional values per serving: KCAL: 230; Fibre: 2g; C 5g; P 29g; F 10g.

# Slow Cooker Chicken Salad Topper.

Another great recipe to put on as you work. Just remember to time it to turn off after 6 hours.

Serves 8. Prep time: 20 minutes. Cooking: slow cooker 6 hours on low.

Ingredients:
- 3 breasts diced chicken
- 4 chopped red and green peppers
- 2 cups tomatoes
- 1 chopped onion
- ½ cup chili
- 2 cloves chopped garlic
- 1 teaspoon olive oil

Directions:
1. Pan fry the onions and garlic. Put in slow cooker.
2. Add all over ingredients.
3. Cook for 6 hours on low.

Nutritional values per serving: KCAL: 250; Fibre: 5g; C 9g; P 25g; F 10g.

## Chicken with Tomato Mediterranean Sauce.

You can still enjoy some sweetness on a ketogenic diet, as this recipe proves.

Serves 6. Prep time: 5 minutes. Cooking: bake for 45 minutes.

Ingredients:
- 2kg boneless chicken thighs
- 2 cans of tomatoes
- 100g pitted black olives
- 3 teaspoons paprika
- 1 tablespoon minced garlic
- 1 teaspoon olive oil
- salt and pepper

Directions:
1. Put the chicken in the slow cooker.
2. Mix the remaining ingredients together.
3. Pour the sauce over the chicken.
4. Bake until cooked through.

Nutritional values per serving: KCAL: 270; Fibre: 10g; C 5g; P 29g; F 13g.

## Osso Bucco – Bone Soup.

Bone broth is all the rage, and for good reason. Bone marrow is an amazing health tonic. So reap the benefits of bones and meat in this tasty soup.

Serves 8. Prep time: 30 minutes. Cooking: boil 6h.

Ingredients:
- 1.5kg bone-in beef, from tail or shank
- 2 chopped onions
- 100g chopped celery
- 100g chopped carrot
- 1 can chopped tomatoes
- 150ml red wine
- 8 chopped garlic cloves
- ¼ ounce mushrooms
- 1 tablespoon oil, split
- parsley 1tsp, lemon zest 1tsp, bay leaf 1
- salt and pepper

Directions:
1. Put the pot on high heat with half a tablespoon of oil and the onions.
2. After five minutes, add the remaining oil and the beef.
3. After turning the beef for 10 minutes to brown it a little, add the remaining ingredients.
4. Cover with stock or water and simmer on low for 6 hours.

Nutritional values per serving: KCAL: 186; Fibre: 5g; C 9g; P 24g; F 6g.

# Thai Chicken Curry For Slow Cooker.

This Thai curry is flavourful and will be ready for you when you get home.

Serves 8. Prep time: 5 minutes. Cooking: 8 hours on low in a slow cooker.

Ingredients:
- 1kg chopped chicken breast
- 2 minced onions
- 1 can of coconut milk
- 1 cup chicken stock
- ½ cup fresh basil leaves
- 3 tablespoons red curry paste
- 4 minced garlic cloves
- 2 tablespoons lime juice
- 2 tablespoons oyster sauce
- 1 shredded chili pepper
- salt

Directions:
1. Mix all the ingredients in the slow cooker.
2. Cook on low for 8 hours.

Nutritional values per serving: KCAL: 200; Fibre: 4g; C 10g; P 27.4g; F 5.5g.

# Chili Orange Shrimp.

Shrimp is very low in everything except protein, making it a great protein boost, and this sautee is so fast!

Serves 4. Prep time: 5 minutes. Cooking: 5-minute sautee.

Ingredients:
- 1kg peeled and deveined shrimp
- 2/3 cup of cream
- 1 chipotle chili
- 1 teaspoon orange zest
- cinnamon
- 5 spice
- salt and pepper

Directions:
1. Blend the half and half, chile, orange, salt, and pepper.
2. Put in a frying pan with the shrimp. Sautee 5 minutes.

Nutritional values per serving: KCAL: 186; Fibre: 0g; C 3g; P 28g; F 6g.

## Alternatives to Carbs

Sometimes we will get a craving for carbs, not because of illness or candida or emotional attachments, but because we just like the food. Whether you want a cake, are craving shepherd's pie, or miss the crunch of cookies and crackers, there are loads of ways of recreating the textures of our favourite carbs and making ketogenic versions of our favourite snacks and comfort foods.

# Root vegetable mash

As we have already mentioned, many root vegetables are actually very low in carbs. But they still have that earthy, rich, heavy quality that makes potatoes so nice. If you want mashed potatoes as a side dish, or want to make a dish that involves a mashed potato topping, such as shepherd's pie or cottage pie, then consider swapping the potato for a root vegetable mash. Some popular blends are carrot and swede, turnips in butter, and swede and celeriac.

Recipe:
1. Boil your root vegetable of choice until tender.
2. For softer root vegetables, like carrots and swedes, simply mash. For tougher root vegetables use a blender.
3. Stir in seasonings as desired.

# Root vegetable chips

Likewise, if you want something crispy and delicious like potato fries or chips, then you could always make root vegetable chips. Many people select a baked option, as they are avoiding fat, but on a ketogenic diet you could happily slice some root vegetables nice and thin and then deep fry them and toss them in salt and herbs for a truly satisfying crunch.

Recipe:

1. Use a guillotine to slice root vegetables very finely. Salt and place between paper towels to absorb moisture.
2. Heat a healthy oil like coconut or lard, about 1 inch deep, in a pan.
3. When to temperature, drop the vegetable slices in one at a time until the pan is half full.
4. Stir, remove when crisp.
5. Repeat 3 and 4 until no more chips remain.

# Vegetable breads

It's a little known fact that eggs hold almost anything together, and baking powder makes almost anything bubble and rise. Consider turning a vegetable mash or vegetable smoothie into a loaf you can use for sandwiches and dipping. There are countless different recipes online, but the basic idea is to make a thick vegetable puree, add one egg and one teaspoon of baking powder per cup of puree, mix well, and bake until firm.

Recipe:

1. Boil, then blend your vegetable. If it is watery, like zucchini, then do not add water. If it is dry, like turnip, add water until the paste is smooth.
2. Season and leave to cool.
3. Preheat oven to 200C. Line or grease a bread tin.
4. Whisk in one egg and one teaspoon of baking powder per cupful of puree.
5. Pour into bread tin and put in the oven.
6. Use a knife or skewer to check how your bread is doing. Remove when the knife or skewer comes out clean

# Berries

Berries may be fruit and still carry some carbs, but if you're looking for a sweet and tasty snack that will not put you out of ketosis, they are your best natural bet. Besides, they are rich in vitamin C and antioxidants, meaning they are great for you.

Recipe:
1. Mix blackberries, blueberries, and currants in your blender. Add the same amount of cucumber and a small squeeze of lemon.
2. Blend. Add sweetener if you like (see below).
3. Use for sweet cravings.

# Artificial sweeteners

If you're not too bothered about whether your food is natural or artificial, but you definitely don't want to risk leaving ketosis, then artificial sweeteners may be your only option. As we have already discussed, they are not ideal, but they can be very helpful. Buy powdered sweeteners as then you can use them in puddings and smoothies as well as drinks. This includes artificially sweetened fizzy drinks, too.

Recipe 2: Cloud bread muffins.

Cloud bread is an amazing mix of eggs and cheese that also makes for a low carb sandwich bread.

1. Preheat oven to 200C.
2. Separate 5 egg yolks and whites. Whisk whites until firm.
3. Mix the yolks with 200g of soft cheese.
4. Gently fold cheese and whites together. Add two tablespoons of sweetener.
5. Dollop onto baking paper. Put in oven.
6. When breads begin to brown, remove and leave to cool.

# Seasoning Your Food

The secret to enjoying your meals on almost any diet is to season them well. Many of our favourite condiments are based on carbs, or full of sugars and syrups. But that doesn't mean ketogenic meals need to be flavourless. You can use dry rubs, hot spices, sweet and fragrant herbs, mustards, curries, dressings and vinegars to add a good level of flavour to your meals. And, from time to time, a tablespoon or two of a sugary condiment won't kick you out of ketosis either.

**Spice mixes.** If you're not already skilled at mixing spices, it will be a relief to know that almost every spice mix you have ever tasted can be bought already mixed in a bag. Some great ones are herbes du provence, Italian herbs, chinese five spice, and Moroccan spice blends. You can also get bouillon and stocks that are low in carbs but high in flavour.

**Dry rubs.** For roasting your meats, consider applying a dry rub. Once again, you can buy ready-made dry rub mixes in jars and tins, so there's no need to make one yourself. These mixes are very rich and you can really elevate your meals without much effort. What is more, if you don't want to use them dry you can add some water and turn them into a marinade for your meats.

**Chili sauce.** Chili sauce is a lifesaver. Avoid sweet chili sauces and mixed ones with sugars, naturally. But this hot condiment can be added to stews and soups and stir fries, and put on the side of dishes, ready for dipping, and will make you not particularly miss the old sweet sauces you used to have all the time. It's not the same, but it's a very good substitute.

**Curry pastes.** When making a curry it can be so easy to get it wrong. Rather than mix your own curry, or use those watered down sauces, consider getting jars of curry paste. This is a mix of herbs and spices that will give you an instant curry, whether you want a korma or a vindaloo. Some do have sugars, so read the ingredients first. But most are just pure spice.

**Pesto.** A pesto is a great way of turning a carb alternative into something rich and flavourful. Often our carb alternatives, like zucchini noodles, are fairly bland and watery. A pesto is a mix of crushed nuts and herbs that will cling to our carb alternative and turn it into a much more rewarding part of our plate. This is especially true when we are having raw vegetables, like a slaw.

**Aioli.** Aioli is a fancy word, but really it just means garlic in olive oil. Get some crushed garlic or garlic paste, mix it half and half with olive oil, and you have aioli. This makes for a healthy and delicious seasoning for salads, dip for meats, and a generally great fat booster.

**Mayonnaise.** You don't necessarily want to buy mayonnaise in stores, as most of it is made with unhealthy refined oils that are no good for you. But mayonnaise really is just oil and eggs, so whether you find a brand that makes a natural mayonnaise, or mix your own, it can be a great addition to a ketogenic diet. It is delicious and will turn your simple salads into something amazing.

**Dressings.** If you aren't sure about aioli or mayonnaise, why not experiment with your own dressings? My general dressing formula is one part oil such as olive oil or coconut oil, one part vinegary food like balsamic vinegar or mustard, one part herbs and spices. Mix these ingredients up in a screw top jar, shake them roughly, and you'll have a dressing for your salads. You can experiment with these dressings until you find the right one for you. They also keep well, due to their high vinegar content.

# Eating Keto Out and About

We can't always stay in and live entirely off home-cooked meals. If we could, diets wouldn't be so hard in the first place. It can really help if the first week you go keto is spent eating entirely from home, as this helps you beat those early carb cravings and get into the groove of things. But sooner or later you need to start going out with friends and family again. So how do we plan our meals when we're eating at a restaurant?

Here is where a ketogenic diet again has an edge over many other low carb diets. Because a ketogenic diet focuses on staying in ketosis, there are no bad or evil foods you absolutely have to avoid. My rule of thumb would be not to worry about incidental carbs, such as sugars in sauces or breading on proteins. Instead, order something that is high in protein and fat, and as long as you stay in ketosis, don't worry about the hidden carbs. Some great ideas for ketogenic meals you can eat out and about include:

**Salads.** It's hard to mess with a salad. Some have a higher carb content, but those are usually the ones with carbs directly mentioned in their names. So long as you avoid pasta salads and potato salads, and choose cold salads over warm salads, you will get a fairly healthy meal.

**Burgers without buns.** There is no rule saying you have to order things exactly as they are on the menu, or eat them exactly as they arrive. Consider ordering a burger with all the toppings, but no bun, and eating it with a knife and fork.

**Rotisserie chickens.** Rotisserie chickens are a great way to eat healthy on a meal out. They are almost entirely pure meat, you get great value for money, and you won't feel that you are depriving yourself as you are getting to indulge.

**Steak and eggs.** Another great one if you don't want to feel left out. Steak and eggs is a nice, enjoyable meal to have when dining out, but it won't push you out of ketosis.

**Bacon and eggs.** For a breakfast option, bacon and eggs can be hard to beat. Two healthy, carb-free protein sources, both fairly high in natural fats. This breakfast will fill you up and make you happy. Just avoid eating any sides, or ask for it without them.

**Many fish dishes.** For some reason it seems to be assumed that the person ordering fish will be on a diet. Which works great for us. Just ask in advance to make sure the fish isn't breaded or battered, and ask them to swap any fries for a side salad instead.

**Ratatouille and other vegetable stews.** Many vegetable stews served in restaurants are very low in carbs and calories, and very healthy. From ratatouille to pumpkin stew, you will have plenty of low-carb options. This is especially true of Chinese food, where carbs are otherwise hard to avoid.

On the flip side, when trying to stay keto there are some foods you never want to order. These foods are almost always high in carbs.

**Anything with grains, pulses, or potatoes as a focal point.** It should go without saying, but: if a food's main focus is grains, pulses, or potatoes, it is going to be high carb.

**Anything with fruits.** Even a small amount of fruit can pack a load of sugar, and often fruity dishes have added sugars to make them even sweeter. Not worth the risk.

**Anything that has been blended.** The issue with blended foods like smoothies and soups is that you can't truly tell what's in them any more. Stick to stews, where you can see what you're eating.

**Sausages.** Most restaurant sausages have an abysmally low amount of real meat in them. Most of the time they will have loads of fillers, like corn or wheat. When eating out, it's safer to just avoid.

**Meat substitutes.** Unfortunately, the case is the same with meat substitutes as it is with sausages. Of course there are many low carb meat substitutes. But they are not guaranteed to be the ones the restaurant is using.

**Food you've never heard of.** If you really have no clue what it is, either look it up on your phone or avoid. Better safe than sorry!

# Chapter Eleven: Ketogenic diet FAQs.

When considering starting a highly specific diet, it is normal to have some questions. And any diet worth its salt should provide clear, sensible answers to those questions. So, to help you out, here is a list of Ketogenic diet FAQs, with their most concise answers.

**How is keto any different from any other low carb diet?**
All diets encourage slight ketosis for weight loss, and all low carb diets dissuade us from eating carb sources. A ketogenic diet is different because it doesn't focus on what you put on your plate, but what you get out of it. You aren't measuring calories or carb levels, but the physical state of your body. This is a much more intuitive, reliable way of dieting than just paying attention to what goes in our mouths,

**Do I need to eat a specialist diet?**
Not at all! Many diet writers will try and tie their diet into a product range, convincing you that you can only do the diet right if every meal comes out of a box or a bottle. The fact is, if you follow this diet correctly you will not be any more successful whether you buy ketogenic ready meals or whether you eat real foods.

**Will I need supplements?**
In an ideal world, no. But if you find that you are having a hard time eating enough fat, protein, vitamins, or fibre, and, for whatever reason, you can't eat the foods you need to replenish them, you might need supplements.

### Will I miss eating carbs?

Not going to lie: of course you will. Whether it's a craving, or you just pass your favourite cake shop, or your friend is eating some pizza, you will want carbs sometimes. That is why we apply the 80/20 principle: so you can enjoy carbs from time to time without compromising all your hard work.

### Can I go keto if I am vegan?

It is definitely possible to go keto on a vegetarian or pescetarian diet, as any animal fats will provide the right balance to keep you healthy through ketosis. When vegan it is possible, but a little harder work. You would do well to investigate various tasty fat sources and focus on making rich vegan dressings for full leafy salads.

### Can I go keto if I am diabetic?

Ketogenic diets are in fact often prescribed to diabetics as a way of controlling blood sugar levels. However you can't prescribe yourself one. Talk with your doctor about what is best for you.

### Will I need to change my lifestyle?

You don't have to, but it will help. You can lose weight by just staying in a calorie deficit in ketosis, and reduce inflammation by eating fewer sugars. But if you exercise, avoid drugs, drink moderately, and make sure you breathe fresh air and take time to relax, the benefits of this diet will be multiplied.

### What if keto doesn't work out for me?

Then it doesn't. It is your diet's job to work for you, not your job to work for your diet. If you do everything right, stick it out, and still don't feel any improvements after a few weeks, or start feeling side effects, then this diet may not be for you. Fear not: there are countless diets out there which could be perfect for your body and lifestyle.

## Conclusion.

In conclusion, a ketogenic diet can be an amazing thing... when done correctly. I'm sure it is now clear to you how much good a ketogenic diet can do for an average, mostly healthy person, and for many people with health complaints too. Hopefully this book has also left you confident enough to give a ketogenic diet a go, and with all your questions answered.

Some may remain skeptical, and I understand this. We have been sold so many rubbish diets, it's no surprise when we roll our eyes at a new one. But ketosis isn't some fad, it's a medical reality. So, rather than live in doubt, at least give this diet a go. What's the worst that could happen?

# Meal Prep

Beginner's Guide to 70+ Quick and Easy Low Carb Keto Recipes to burn Fat and Lose Weight Fast

# Introduction

Everyone on the Keto Diet wants to enjoy high quality, healthy, and delicious home cooked meals every day. However, not everyone knows that this is possible, which is why they would sometimes resort to low quality, unhealthy alternatives such as cheap take outs or commercially produced, highly processed meals.

Those looking for better strategies to help them maintain the Keto Diet safely and effectively, however, should look no further because this book can help them achieve the goal of having healthy and delicious home cooked keto meals prepared at home. Every. Single. Day.

How? Well, that is because this book contains the steps to effectively meal prepping at home *and,* best of all, over 70 meal prep-friendly, low carb keto dishes for breakfast, lunch, dinner, snacks, smoothies, and even desserts! It also includes a suggested comprehensive 30-day keto meal plan for those who want to make things even easier for them.

Start meal prepping your low carb keto meals right now by turning to Chapter 1!

# Chapter 1 – The Basics and Benefits of Low Carb Keto Meal Prepping

The Ketogenic Diet, or Keto, is fast becoming the alternative diet for many people. It has helped many lose weight, overcome PCOS (polycystic ovarian syndrome), enhance their athletic performance, and manage Alzheimer's disease and other neurological conditions.

If you are someone who is currently on the Keto diet, then you would understand how difficult it can be to maintain, especially since we are often surrounded by high carb food. Keto dieters more often than not would need to prepare their own meals at home to ensure their enjoyment of delicious, healthy, low carb and high fat food.

The good news, however, is that you can choose to **meal prep** your low carb keto meals. That way, can save a lot of money, time, and effort as you continue to be on the keto diet. Meal prepping is a practical way to prepare food at home because it enables you to cook large batches for only a few times per week (sometimes even once a week) and then store individual portions of the food properly in the refrigerator or freezer. Then, throughout the week, all you will have to do is reheat those servings and enjoy them. Best of all, some foods, such as salads and snacks, do not even need reheating at all.

# How to Meal Prep the Right Way

Some people have quit meal prepping simply because they do not follow a practical and efficient process. You can avoid becoming one of them by creating one, and these guidelines can help you do so.

### 1: Choose where and when to do your weekly grocery shopping

Where would you like to buy your ingredients? Take note of the closest markets in your area that offer the best quality your food budget can afford. Then, determine the best day and time to purchase all the ingredients you need there. For instance, if your free day is on a Saturday morning and you know not a lot of people do their grocery shopping at 10 a.m. in that market, then you can schedule your weekly trips then.

### 2: Create a grocery list template.

Whether it is on your phone or a physical list, you should have a template on which to list down the ingredients you need for the recipes you will be meal prepping. Take note of the amount, generic names, and brands if you must. Then, sit down with your chosen recipes for the week and take note.

### 3: Shop in bulk.

Once you have a list of the ingredients you need, all you have to do is buy them during your chosen date and time. Then, store them appropriately in your kitchen pantry and refrigerator as soon as you get home.

### 4: Choose two Meal Prep Days.

Before you go grocery shopping, make sure you have already chosen your meal prep day for the week. Is it going to be on a Sunday afternoon? If so, then make sure you have bought the ingredients a day before. That way, you will not be so exhausted by the time you start cooking.

### 5: *Prepare your individual food containers.*
You will make your own life so much easier if you divide your meal prepped meals into individual containers because you will then be able to do a "grab and go" system throughout the week. Choose guaranteed food-safe, airtight containers suitable for the types of foods you want to enjoy. Also, label the containers so you would not end up storing your delicate muffins in one that smells strongly of garlic and pepper.

There you have it: meal prepping made easy. If you are not the only one who will enjoy these meal prepped meals, then you can definitely work together with whoever you are sharing them with. That way, you can cut on cost and time so much more effectively.

## Common Mistakes in Meal Prepping

There are definitely safety measures to take when meal prepping. After all, you are dealing with something that you put into your body. So, here are some common mistakes you must avoid while meal prepping your low carb Keto meals.

### Mistake 1: Storing cooked food for more than 4 days in the fridge.
The safest maximum number of days for storing most cooked food in the refrigerator (40 degrees F or lower) is 4 days. The food should also be stored in an airtight container to significantly slow down oxidation. Any longer than 4 days and you might risk food poisoning.

## Mistake 2: Reheating food more than once

Cooked food should never be reheated more than once. Otherwise, you could risk not just losing the nutritional value and flavor but also the chance of food poisoning. You should also reheat the food until the internal temperature reaches 165 degrees F to ensure that it is completely thawed and safe to eat.

## Mistake 3: Going to the grocery store without a detailed list

You could waste a lot of money and food when you overbuy certain ingredients. It is therefore critical for you to take note of the amount required for the meal prep before you step into the grocery store.

## Mistake 4: Storing food improperly

Oxygen quickly breaks down the food and causes bacteria to flourish, that is why you must minimize the food's exposure to oxygen as soon as it is cool enough to be stored. This can be achieved by using airtight containers and freezer bags. You can also do the water immersion technique to make bagged food airtight before sealing. Check any online video on how to do this.

## Mistake 5: Failing to add variety

It is important to eat different food within the week for two reasons. First is, you could easily grow bored with the same meals every day. Second is, you will not be able to give your body a variety of nutrients if you eat the same types of food daily. So, do not hesitate to try other recipes. Better yet, always include a fresh salad with most of your meals so you will not only add variety to flavor, but also to nutrients.

At this point, you must be ready to start low carb Keto meal prepping. So, without further ado, go ahead and get started!

# Chapter 2 – 30-Day Low Carb Keto Meal Plan

In the following pages is a suggested 30-day list of meal plans you can follow, based on the recipes found in this book. Of course, you can always make changes based on your personal taste and preferences, so feel free to adjust when needed.

Day 1

Breakfast: Savory Cheddar Pancakes

Smoothie: Creamy Matcha Green Tea Smoothie

Lunch: Savory Beef Balls with Asian Style Dip

Snacks: Avocado, Cream Cheese and Cucumber Bites

Dinner: Deviled Eggs with Chopped Bacon

Dessert: Cocoa Nibbles with Cream Cheese

Day 2

Breakfast: Savory Cheddar Pancakes

Smoothie: Creamy Matcha Green Tea Smoothie

Lunch: Savory Beef Balls with Asian Style Dip

Snacks: Avocado, Cream Cheese and Cucumber Bites

Dinner: Deviled Eggs with Chopped Bacon

Dessert: Cocoa Nibbles with Cream Cheese

Day 3

Breakfast: Chia Cinnamon Vanilla Granola

Smoothie: Peanut Butter Choco Smoothie

Lunch: Savory Beef Balls with Asian Style Dip

Snacks: Avocado, Cream Cheese and Cucumber Bites

Dinner: Keto Caesar Salad

Dessert: Cocoa Nibbles with Cream Cheese

Day 4

Breakfast: Chia Cinnamon Vanilla Granola

Smoothie: Peanut Butter Choco Smoothie

Lunch: Chicken Curry with Oil-Roasted Peanuts

Snacks: Ham 'n' Cheese Puffs

Dinner: Keto Caesar Salad

Dessert: Creamy Vanilla Pudding

Day 5

Breakfast: Chia Cinnamon Vanilla Granola

Smoothie: Strawberries and Cream Smoothie

Lunch: Chicken Curry with Oil-Roasted Peanuts

Snacks: Ham 'n' Cheese Puffs

Dinner: Fried Cheesy Avocado Wedges

Dessert: Creamy Vanilla Pudding

Day 6

Breakfast: Cheese and Sausage in Portobello Breakfast Burgers

Smoothie: Strawberries and Cream Smoothie

Lunch: Baked Parmesan Chicken Nuggets in Mozzarella Marinara Sauce

Snacks: Ham 'n' Cheese Puffs

Dinner: Fried Cheesy Avocado Wedges

Dessert: Creamy Vanilla Pudding

Day 7

Breakfast: Cheese and Sausage in Portobello Breakfast Burgers

Smoothie: Zesty Green Smoothie

Lunch: Baked Parmesan Chicken Nuggets in Mozzarella Marinara Sauce

Snacks: Walnut Parmesan Bites

Dinner: Simple Beef Chili

Dessert: Lemon Poppy Seed Cupcakes

Day 8

Breakfast: Cheesy Keto Quiche

Smoothie: Zesty Green Smoothie

Lunch: Zucchini Beef Lasagna

Snacks: Walnut Parmesan Bites

Dinner: Simple Beef Chili

Dessert: Lemon Poppy Seed Cupcakes

Day 9

Breakfast: Cheesy Keto Quiche

Smoothie: Chia Seeds and Crisp Greens Smoothie

Lunch: Zucchini Beef Lasagna

Snacks: Walnut Parmesan Bites

Dinner: Low Carb Hearty Pot Roast

Dessert: Lemon Poppy Seed Cupcakes

Day 10

Breakfast: Blueberry Breakfast Scones

Smoothie: Chia Seeds and Crisp Greens Smoothie

Lunch: Chicken Bell Pepper Kebabs

Snacks: Cream Cheese Bacon Stuffed Jalapenos

Dinner: Low Carb Hearty Pot Roast

Dessert: Keto Choco Brownies

Day 11

Breakfast: Blueberry Breakfast Scones

Smoothie: Buttered Coffee Smoothie

Lunch: Chicken Bell Pepper Kebabs

Snacks: Cream Cheese Bacon Stuffed Jalapenos

Dinner: Miso Beef and Tender Zucchini

Dessert: Keto Choco Brownies

Day 12

Breakfast: Cinnamon Coconut Porridge

Smoothie: Buttered Coffee Smoothie

Lunch: Chicken Bell Pepper Kebabs

Snacks: Cream Cheese Bacon Stuffed Jalapenos

Dinner: Miso Beef and Tender Zucchini

Dessert: Keto Choco Brownies

Day 13

Breakfast: Cinnamon Coconut Porridge

Smoothie: Smooth Vanilla Smoothie

Lunch: Easy Grilled Shrimp with Avocado, Tomato and Onion Salad

Snacks: Low Carb Guacamole

Dinner: Roasted Garlic Butter Cod with Bok Choy

Dessert: No Bake Coconut Macaroons

Day 14

Breakfast: Easy Scotch Eggs

Smoothie: Smooth Vanilla Smoothie

Lunch: Easy Grilled Shrimp with Avocado, Tomato and Onion Salad

Snacks: Low Carb Guacamole

Dinner: Roasted Garlic Butter Cod with Bok Choy

Dessert: No Bake Coconut Macaroons

Day 15

Breakfast: Easy Scotch Eggs

Smoothie: Avocado Coco Smoothie

Lunch: Mediterranean Style Tuna Salad

Snacks: Low Carb Guacamole

Dinner: Creamy Chicken Soup

Dessert: No Bake Coconut Macaroons

Day 16

Breakfast: Easy Scotch Eggs

Smoothie: Avocado Coco Smoothie

Lunch: Mediterranean Style Tuna Salad

Snacks:

Dinner: Creamy Chicken Soup

Dessert: Raspberry Cream Cheese Pops

Day 17

Breakfast: Easy Breakfast Tacos

Smoothie: Creamy Matcha Green Tea Smoothie

Lunch: Creamy Cauli Mac 'n' Cheese

Snacks: Smoked Salmon and Dill Spread

Dinner: Ginger Sesame Halibut

Dessert: Raspberry Cream Cheese Pops

Day 18

Breakfast: Easy Breakfast Tacos

Smoothie: Creamy Matcha Green Tea Smoothie

Lunch: Creamy Cauli Mac 'n' Cheese

Snacks: Smoked Salmon and Dill Spread

Dinner: Ginger Sesame Halibut

Dessert: Raspberry Cream Cheese Pops

Day 19

Breakfast: Bacon and Ricotta Breakfast Muffins

Smoothie: Peanut Butter Choco Smoothie

Lunch: Balsamic Herbed Pork Tenderloin

Snacks: Smoked Salmon and Dill Spread

Dinner: Hearty Beef and Mushroom Stew

Dessert: Coco Peanut Butter Bites

Day 20

Breakfast: Bacon and Ricotta Breakfast Muffins

Smoothie: Peanut Butter Choco Smoothie

Lunch: Balsamic Herbed Pork Tenderloin

Snacks: Coco Lime Fat Bombs

Dinner: Hearty Beef and Mushroom Stew

Dessert: Coco Peanut Butter Bites

Day 21

Breakfast: Bacon and Ricotta Breakfast Muffins

Smoothie: Strawberries and Cream Smoothie

Lunch: Sardine and Garden Salad

Snacks: Coco Lime Fat Bombs

Dinner: Goat Cheese and Smoked Onion Pizza

Dessert: Coco Peanut Butter Bites

Day 22

Breakfast: Keto Mini Waffles

Smoothie: Strawberries and Cream Smoothie

Lunch: Sardine and Garden Salad

Snacks: Coco Lime Fat Bombs

Dinner: Goat Cheese and Smoked Onion Pizza

Dessert: Cocoa Nibbles with Cream Cheese

Day 23

Breakfast: Keto Mini Waffles

Smoothie: Zesty Green Smoothie

Lunch: Herbed Parmesan Chicken Fingers

Snacks: Coco Lemon Fat Bombs

Dinner: Savory Butternut Squash Soup

Dessert: Cocoa Nibbles with Cream Cheese

Day 24

Breakfast: Bacon and Ricotta Breakfast Muffins

Smoothie: Zesty Green Smoothie

Lunch: Herbed Parmesan Chicken Fingers

Snacks: Coco Lemon Fat Bombs

Dinner: Savory Butternut Squash Soup

Dessert: Cocoa Nibbles with Cream Cheese

Day 25

Breakfast: Bacon and Ricotta Breakfast Muffins

Smoothie: Chia Seeds and Crisp Greens Smoothie

Lunch: Ham, Onion and Green Bean Salad

Snacks: Coco Lemon Fat Bombs

Dinner: Savory Butternut Squash Soup

Dessert: Creamy Vanilla Pudding

Day 26

Breakfast: Creamy Herbed Baked Eggs

Smoothie: Chia Seeds and Crisp Greens Smoothie

Lunch: Ham, Onion and Green Bean Salad

Snacks: Roasted Eggplant Spread

Dinner: Deviled Eggs with Chopped Bacon

Dessert: Creamy Vanilla Pudding

Day 27

Breakfast: Creamy Herbed Baked Eggs

Smoothie: Smooth Vanilla Smoothie

Lunch: Cheesy Avocado Beef Patties

Snacks: Choco Peanut Fat Bombs

Dinner: Deviled Eggs with Chopped Bacon

Dessert: Creamy Vanilla Pudding

Day 28

Breakfast: Keto Bread and Cinnamon Butter

Smoothie: Smooth Vanilla Smoothie

Lunch: Cheesy Avocado Beef Patties

Snacks: Cauli Cheddar Bites

Dinner: Deviled Eggs with Chopped Bacon

Dessert: Lemon Poppy Seed Cupcakes

Day 29

Breakfast: Keto Bread and Cinnamon Butter

Smoothie: Avocado Coco Smoothie

Lunch: Cheesy Sausage, Mushroom and Spaghetti Squash Casserole

Snacks: Cauli Cheddar Bites

Dinner: Keto Caesar Salad

Dessert: Lemon Poppy Seed Cupcakes

Day 30

Breakfast: Keto Bread and Cinnamon Butter

Smoothie: Avocado Coco Smoothie

Lunch: Cheesy Sausage, Mushroom and Spaghetti Squash Casserole

Snacks: Cauli Cheddar Bites

Dinner: Keto Caesar Salad

Dessert: Lemon Poppy Seed Cupcakes

# Chapter 3 – Keto Meal Prep Breakfast Recipes

### Recipe #1: Savory Cheddar Pancakes

*Number of Servings: 4*
*Serving Size: 2 pancakes*

*Prep Time: 15 minutes*
*Cook Time: 10 minutes*

Ingredients:
- 4 large egg whites
- 4 oz. grated cheddar cheese
- 2 cups almond meal
- 4 Tbsp. olive oil
- 1 Tbsp. chopped green onion
- 1 tsp. baking powder

Cooking Directions:
1. Combine the almond meal, water, grated cheddar cheese, green onion, and garlic in a large bowl. Mix well and set aside.
2. Whisk the egg whites in a separate bowl together with the baking powder, then add the almond meal mixture. Beat everything well until smooth.
3. Place a pancake griddle or nonstick skillet over medium high flame and heat through. Add a bit of the olive oil and swirl to coat.
4. Once hot, ladle in an eighth of the batter into the hot skillet and cook for 1 minute per side, or until set.

5. Transfer to a platter then repeat with the remaining batter. Place in an airtight container and refrigerate for up to 3 days. Reheat before serving.

*Nutritional Facts per Serving:*

| | | |
|---|---|---|
| Energy (calories) | 257 | kcal |
| Protein | 11 | g |
| Fat | 24 | g |
| Net Carbohydrates | 2 | g |
| Fiber | 0.1 | g |
| Sugars, total | 0.4 | g |

# Recipe #2: Chia Cinnamon Vanilla Granola

*Number of Servings: 6*
*Serving Size: ½ cup*

*Prep Time: 20 minutes*
*Cook Time: 25 minutes*

Ingredients:
- 56 grams whey protein powder
- 1 cup macadamia nuts
- ¼ cup water
- 4 Tbsp. flaxseed meal
- 4 Tbsp. whole chia seeds
- 4 Tbsp. coconut oil, melted
- 3 Tbsp. water
- 4 tsp. stevia
- 2 tsp. cinnamon
- 1 tsp. pure vanilla extract
- ¼ tsp. fine sea salt

Cooking Directions:
1. Set the oven to 350 degrees F to preheat. Line a baking sheet with baking paper and set aside.
2. Mix together the vanilla extract, water, and chia seeds in a large bowl. Set aside for 5 minutes, or until the mixture becomes gelatinous.
3. Pour the macadamia nuts into a food processor then add the flaxseed meal, protein powder, stevia, salt, and cinnamon. Pulse until the mixture is fine and the nuts are grounded.
4. Pour the gelatinous chia seed mixture into the food processor, then add about 1 ½ tablespoons of water

and the coconut oil. Blend until the mixture is smooth. Set aside.
5. Using a tablespoon, transfer the mixture onto the prepared baking sheet. Then, transfer to the oven and bake for 15 minutes.
6. Once baked, remove from the oven and break into small pieces. Spread out on the pan.
7. Bake for an additional 10 minutes, or until the granola is dry and golden brown. Set on a cooling rack and allow to cool completely.
8. Transfer to an airtight container and store for up to 1 week in the refrigerator. Best served with warm milk.

*Nutritional Facts per Serving:*

| | | |
|---|---|---|
| Energy (calories) | 336 | kcal |
| Protein | 9 | g |
| Fat | 31 | g |
| Net Carbohydrates | 11 | g |
| Fiber | 6 | g |
| Sugars, total | 1.3 | g |

# Recipe #3: Cheese and Sausage in Portobello Breakfast Burgers

*Number of Servings: 4*
*Serving Size: 1 patty*

*Prep Time: 25 minutes*
*Cook Time: 20 minutes*

Ingredients:
- 8 Portobello mushroom caps
- 4 slices American cheese, 2 oz. each
- ¼ cup breakfast sausage
- 4 Tbsp. olive oil

Cooking Directions:
1. Rinse the mushroom caps thoroughly, removing and discarding the stems and gills. Blot dry with paper towels and set aside.
2. Place a large cast iron skillet over medium flame and heat through. Once hot, add a quarter of the olive oil and swirl to coat.
3. Add two of the Portobello mushroom caps and cook for 5 minutes per side, or until browned all over. Transfer to a platter and repeat with the remaining mushroom caps. Set aside.
4. Divide the breakfast sausage into four patties.
5. Wipe the skillet clean and reheat over medium flame. Add half of the remaining olive oil and swirl to coat. Add two of the patties and cook for about 2 to 3 minutes per side, or until cooked through.
6. Add a slice of American cheese on each patty, then cover the pan and cook until the cheese is melted.

7. Slice the patties with the melted cheese into the mushroom caps. Repeat with the remaining patties and cheese slices until four patties have patties.
8. Cover the top of the mushroom caps with the other patties until you have four "burgers."
9. Wrap each "burger" in aluminum foil and refrigerate for up to 3 days, or freeze for up to 3 weeks. Reheat before serving.

*Nutritional Facts per Serving:*

| | | |
|---|---|---|
| Energy (calories) | 504 | kcal |
| Protein | 24 | g |
| Fat | 41 | g |
| Net Carbohydrates | 10 | g |
| Fiber | 3 | g |
| Sugars, total | 7 | g |

# Recipe #4: Cheesy Keto Quiche

*Number of Servings: 8*
*Serving Size: 1/8 of the recipe*

*Prep Time: 15 minutes*
*Cook Time: 1 hour*

Ingredients:
*For the Crust:*
- 2 large raw egg whites
- 1 cup almond flour
- 2/3 cup dry roasted macadamia nuts
- ¼ cup and 1 Tbsp. extra virgin olive oil
- ½ tsp. fine sea salt
- Nonstick cooking spray

*For the Filling:*
- 6 large eggs
- 1 cup 36 percent heavy cream
- ½ cup mild cheddar cheese
- Fine sea salt, to taste

Cooking Directions:
1. Set the oven to 350 degrees F to preheat. Lightly coat a 9-inch pie pan with nonstick cooking spray and set aside.
2. Prepare the crust a day ahead by combining all the ingredients in a bowl until the mixture turns into a dough. Transfer the dough onto the prepared pie pan and spread out until completely covered. If needed, transfer to the freezer and chill for 10 minutes to set.
3. Bake the crust for 25 minutes in the preheated oven until golden brown. Then, transfer to a cooling rack

and let cool completely. Cover and refrigerate until ready to cook the quiche.
4. Prepare the quiche filling by combining the eggs, cheese, and heavy cream in a large bowl. Add a pinch of salt and mix well until smooth.
5. Pour the mixture into the prepared pie crust. Bake for 25 minutes, or until the quiche is just set. Insert a toothpick in the center of the quiche; if it comes out clean, it is ready.
6. Place the quiche on a cooling rack and allow to set for about 10 minutes. Slice and serve. Store in the refrigerator in an airtight container for up to 3 days.

*Nutritional Facts per Serving:*

| | | |
|---|---|---|
| Energy (calories) | 166 | kcal |
| Protein | 2 | g |
| Fat | 17 | g |
| Net Carbohydrates | 2 | g |
| Fiber | 1 | g |
| Sugars, total | 0.94 | g |

# Recipe #5: Blueberry Breakfast Scones

*Number of Servings: 12*
*Serving Size: 1 scone*

*Prep Time: 10 minutes*
*Cook Time: 15 minutes*

Ingredients:
- 3 large eggs, beaten
- 1 ½ cups almond flour
- ¾ cup fresh or frozen raspberries
- ½ cup stevia
- 2 tsp. pure vanilla extract
- 2 tsp. baking powder

Cooking Directions:
1. Set the oven to 375 degrees F to preheat. Line a baking sheet with baking paper and set aside.
2. In a large mixing bowl, beat the eggs together with the stevia, vanilla extract, baking powder, and then almond flour.
3. Fold the raspberries into the batter until evenly combined.
4. Scoop the batter onto the prepared baking sheet, about 3 tablespoons per mound. Ensure there is at least 2 inches of space between each scone.
5. Bake the scones for 15 minutes, or until golden brown.
6. Transfer the scones to a cooling rack and allow to set for 10 minutes. Then, transfer to an airtight container and store in a cool dry place for up to 3 days, or refrigerate for up to 5 days. Reheat before serving.

*Nutritional Facts per Serving:*

| | | |
|---|---|---|
| Energy (calories) | 133 | kcal |
| Protein | 2 | g |
| Fat | 8 | g |
| Net Carbohydrates | 4 | g |
| Fiber | 2 | g |
| Sugars, total | 2 | g |

# Recipe #6: Cinnamon Coconut Porridge

*Number of Servings: 4*
*Serving Size: ½ cup*

*Prep Time: 5 minutes*
*Cook Time: 5 minutes*

Ingredients:
- 2 cups water
- 1 cup 36 percent heavy cream
- ½ cup unsweetened dried shredded coconut
- 2 Tbsp. oat bran
- 2 Tbsp. flaxseed meal
- 1 Tbsp. butter
- 1 ½ tsp. stevia
- 1 tsp. cinnamon
- Fine sea salt, to taste

Cooking Directions:
1. Combine all the ingredients in a small pot and mix well until smooth.
2. Place the pot over medium low flame and bring to a slow boil. Once boiling, stir well and remove from the heat.
3. Divide into four equal servings and set aside for 10 minutes to thicken. Best served warm. Store in mason jars, seal tightly, and refrigerate for up to 2 days.

*Nutritional Facts per Serving:*

| | | |
|---|---|---|
| Energy (calories) | 171 | kcal |
| Protein | 2 | g |
| Fat | 16 | g |
| Net Carbohydrates | 6 | g |
| Fiber | 2.5 | g |
| Sugars, total | 1.76 | g |

# Recipe #7: Easy Scotch Eggs

*Number of Servings: 6*
*Serving Size: 1 scotch egg*

*Prep Time: 15 minutes*
*Cook Time: 25 minutes*

Ingredients:
- 6 hardboiled eggs, peeled
- 1 ½ cups breakfast sausage
- 1 ½ tsp. garlic powder
- 1/3 tsp. fine sea salt
- ½ tsp. freshly ground black pepper

Cooking Directions:
1. Set the oven to 400 degrees F to preheat.
2. Spread a large sheet of baking paper on a clean dry surface.
3. Place the breakfast sausage in a large bowl and add the salt, pepper, and garlic powder. Mix well with clean hands.
4. Divide the breakfast sausage mixture into 6 equal balls and arrange on the sheet of baking paper. Flatten the sausage balls out, then place a hardboiled egg on top. Wrap the egg with the sausage mixture.
5. Arrange the sausage-coated eggs on a dry baking sheet and bake in the preheated oven for 25 minutes.
6. Arrange the scotch eggs on a cooling rack and let set for 5 minutes. Store in an airtight container and refrigerate for up to 4 days. Reheat before serving.

*Nutritional Facts per Serving:*

| | | |
|---|---|---|
| Energy (calories) | 258 | kcal |
| Protein | 17 | g |
| Fat | 21 | g |
| Net Carbohydrates | 1 | g |
| Fiber | 0 | g |
| Sugars, total | 1 | g |

# Recipe #8: Easy Breakfast Tacos

*Number of Servings: 2*
*Serving Size: ½ of the recipe*

*Prep Time: 10 minutes*
*Cook Time: 5 minutes*

Ingredients:
- 2 low carb tortillas, about 36 grams each
- 4 large eggs
- ½ avocado, pitted, peeled and sliced into thin pieces
- 2 Tbsp. mayonnaise
- 1 Tbsp. butter
- 4 fresh cilantro sprigs
- Tabasco sauce, to taste
- Sea salt, to taste
- Freshly ground black pepper, to taste

Cooking Directions:
1. Whisk the eggs in a bowl until smooth. Set aside.
2. Place a nonstick skillet over medium flame and heat through. Once hot, add the butter and swirl to coat.
3. Add the egg and tilt until the eggs are spread out. Cook until done, then transfer to a bowl. Set aside.
4. Warm the tortillas over low flame, then place on a platter and spread the mayonnaise on one side of each tortilla.
5. Divide the egg between the two tortillas, then add the sliced avocado, and cilantro. Season with salt and pepper, then add the pepper sauce. Roll up the tortillas and serve.
6. To store, add lime juice all over the avocado first before placing in the tortilla. Wrap tightly in aluminum foil

and store in the freezer for up to 1 day. Reheat in a toaster oven before serving.

*Nutritional Facts per Serving:*

| | | |
|---|---|---|
| Energy (calories) | 289 | kcal |
| Protein | 7 | g |
| Fat | 27 | g |
| Net Carbohydrates | 6 | g |
| Fiber | 4 | g |
| Sugars, total | 0.67 | g |

# Recipe #9: Bacon and Ricotta Breakfast Muffins

*Number of Servings: 6*
*Serving Size: 2 muffins*

*Prep Time: 15 minutes*
*Cook Time: 30 minutes*

Ingredients:
- 2 large eggs
- 1 lb. ricotta cheese
- 10 oz. baby spinach, rinsed and drained thoroughly
- 7 oz. bacon
- 2 oz. chopped toasted pine nuts
- 1 cup freshly grated Parmesan cheese
- ½ cup thick plain Greek yogurt
- Sea salt, to taste
- Freshly ground black pepper, to taste
- Nonstick cooking spray, as needed

Cooking Directions:
1. Set the oven to 350 degrees F to preheat. Lightly coat a 12 cup muffin tin with nonstick cooking spray and set aside.
2. Bring a saucepan of water to a boil, then add the spinach and blanch for 30 minutes, or until wilted. Drain well and set aside in a colander.
3. Meanwhile, dice the bacon and set aside.
4. Once the spinach is drained, finely chop then transfer to a large bowl. Add the ricotta cheese, pine nuts, Parmesan cheese, yogurt, eggs, and bacon. Mix very well until evenly combined.

5. Divide the mixture among the muffin cups, then bake for 30 minutes or until golden brown.
6. Place on a cooling rack and allow to cool slightly. Store in an airtight container and refrigerate for up to 3 days, or freeze for up to 3 weeks. Reheat in the microwave before serving.

*Nutritional Facts per Serving:*

| | | |
|---|---|---|
| Energy (calories) | 440 | kcal |
| Protein | 27 | g |
| Fat | 29 | g |
| Net Carbohydrates | 22 | g |
| Fiber | 4 | g |
| Sugars, total | 3 | g |

# Recipe #10: Keto Mini Waffles

*Number of Servings: 8*
*Serving Size: 1 waffle*

*Prep Time: 15 minutes*
*Cook Time: 10 minutes*

Ingredients:
- 2 large eggs
- ½ cup almond flour
- 4 Tbsp. full fat sour cream
- 2 Tbsp. melted grass-fed butter
- 4 tsp. arrowroot flour
- 2 tsp. cider vinegar
- 1 ½ tsp. stevia
- ¼ tsp. baking powder
- ¼ tsp. baking soda
- 1/8 tsp. xanthan gum
- 1/8 tsp. fine sea salt

Cooking Directions:
1. Combine the sour cream, egg, and vinegar with the melted butter in a bowl. Mix well.
2. Sift the dry ingredients into the sour cream and egg mixture. Then, stir gently until smooth.
3. Preheat a mini-waffle iron set on low. Once hot, cook the batter into 8 mini-waffles (or 4 regular-sized waffles) until firm.
4. Transfer to a tray and serve warm. May be stored in the freezer for up to 2 weeks. Reheat in the waffle iron before serving.

*Nutritional Facts per Serving:*

| | | |
|---|---|---|
| Energy (calories) | 49 | kcal |
| Protein | 1 | g |
| Fat | 4 | g |
| Net Carbohydrates | 2 | g |
| Fiber | 0.1 | g |
| Sugars, total | 0.06 | g |

# Recipe #11: Creamy Herbed Baked Eggs

*Number of Servings: 4*
*Serving Size: ¼ of the recipe*

*Prep Time: 10 minutes*
*Cook Time: 20 minutes*

Ingredients:
- 4 large eggs
- 60 grams 36 percent heavy cream
- 2 Tbsp. grass-fed butter, at room temperature
- 4 tsp. chopped fresh parsley
- 4 tsp. chopped fresh chives
- Sea salt, to taste
- Freshly ground black pepper, to taste

Cooking Directions:
1. Set the oven to 350 degrees F to preheat. Use 1 tablespoon of butter to coat four 1-cup ovenproof ramekins.
2. Crack an egg into each ramekin, then divide the heavy cream among them. Top with the fresh parsley and chives. Season with salt and pepper.
3. Arrange the ramekins on a baking sheet and bake for 20 minutes, or until the eggs are set.
4. Transfer to a cooling rack and let stand for 5 minutes before serving. To store, cover with aluminum foil and refrigerate for up to 2 days. Reheat in the microwave before serving.

*Nutritional Facts per Serving:*

| | | |
|---|---|---|
| Energy (calories) | 158 | kcal |
| Protein | 3 | g |
| Fat | 16 | g |
| Net Carbohydrates | 1 | g |
| Fiber | 0.1 | g |
| Sugars, total | 0.5 | g |

# Recipe #12: Keto Bread

*Number of Servings: 6*
*Serving Size: 1/6 of the recipe*

*Prep Time: 1 hour and 30 minutes*
*Cook Time: 1 hour*

Ingredients:
- 3 large eggs
- 1/3 cup full fat cream cheese, at room temperature
- 4 ½ Tbsp. flaxseed meal
- 1 ½ Tbsp. and 1 ½ tsp. melted coconut oil
- 6 tsp. psyllium powder
- 3 tsp. coconut flour
- 3 tsp. cider vinegar
- 3 tsp. warm water
- 2 ¼ tsp. stevia
- 1/3 tsp. baking soda
- 1/3 tsp. baking powder
- 1/6 tsp. xanthan gum
- 1/6 tsp. fine sea salt

Cooking Directions:
1. Set the oven to 350 degrees F to preheat. Cover a baking sheet with baking paper and set aside.
2. Mix together all the dry ingredients in a bowl very well, then set aside.
3. In a separate bowl, whisk together all the wet ingredients. Then, gradually mix in the dry ingredients until smooth.
4. Divide the mixture into six equal sized rolls then arrange on the prepared baking sheet. Cover with a

clean kitchen towel and let rise for about 30 minutes to an hour.

5. Once the rolls have risen to double their size, bake the rolls for 40 minutes. Insert a toothpick in the center of one roll; if it comes out clean, it is ready.
6. Transfer the rolls on a cooling rack and allow to cool slightly. Best served right away. May be stored for up to 3 days in an airtight container away from direct sunlight.

*Nutritional Facts per Serving:*

| | | |
|---|---|---|
| Energy (calories) | 106 | kcal |
| Protein | 4 | g |
| Fat | 9 | g |
| Net Carbohydrates | 4 | g |
| Fiber | 2 | g |
| Sugars, total | 1 | g |

# Chapter 4 – Keto Meal Prep Lunch Recipes

## Recipe #1: Savory Beef Balls with Asian Style Dip

*Number of Servings: 5*
*Serving Size: 6 meatballs*

*Prep Time: 15 minutes*
*Cook Time: 15 minutes*

Ingredients:
- 1 lb. organic ground beef
- 1 large egg
- 1 small red onion, peeled and minced
- 2 garlic cloves, peeled and minced
- ½ tsp. sea salt
- Freshly ground black pepper, to taste

*For the Sauce:*
- 1 garlic clove, peeled and minced
- ¼ cup light soy sauce
- 2 Tbsp. rice wine vinegar
- 1 Tbsp. freshly grated ginger
- 1 Tbsp. chopped green onion
- Liquid stevia, to taste
- Nonstick cooking spray, as needed

Cooking Directions:
1. Set the oven to 425 degrees F to preheat. Lightly coat a baking sheet with nonstick cooking spray and set aside.

2. Place the ground beef in a large mixing bowl and add the egg, onion, salt, garlic, and a generous pinch of black pepper. Mix everything well with clean hands.
3. Make about 40 1-inch sized balls from the meat mixture and arrange them on the prepared baking sheet.
4. Bake the meatballs in the preheated oven for about 12 minutes, or until browned all over but still moist.
5. While the meatballs are cooking, combine all the sauce ingredients in a dipping bowl and stir well.
6. Once the meatballs are cooked, transfer them to an airtight container and allow to cool slightly before sealing. Store the dipping sauce in a separate airtight container.
7. Refrigerate the meatballs and sauce for up to 3 days, or freeze for up to 3 weeks. Reheat before serving.

*Nutritional Facts per Serving:*

| | | |
|---|---|---|
| Energy (calories) | 238 | kcal |
| Protein | 24 | g |
| Fat | 14 | g |
| Net Carbohydrates | 3 | g |
| Fiber | 0.4 | g |
| Sugars, total | 0.8 | g |

# Recipe #2: Chicken Curry with Oil-Roasted Peanuts

*Number of Servings: 3*
*Serving Size: 1/3 of the recipe*

*Prep Time: 15 minutes*
*Cook Time: 20 minutes*

Ingredients:
- 1 garlic clove, peeled and minced
- 7.5 oz. full fat unsweetened coconut milk
- ½ lb. chicken breast, sliced into thin strips
- ¼ cup diced yellow onion
- ¼ cup water
- ¼ cup oil roasted peanuts
- 2 Tbsp. chopped fresh cilantro
- 1 ½ Tbsp. melted coconut oil
- 1 ½ Tbsp. melted palm oil
- ½ Tbsp. curry powder
- 1 tsp. minced fresh ginger
- Sea salt, to taste
- Red pepper flakes, to taste

Cooking Directions:
1. Place a saucepan over medium flame and add the coconut and palm oil. Swirl to combine.
2. Stir in the onion and curry powder then sauté until the onions are tender.
3. Stir in the sliced chicken and sauté until the chicken is cooked through. Then, add the ginger and garlic and sauté until fragrant.
4. Add the water and coconut milk then bring to a boil.

5. Once boiling, reduce to simmer and stir in the peanuts. Continue to simmer until the curry is thickened and the chicken is completely cooked.
6. Remove the curry from heat and stir in the cilantro. Season to taste with salt and red pepper flakes.
7. Divide between two airtight containers and allow to cool slightly. Cover and refrigerate for up to 3 days. Reheat before serving.

*Nutritional Facts per Serving:*

| | | |
|---|---|---|
| Energy (calories) | 586 | kcal |
| Protein | 18 | g |
| Fat | 56 | g |
| Net Carbohydrates | 6 | g |
| Fiber | 2 | g |
| Sugars, total | 3 | g |

# Recipe #3: Baked Parmesan Chicken Nuggets in Mozzarella Marinara Sauce

*Number of Servings: 6*
*Serving Size: 4 nuggets*

*Prep Time: 20 minutes*
*Cook Time: 45 minutes*

Ingredients:
- 1 lb. finely minced chicken breast
- 3 oz. fresh mozzarella cheese
- 1 cup almond flour
- 1 cup marinara sauce, no sugar added
- ½ cup full cream milk
- ½ cup freshly grated Parmesan cheese
- 1 tsp. fine sea salt
- ½ tsp. dried oregano
- Freshly ground black pepper, to taste
- Nonstick cooking spray, as needed

Cooking Directions:
1. Set the oven to 350 degrees F to preheat. Lightly coat a large baking dish and set aside.
2. In a large mixing bowl, combine half the almond flour with the milk, parmesan cheese, salt, and a pinch of black pepper. Mix everything well.
3. Add the minced chicken into the almond flour mixture and mix well until evenly combined.
4. Divide the mixture into 24 equal balls then dredge the balls in the reserved almond flour.
5. Arrange the balls on the prepared baking dish, then bake for 10 minutes.

6. After 10 minutes, turn over the balls and bake for an additional 10 minutes.
7. Once the balls are baked, pour the marinara sauce over them then dot with pieces of mozzarella cheese.
8. Bake for an additional 12 to 15 minutes, or until the cheese is melted.
9. Remove from the oven and top with dried oregano.
10. Allow to cool slightly, then cover and refrigerate for up to 3 days. Reheat before serving.

*Nutritional Facts per Serving:*

| | | |
|---|---|---|
| Energy (calories) | 282 | kcal |
| Protein | 33 | g |
| Fat | 12 | g |
| Net Carbohydrates | 11 | g |
| Fiber | 3 | g |
| Sugars, total | 4 | g |

# Recipe #4: Zucchini Beef Lasagna

*Number of Servings: 10*
*Serving Size: 1/10 of the recipe*

*Prep Time: 20 minutes*
*Cook Time: 1 hour*

Ingredients:
- 2 large zucchinis
- 1 large yellow onion, chopped
- 2 garlic cloves, peeled and minced
- 1 lb. 75 percent lean ground beef
- 2 cups no sugar organic pasta sauce
- 1 cup ricotta cheese
- ½ cup shredded Parmesan cheese
- 8 Tbsp. shredded mozzarella cheese
- 2 Tbsp. chopped fresh oregano
- 2 Tbsp. olive oil
- 1 Tbsp. chopped fresh basil
- ¼ tsp. fine sea salt
- ¼ tsp. freshly ground black pepper

Cooking Directions:
1. Set the oven to 375 degrees F to preheat.
2. Place a saucepan over medium high flame and heat through. Once hot, add the olive oil and swirl to coat.
3. Sauté the onion in the saucepan until tender, then stir in the garlic and sauté until fragrant.
4. Add the ground beef to the saucepan and stir, breaking up, until browned all over.
5. Stir in the pasta sauce then bring to a simmer. Once simmering, reduce to low flame and stir in the basil, oregano, and salt. Mix well then set aside.

6. Halve the zucchinis lengthwise, then slice into extra thin strips, about 1/8 inch thick.
7. Arrange 6 zucchini slices on the bottom of the baking dish, then add a quarter of the meat sauce on top. Add ¼ cup of the ricotta cheese with 2 tablespoons or mozzarella cheese. Repeat, ensuring the zucchini slices crisscross.
8. Once the lasagna is assembled, top with Parmesan cheese and black pepper. Bake in the oven for 1 hour, or until the top is browned and bubbling.
9. Carefully remove the lasagna from the oven and place on the kitchen counter. Allow to set for about 15 minutes, then slice into 10 equal servings.
10. Allow to cool slightly, then cover and refrigerate for up to 4 days. Reheat before serving.

*Nutritional Facts per Serving:*

| | | |
|---|---|---|
| Energy (calories) | 366 | kcal |
| Protein | 46 | g |
| Fat | 15 | g |
| Net Carbohydrates | 12 | g |
| Fiber | 4 | g |
| Sugars, total | 6 | g |

# Recipe #5: Chicken Bell Pepper Kebabs

*Number of Servings: 4*
*Serving Size: 2 kebabs*

*Prep Time: 15 minutes*
*Cook Time: 12 minutes*

Ingredients:
- 2 lbs. boneless and skinless chicken breasts
- 3 garlic cloves, peeled and crushed
- 1 large red bell pepper, stemmed, seeded, and sliced into bite-sized chunks
- 1 large green bell pepper, stemmed, seeded, and sliced into bite-sized chunks
- ¾ cup olive oil
- 2 ½ Tbsp. freshly squeezed lemon juice
- 1 Tbsp. chopped fresh parsley
- 2 ½ tsp. freshly grated lemon zest
- Sea salt, to taste
- Freshly ground black pepper, to taste

Cooking Directions:
1. If using wooden skewers, then soak in ice water.
2. Rinse the chicken breasts thoroughly then blot dry with paper towels and set aside.
3. Chop the chicken breasts into bite-sized chunks then set aside.
4. Combine ¼ cup of the olive oil with the crushed garlic, and lemon zest. Mix well, then stir in the parsley with a pinch of salt and pepper. Mix well.
5. Place the chicken cubes into the mixture and toss several times to coat. Once mixed, cover and refrigerate for up to 12 hours to marinate.

6. Once ready to cook, combine the remaining olive oil with the lemon juice then season to taste with salt and pepper.
7. Set the broiler or grill to medium to preheat.
8. Skewer the chicken and bell peppers, alternating the three. Then, coat the kebabs in the lemon and olive oil mixture.
9. Broil the skewered chicken and pepper for 10 minutes, turning and basting occasionally. Once the chicken is cooked and the bell peppers are browned, transfer to a platter.
10. Allow the chicken and bell pepper kebabs to cool slightly, then store in an airtight container and refrigerate for up to 3 days. Reheat before serving.

*Nutritional Facts per Serving:*

| | | |
|---|---|---|
| Energy (calories) | 287 | kcal |
| Protein | 52 | g |
| Fat | 20 | g |
| Net Carbohydrates | 4 | g |
| Fiber | 0.5 | g |
| Sugars, total | 1.4 | g |

# Recipe #6: Easy Grilled Shrimp with Avocado, Tomato and Onion Salad

*Number of Servings: 6*
*Serving Size: 1/6 of the recipe*

*Prep Time: 20 minutes*
*Cook Time: 5 minutes*

Ingredients:
- 2 avocados, pitted, peeled and cubed
- 2 lb. shrimp, peeled and deveined
- ½ cup chopped tomato
- ½ cup chopped bell pepper
- ½ cup chopped onion
- 4 Tbsp. olive oil
- 2 tsp. freshly squeezed lime juice
- 1 tsp. garlic powder
- 1 tsp. fine sea salt
- ¼ tsp. freshly ground black pepper

Cooking Directions:
1. Place a grill over medium high flame and heat through.
2. Meanwhile, combine the garlic powder, half the salt and pepper, and olive oil in a large bowl. Add the shrimp and toss well to coat. Set aside.
3. In a salad bowl, combine the bell pepper, tomato, onion, avocado, and lime juice. Season with the remaining salt and toss gently to coat. Cover and refrigerate until ready to serve.
4. Cook the shrimp in the hot grill for 3 minutes per side, or until cooked through.

5. Divide the shrimp into individual servings, followed by the salad. Cover and refrigerate for up to 3 days. Reheat the shrimp before serving.

*Nutritional Facts per Serving:*

| | | |
|---|---|---|
| Energy (calories) | 409 | kcal |
| Protein | 36 | g |
| Fat | 25 | g |
| Net Carbohydrates | 11 | g |
| Fiber | 5 | g |
| Sugars, total | 5 | g |

# Recipe #7: Mediterranean Style Tuna Salad

*Number of Servings: 6*
*Serving Size: ½ cup*

*Prep Time: 15 minutes*

Ingredients:
- 300 grams endives, leaves separated
- 15 oz. solid white albacore tuna packed in oil, drained
- 1 ½ cups crumbled feta cheese
- ¾ cup extra virgin olive oil
- ¾ cup diced roasted red peppers
- 1/3 cup quartered green olives
- 1/3 cup chopped fresh parsley
- 1 ½ Tbsp. freshly squeezed lemon juice
- 1 ½ Tbsp. drained capers
- Red pepper flakes, to taste
- Fine sea salt, to taste
- Freshly ground black pepper, to taste

Cooking Directions:
1. Place the tuna in a bowl and crumble. Fold in the feta cheese, roasted red peppers, green olives, capers, parsley, lemon juice, and olive oil. Mix well.
2. Season the tuna mixture to taste with salt, pepper, and red pepper flakes then mix well to combine.
3. Divide the salad into six equal portions in airtight containers then add the endive leaves. Cover and refrigerate for up to 3 days. Serve chilled.

*Nutritional Facts per Serving:*

| | | |
|---|---|---|
| Energy (calories) | 352 | kcal |
| Protein | 25 | g |
| Fat | 26 | g |
| Net Carbohydrates | 5 | g |
| Fiber | 2 | g |
| Sugars, total | 3 | g |

# Recipe #8: Creamy Cauli Mac 'n' Cheese

*Number of Servings: 4*
*Serving Size: ¼ of the recipe*

*Prep Time: 10 minutes*
*Cook Time: 30 minutes*

Ingredients:
- 1 small cauliflower head, chopped into small florets
- ½ cup heavy cream
- ½ cup shredded Cheddar cheese
- ¼ cup shredded mozzarella cheese
- ¼ cup shredded Parmesan cheese
- ¼ cup cubed cream cheese
- ½ tsp. fine sea salt
- ¼ tsp. minced garlic
- 1/8 tsp. freshly ground black pepper
- Nonstick cooking spray, as needed

Cooking Directions:
1. Set the oven to 400 degrees F to preheat.
2. Fill a small pot with water, cover and place over high flame. Bring to a boil, then add ¼ teaspoon of salt.
3. Add the cauliflower florets to the boiling water, then boil for about 3 minutes. Drain then place on a platter lined with paper towels and set aside.
4. Place a skillet over medium flame and add the heavy cream. Bring to a simmer, then stir in the cream cheese until smooth.
5. Stir in the Cheddar cheese, garlic, and mozzarella cheese, then stir until melted.

6. Turn off the heat and mix in the cauliflower. Stir until the cauliflower is completely coated. Season with salt and pepper.
7. Lightly coat a small baking dish with nonstick cooking spray. Add the cauliflower and cheese mixture, then sprinkle the Parmesan cheese on top.
8. Bake the mac and cheese for 15 minutes, or until the top is golden brown.
9. Place on a cooling rack and allow to cool slightly. Slice into four equal servings, then cover and refrigerate for up to 3 days. Reheat before serving.

*Nutritional Facts per Serving:*

| | | |
|---|---|---|
| Energy (calories) | 198 | kcal |
| Protein | 10 | g |
| Fat | 17 | g |
| Net Carbohydrates | 3 | g |
| Fiber | 0.9 | g |
| Sugars, total | 2 | g |

# Recipe #9: Balsamic Herbed Pork Tenderloin

*Number of Servings: 2*
*Serving Size: ½ of the recipe*

*Prep Time: 15 minutes*
*Cook Time: 20 minutes*

Ingredients:
- ¾ lb. pork tenderloin, sliced into 1 ½ inch thick medallions
- 1 garlic clove, peeled and minced
- 1 small shallot, minced
- 3 Tbsp. butter
- 2 Tbsp. balsamic vinegar
- 1 ½ Tbsp. olive oil
- ¾ tsp. soy sauce
- 3 fresh rosemary sprigs
- 3 fresh thyme sprigs
- Sea salt, to taste
- Freshly ground black pepper, to taste

Cooking Directions:
1. Set the oven to 475 degrees F to preheat.
2. Blot the pork medallions dry with paper towels then season with salt and pepper.
3. Place an ovenproof skillet over medium high flame and heat through. Once hot, add the olive oil and ¾ tablespoon of butter then swirl to coat.
4. Add the garlic and shallot then sauté until fragrant. Add the pork medallions and sear for 2 minutes per side.

5. Stir in the balsamic vinegar, soy sauce, thyme, rosemary, and remaining butter. Stir well to combine, then spoon the mixture over the pork.
6. Simmer for 2 minutes, then bake for 5 minutes.
7. After 5 minutes, turn over the pork medallions and cook for an added 5 minutes, or until the internal temperature of the pork is 150 degrees F.
8. Transfer the pork to a platter and let rest for 3 minutes. Then, divide into individual servings and spoon the sauce on top. Cover and refrigerate for up to 3 days.

*Nutritional Facts per Serving:*

| | | |
|---|---|---|
| Energy (calories) | 508 | kcal |
| Protein | 45 | g |
| Fat | 34 | g |
| Net Carbohydrates | 4 | g |
| Fiber | 0.1 | g |
| Sugars, total | 3 | g |

# Recipe #10: Keto Squash-getti with Herbed Meatballs

*Number of Servings: 6*
*Serving Size: 1/6 of the recipe*

*Prep Time: 20 minutes*
*Cook Time: 30 minutes*

Ingredients:
- 1 extra large or 2 medium spaghetti squash
- ¾ cup chopped fresh parsley
- 4 ½ Tbsp. water
- 3 Tbsp. olive oil

*For the Herbed Meatballs*
- 2 garlic cloves, peeled and minced
- ¾ lb. lean ground beef, 80 percent
- ¾ lb. ground pork
- 1 ½ cup organic pasta sauce, no sugar added
- ¾ cup shredded Parmesan cheese
- 3 Tbsp. chopped fresh oregano
- 3 Tbsp. chopped fresh basil
- ¾ tsp. onion powder
- 1/3 tsp. fine sea salt
- 1/3 tsp. freshly ground black pepper

Cooking Directions:
1. Halve the spaghetti squash lengthwise. Scoop out and discard the seeds, then place on a microwaveable dish, cut side face down. Microwave for 12 minutes on high.
2. Carefully scoop out the squash mixture from the shells using a large fork and transfer to a bowl.

3. Place a skillet over medium high flame and heat through. Add 1 ½ tablespoons of olive oil and swirl to coat.
4. Add the squash and stir well until browned. Transfer to a bowl and fold in 1/3 cup of parsley. Set aside.
5. Pour the remaining parsley in a large bowl, then mix in the pork, beef, oregano, basil, garlic, onion powder, 1/3 cup of the Parmesan cheese, and salt and pepper. Mix well with clean hands.
6. Divide the mixture into 18 equal sized balls, then arrange on a platter.
7. Place a heavy duty skillet over medium high flame and heat through. Once hot, add the remaining olive oil and swirl to coat.
8. Cook the meatballs, in batches, if needed, for 2 minutes per side, or until cooked through.
9. Once all the meatballs are cooked, return them all to the skillet and add the pasta sauce. Bring to a simmer, then stir and reduce to low flame. Simmer for 15 minutes.
10. Divide the spaghetti squash into individual servings then divide the meatballs as well. Sprinkle with the remaining Parmesan cheese, then let cool slightly. Cover and refrigerate for up to 3 days. Reheat before serving.

*Nutritional Facts per Serving:*

| | | |
|---|---|---|
| Energy (calories) | 460 | kcal |
| Protein | 43 | g |
| Fat | 28 | g |
| Net Carbohydrates | 11 | g |
| Fiber | 1 | g |
| Sugars, total | 9 | g |

# Recipe #11: Sardine and Garden Salad

*Number of Servings: 3*
*Serving Size: 1/3 of the recipe*

*Prep Time: 15 minutes*

Ingredients:
- 1 cucumber, quartered and diced
- 2 large tomatoes, diced
- 1 small red onion, peeled and minced
- 2 sardine fillets packed in oil, drained and chopped
- 2 sardine fillets packed in oil, drained
- 2 cups arugula leaves, chopped
- ¼ cup chopped fresh flat leaf parsley

*For the dressing:*
- 2 Tbsp. extra virgin olive oil
- ½ Tbsp. freshly squeezed lemon juice
- Sea salt, to taste
- Freshly ground black pepper, to taste

Cooking Directions:
1. Combine the ingredients for the dressing in a bowl and set aside.
2. Toss together the chopped sardines, vegetables, and herbs in a bowl. Mix well, then divide into individual servings.
3. Divide the whole sardine fillets among the servings.
4. Drizzle the dressing over the salads, then cover and refrigerate for up to 3 days.

*Nutritional Facts per Serving:*

| | | |
|---|---|---|
| Energy (calories) | 150 | kcal |
| Protein | 6 | g |
| Fat | 11 | g |
| Net Carbohydrates | 8 | g |
| Fiber | 2 | g |
| Sugars, total | 5 | g |

# Recipe #12: Herbed Parmesan Chicken Fingers

*Number of Servings: 6*
*Serving Size: 4 chicken fingers*

*Prep Time: 15 minutes*
*Cook Time: 30 minutes*

Ingredients:
- 2 lbs. boneless and skinless chicken breast
- 4 garlic cloves, peeled and chopped
- 4 oz. butter
- 1 cup freshly grated Parmesan cheese
- 2 Tbsp. chopped fresh thyme
- 1 tsp. chili pepper flakes
- Sea salt, to taste
- Freshly ground black pepper, to taste
- Nonstick cooking spray

Cooking Directions:
1. Set the oven to 350 degrees F to preheat. Lightly coat a baking sheet with nonstick cooking spray and set aside.
2. Place a saucepan over medium flame and heat through. Add the butter and swirl to melt.
3. Stir the garlic into the saucepan and sauté until fragrant. Remove from heat and set aside for 15 minutes.
4. Combine the thyme, Parmesan cheese, chili pepper, and a pinch of salt and pepper. Stir well to combine then set aside.
5. Rinse the chicken breast thoroughly then blot dry with paper towels. Slice into 24 fingers, then coat in the garlic butter mixture.

6. Dredge the chicken fingers in the cheesy mixture then arrange on the prepared baking sheet.
7. Bake for 25 to 30 minutes, or until the chicken fingers are golden brown and cooked through.
8. Transfer the chicken fingers to a cooling rack and allow to cool completely. Store in an airtight container and refrigerate for up to 3 days. Reheat before serving.

*Nutritional Facts per Serving:*

| | | |
|---|---|---|
| Energy (calories) | 370 | kcal |
| Protein | 40 | g |
| Fat | 20 | g |
| Net Carbohydrates | 6 | g |
| Fiber | 0.2 | g |
| Sugars, total | 0.2 | g |

# Recipe #13: Ham, Onion and Green Bean Salad

*Number of Servings: 3*
*Serving Size: 1/3 of the recipe*

*Prep Time: 15 minutes*

Ingredients:
- ½ lb. trimmed green beans, steamed
- 1 small white onion, peeled and minced
- 1 roasted red bell pepper, drained and diced
- 1 oz. Spanish ham, chopped
- 1 small hardboiled egg, chopped
- 2 ½ Tbsp. fresh flat leaf parsley
- 2 Tbsp. extra virgin olive oil
- 1 ½ Tbsp. red wine vinegar
- Sea salt, to taste
- Freshly ground black pepper, to taste

Cooking Directions:
1. Rinse and drain the steamed green beans. Blot dry with paper towels and set aside.
2. Combine the olive oil, vinegar, and a dash of salt and pepper. Mix well.
3. Divide the green beans into individual servings, followed by the minced onion, ham, peppers, egg, and parsley. Add the dressing.
4. Cover and refrigerate for up to 2 days. Reheat before serving, if desired.

*Nutritional Facts per Serving:*

| | | |
|---|---|---|
| Energy (calories) | 102 | kcal |
| Protein | 4 | g |
| Fat | 8 | g |
| Net Carbohydrates | 5 | g |
| Fiber | 2 | g |
| Sugars, total | 2 | g |

# Recipe #14: Cheesy Avocado Beef Patties

*Number of Servings: 2*
*Serving Size: 1 patty*

*Prep Time: 15 minutes*
*Cook Time: 10 minutes*

Ingredients:
- ½ lb. 85 percent lean ground beef
- 1 small avocado, pitted and peeled
- 2 slices yellow cheddar cheese
- Sea salt, to taste
- Freshly ground black pepper, to taste

Cooking Directions:
1. Preheat the broiler or grill to high.
2. Divide the ground beef into two equal sized patties. Season with salt and pepper.
3. Grill or broil the beef patties for about 5 minutes per side, or until cooked through.
4. Transfer the patties to a platter and add the cheese. To store, wrap in aluminum foil and refrigerate for up to 3 days.
5. Right before serving, reheat the burger patty in a microwave oven. Slice the avocado into thin strips and place on top of the patty. Serve warm, preferably with a light, low carb salad.

*Nutritional Facts per Serving:*

| | | |
|---|---|---|
| Energy (calories) | 568 | kcal |
| Protein | 38 | g |
| Fat | 43 | g |
| Net Carbohydrates | 9 | g |
| Fiber | 7 | g |
| Sugars, total | 0.74 | g |

# Recipe #15: Cheesy Sausage, Mushroom and Spaghetti Squash Casserole

*Number of Servings: 10*
*Serving Size: 1/10 of the recipe*

*Prep Time: 30 minutes*
*Cook Time: 1 ½ hours*

Ingredients:
- 1 large spaghetti squash
- 1 large onion, peeled and minced
- ½ lb. lean organic ground beef, 80 percent
- ½ lb. Italian sausage
- ½ lb. chicken or turkey sausage
- ½ lb. sliced mushrooms
- 18 oz. diced tomatoes
- 8 oz. freshly grated Parmesan cheese
- 6 oz. organic tomato paste
- 4 oz. mozzarella cheese
- 4 oz. ricotta cheese
- ½ cup butter
- ½ cup red wine
- ½ tsp. sea salt
- ½ tsp. freshly ground black pepper

Cooking Directions:
1. Set the oven to 350 degrees F to preheat.
2. Pierce the spaghetti squash all over with a sharp then place in the microwave and microwave on high for about 20 minutes. set aside to cool.

3. Melt the butter in a skillet over medium high flame. Sauté the ground beef and sausages until cooked through and crumbled.
4. Add the red wine and simmer until liquid is reduced. Then, stir in the onion and garlic. Sauté until tender.
5. Add the mushrooms and sauté until tender. Stir in the diced tomatoes, tomato paste, and seasonings. Sauté until combined.
6. Halve the spaghetti squash and scrape out the flesh. Set aside.
7. Spread half the spaghetti squash in a baking dish then add 2 ounces each of the mozzarella and ricotta, followed by 4 ounces of the Parmesan.
8. Spoon some tomato sauce on top, then add the remaining spaghetti squash. Add the remaining cheeses, then cover the dish.
9. Bake for 20 minutes, then uncover and bake for an additional 20 minutes.
10. Set the oven to broil and broil the casserole for 3 minutes, or until the top is browned and crisp.
11. Place on a cooling rack and let set for 15 minutes. Slice into 10 equal servings, then cover and refrigerate for up to 5 days. Reheat before serving.

*Nutritional Facts per Serving:*

| | | |
|---|---|---|
| Energy (calories) | 402 | kcal |
| Protein | 31 | g |
| Fat | 24 | g |
| Net Carbohydrates | 15 | g |
| Fiber | 2 | g |
| Sugars, total | 2 | g |

# Chapter 5 – Keto Meal Prep Dinner Recipes

## Recipe #1: Deviled Eggs with Chopped Bacon

*Number of Servings: 6*
*Serving Size: 3 stuffed halved eggs*

*Prep Time: 5 minutes*
*Cook Time: 15 minutes*

Ingredients:
- 9 large eggs
- 6 bacon slices, chopped
- 2 ¼ Tbsp. mayonnaise
- 1 ½ Tbsp. mustard
- ¾ tsp. paprika
- 1/6 tsp. fine sea salt
- 1/6 tsp. freshly ground black pepper

Cooking Directions:
1. Place the eggs in a pot and add enough water to cover them by about an inch. Cover and place over high flame. Bring to a boil.
2. Once boiling, reduce to a simmer, then simmer for 3 minutes. Turn off the heat and keep the eggs in the hot water.
3. Meanwhile, place a large skillet over medium high flame and heat through. Once hot, add the bacon and cook until crisp.
4. Transfer the bacon to a plate lined with paper towels and allow to drain.

5. Take the eggs out of the water and transfer to a basin of cold water. Once cool to the touch, carefully peel them.
6. Halve the hardboiled eggs carefully then scoop out the yolks and place in a bowl. Arrange the halves, cut side facing up, on a platter and set aside.
7. Mash the yolks together with the mustard, mayonnaise, salt, and pepper. Add 1/3 teaspoon of the paprika and mix well.
8. Dice the drained crispy bacon. Pour 1/3 cup of the chopped bacon into the bowl of yolk mixture and stir well.
9. Spoon the yolk mixture among the halved egg whites, then divide the reserved bacon among them.
10. Sprinkle with paprika and serve. Store the extra devilled eggs in an airtight container and refrigerate for up to 3 days.

*Nutritional Facts per Serving:*

| | | |
|---|---|---|
| Energy (calories) | 283 | kcal |
| Protein | 20 | g |
| Fat | 21 | g |
| Net Carbohydrates | 3 | g |
| Fiber | 0.5 | g |
| Sugars, total | 2 | g |

# Recipe #2: Keto Caesar Salad

*Number of Servings: 6*
*Serving Size: 2 cups*

*Prep Time: 15 minutes*

Ingredients:
- 12 cups chopped romaine lettuce
- 1/3 cup extra virgin olive oil
- 1/3 cup freshly grated Parmesan cheese
- 3 Tbsp. freshly squeezed lemon juice
- 1 ½ Tbsp. mayonnaise
- 1/3 tsp. anchovy paste
- 1/3 tsp. garlic powder
- Freshly ground black pepper, to taste

Cooking Directions:
1. Combine the lemon juice, olive oil, anchovy paste, garlic powder, and mayonnaise in an airtight container. Whisk well until thoroughly combined. Divide into 6 equal servings in small airtight containers and refrigerate for up to 3 days.
2. In a large bowl, toss together the lettuce and Parmesan cheese. Season lightly with black pepper and toss again to coat. Divide into 6 airtight containers then cover and refrigerate for up to 3 days.
3. Right before serving, add the dressing to the salad. Toss to coat then serve right away.

*Nutritional Facts per Serving:*

| | | |
|---|---|---|
| Energy (calories) | 93 | kcal |
| Protein | 3 | g |
| Fat | 7 | g |
| Net Carbohydrates | 6 | g |
| Fiber | 2 | g |
| Sugars, total | 1 | g |

# Recipe #3: Fried Cheesy Avocado Wedges

*Number of Servings: 4*
*Serving Size: ¼ of the recipe*

*Prep Time: 5 minutes*
*Cook Time: 10 minutes*

Ingredients:
- 2 small eggs
- 1 large avocado
- 1/3 cup ground pork rinds
- 1/3 cup shredded Parmesan cheese
- 1 ½ Tbsp. heavy cream
- 1/3 tsp. garlic powder
- 1/3 tsp. onion powder
- 1/3 tsp. fine sea salt
- 1/3 tsp. freshly ground black pepper
- Sunflower oil, as needed

Cooking Directions:
1. Place a heavy duty skillet over medium flame and add approximately 1 ½ inches of oil. Heat the oil to 375 degrees F.
2. Meanwhile, whisk the eggs in a small bowl then mix in until smooth.
3. Halve the avocado carefully then discard the stone. Scoop out the flesh using a spoon then slice into ½ inch thick wedges.
4. Season the avocado wedges with salt and pepper then set aside.
5. On a plate, combine the pork rinds, onion and garlic powders, and Parmesan cheese. Mix well.

6. Dip the avocado wedges in the egg mixture, then drain and dredge in the pork rind and Parmesan cheese mixture until completely covered.
7. Add the coated wedges in the hot oil and cook for 1 minute per side, or until golden brown.
8. Transfer the wedges to a platter lined with paper towels and let drain. Allow to cool slightly, then transfer to an airtight container and refrigerate for up to 2 days. Reheat before serving in hot oil, if desired.

*Nutritional Facts per Serving:*

| | | |
|---|---|---|
| Energy (calories) | 179 | kcal |
| Protein | 8 | g |
| Fat | 14 | g |
| Net Carbohydrates | 6 | g |
| Fiber | 3 | g |
| Sugars, total | 0.5 | g |

# Recipe #4: Simple Beef Chili

*Number of Servings: 3*
*Serving Size: ½ cup*

*Prep Time: 15 minutes*
*Cook Time: 1 hour*

Ingredients:
- 1 small yellow onion, peeled and diced
- 1 lb. 85 percent ground beef
- 2 cups organic beef broth
- ¼ cup extra virgin olive oil
- 2 Tbsp. flaxseed meal
- 1 Tbsp. chili powder
- 1 tsp. dried oregano
- ½ tsp. cumin seeds
- ¼ tsp. garlic powder
- Sea salt, to taste
- Freshly ground black pepper, to taste

Cooking Directions:
1. Place a heavy duty pot over high flame and heat through. Once hot, add the beef and onion and sauté until the beef is browned.
2. Stir in the chili powder, oregano, cumin seeds, and garlic powder then sauté until combined.
3. Pour in the beef broth, flaxseed meal, and olive oil. Stir to combine, then bring to a boil.
4. Once boiling, reduce to medium high flame and simmer, partially covered, for 1 hour or until the chili is thickened.
5. Remove from heat and cover. Allow to cool, then transfer to airtight containers and refrigerate for up to

3 days. Reheat and season to taste with salt and pepper before serving.

*Nutritional Facts per Serving:*

| | | |
|---|---|---|
| Energy (calories) | 567 | kcal |
| Protein | 41 | g |
| Fat | 36 | g |
| Net Carbohydrates | 18 | g |
| Fiber | 3 | g |
| Sugars, total | 0.3 | g |

## Recipe #5: Low Carb Hearty Pot Roast

*Number of Servings: 3*
*Serving Size: 1/3 of the recipe*

*Prep Time: 35 minutes*
*Cook Time: 5 hours*

Ingredients:
- 2 ½ lb. bottom round rump roast
- 1 small onion, peeled and quartered
- 1 large garlic clove, peeled
- 1 fresh thyme sprig
- 1 turnip, peeled and chopped
- 1 ½ cups beef stock
- 1 cup halved radishes
- 2 Tbsp. heavy cream
- 1 ½ Tbsp. olive oil
- Sea salt, to taste
- Freshly ground black pepper, to taste

Cooking Directions:
1. Set the oven to 475 degrees F.
2. Season the pork all over with salt and pepper.
3. Place a Dutch oven over high flame and add the olive oil. Swirl to coat, then brown the roast all over and set aside.
4. Sauté the onion in the same pot until browned then transfer to the bowl with the pot roast.
5. Add the beef stock, garlic, and thyme, then mix well. Return the roast and onion, then add the radishes and turnips.

6. Place the pot, uncovered, in the oven and set it to 400 degrees F. Cook for 4 to 5 hours, or until the internal temperature of the pot roast is 130 degrees F.
7. Take the roast out of the pot and let cool. Then, transfer the vegetables and roast to a bowl.
8. Place a saucepan over medium flame and add the liquid from the Dutch oven. Stir in the heavy cream then bring to a boil. Then, reduce to a simmer.
9. Slice the pot roast thinly, then divide into individual servings. Divide the vegetables and sauce as well, then let cool slightly. Cover and refrigerate for up to 3 days.

*Nutritional Facts per Serving:*

| | | |
|---|---|---|
| Energy (calories) | 521 | kcal |
| Protein | 69 | g |
| Fat | 25 | g |
| Net Carbohydrates | 6 | g |
| Fiber | 4 | g |
| Sugars, total | 4 | g |

# Recipe #6: Miso Beef and Tender Zucchini

*Number of Servings: 2*
*Serving Size: ½ of the recipe*

*Prep Time: 15 minutes*
*Cook Time: 15 minutes*

Ingredients:
- ½ lb. flank steak
- ½ lb. zucchini, julienned
- 3 oz. butter, at room temperature
- 2 Tbsp. water
- ¼ Tbsp. toasted sesame oil
- 2 tsp. white miso paste
- Sea salt, to taste
- Freshly ground black pepper, to taste

Cooking Directions:
1. Preheat the grill to high.
2. In a bowl, stir together the miso paste and butter until thoroughly combined. Cover then set aside.
3. Blot the flank steak dry with paper towels then season all over with salt and pepper.
4. Grill the flank steak until the internal temperature is at least 160 degrees F, or the beef is cooked through.
5. Transfer the beef to a sheet of aluminum foil and let rest for about 10 minutes.
6. Put the julienned zucchini in a bowl and add 2 tablespoons of water. Cover and steam for 2 minutes or until the zucchini is slightly tender.
7. Drain the zucchini then add the sesame oil. Toss to coat.

8. Slice the beef across the grain very thinly then divide into two portions. Place in an airtight container.
9. Divide the zucchini and add to the side. Spoon the butter mixture on top, then cover and refrigerate for up to 3 days. Reheat in the microwave before serving.

*Nutritional Facts per Serving:*

| | | |
|---|---|---|
| Energy (calories) | 511 | kcal |
| Protein | 28 | g |
| Fat | 43 | g |
| Net Carbohydrates | 5 | g |
| Fiber | 2 | g |
| Sugars, total | 0.3 | g |

# Recipe #7: Roasted Garlic Butter Cod with Bok Choy

*Number of Servings: 3*
*Serving Size: 1 cod fillet*

*Prep Time: 5 minutes*
*Cook Time: 20 minutes*

Ingredients:
- 3 cod fillets, 8 oz. each
- ¾ lb. baby bok choy, halved
- 1/3 cup thinly sliced butter
- 1 ½ Tbsp. minced garlic
- Sea salt, to taste
- Freshly ground black pepper, to taste

Cooking Directions:
1. Set the oven to 400 degrees F to preheat.
2. Cut out 3 sheets of aluminum foil, each large enough to completely cover one cod fillet.
3. Place a cod fillet on each sheet of aluminum foil then add the butter and garlic. Add the bok choy, then season everything with salt and pepper.
4. Fold over the pouches and crimp the edges. Arrange on a baking sheet.
5. Bake for 20 minutes, then transfer to a cooling rack. Let cool slightly, then refrigerate for up to 3 days. Reheat in the oven before serving.

*Nutritional Facts per Serving:*

| | | |
|---|---|---|
| Energy (calories) | 355 | kcal |
| Protein | 37 | g |
| Fat | 21 | g |
| Net Carbohydrates | 3 | g |
| Fiber | 1 | g |
| Sugars, total | 1 | g |

# Recipe #8: Creamy Chicken Soup

*Number of Servings: 4*
*Serving Size: 1 cup*

*Prep Time: 15 minutes*
*Cook Time: 20 minutes*

Ingredients:
- 1 large yellow onion, peeled and diced
- 2 cups organic chicken broth
- 1 cup diced cooked chicken breast
- ½ cup macadamia nuts
- ½ cup water
- ½ cup sliced celery
- ¼ cup diced carrot
- ¼ cup olive oil
- Sea salt, to taste
- Dried herbs de Provence, to taste

Cooking Directions:
1. Place a saucepan over medium flame and heat through. Once hot, add the olive oil and swirl to coat.
2. Sauté the onion, carrot, and celery until the onion is translucent. Then, stir in the macadamia nuts and chicken broth.
3. Bring to a simmer, then reduce to low flame and simmer until the carrot is tender.
4. Turn off the heat and allow the mixture to cool slightly. Then, blend with an immersion blender or high power blender until smooth and the macadamia nuts are pureed. Pour the mixture back into the saucepan.

5. Add ½ cup of water into the soup and stir well to combine. Reheat over medium flame and reheat. Stir in the chicken and stir until reheated.
6. Ladle the soup into individual bowls and allow to cool slightly. Cover and refrigerate for up to 3 days. Reheat before serving.

*Nutritional Facts per Serving:*

| | | |
|---|---|---|
| Energy (calories) | 325 | kcal |
| Protein | 14 | g |
| Fat | 28 | g |
| Net Carbohydrates | 7 | g |
| Fiber | 3 | g |
| Sugars, total | 3 | g |

# Recipe #9: Ginger Sesame Halibut

*Number of Servings: 3*
*Serving Size: 1 halibut fillet*

*Prep Time: 20 minutes*
*Cook Time: 20 minutes*

Ingredients:
- 3 Alaskan halibut fillets, 8 oz. each
- 1 ½ Tbsp. minced fresh ginger
- 1 ½ tsp. soy sauce
- 1 ½ tsp. olive oil
- ¾ tsp. sesame oil
- ¾ tsp. rice wine vinegar

Cooking Directions:
1. Set the oven to 400 degrees F to preheat. Line a baking sheet with aluminum foil and set aside.
2. Combine the sesame and olive oils in a bowl, then stir in the rice vinegar, soy sauce, and ginger.
3. Add the fish fillets and turn several times to coat.
4. Arrange the fish fillets on the prepared baking sheet. Bake for 17 minutes, or until done.
5. Cover each fish fillet with aluminum foil and refrigerate for up to 3 days, or freeze for up to 2 weeks. Reheat before serving.

*Nutritional Facts per Serving:*

| | | |
|---|---|---|
| Energy (calories) | 237 | kcal |
| Protein | 33 | g |
| Fat | 35 | g |
| Net Carbohydrates | 1 | g |
| Fiber | 0.1 | g |
| Sugars, total | 0.6 | g |

# Recipe #10: Hearty Beef and Mushroom Stew

*Number of Servings: 3*
*Serving Size: ½ of the recipe*

*Prep Time: 15 minutes*
*Cook Time: 50 minutes*

Ingredients:
- ½ lb. stew meat, chopped into 1 inch cubes
- ½ lb. sliced baby Portobello mushrooms
- 1 oz. butter
- 2 cups organic beef broth
- ¼ cup extra virgin olive oil
- ¼ cup diced onion
- 2 Tbsp. chopped fresh parsley
- ½ Tbsp. flaxseed meal
- ½ tsp. minced garlic
- ½ tsp. dried thyme
- 1 bay leaf
- Sea salt, to taste
- Freshly ground black pepper, to taste

Cooking Directions:
1. Place a heavy duty pot over medium high flame and heat through. Once hot, add the butter and olive oil and swirl to coat.
2. Add the beef and sauté until all the sides are browned. Then, stir in the mushroom and onion. Sauté until the mushroom is tender and the onion is translucent.
3. Pour in the broth, garlic, bay leaf, thyme, and flaxseed meal then stir to combine. Mix well and bring to a boil.
4. Once boiling, reduce to low flame, cover, and simmer for 45 minutes, or until the beef is extra tender.

5. After 1 hour, discard the bay leaf. Shred the beef using two forks then stir in the parsley. Divide between two airtight containers and refrigerate for up to 3 days. Reheat before serving.

*Nutritional Facts per Serving:*

| | | |
|---|---|---|
| Energy (calories) | 430 | kcal |
| Protein | 25 | g |
| Fat | 28 | g |
| Net Carbohydrates | 19 | g |
| Fiber | 3 | g |
| Sugars, total | 2 | g |

# Recipe #11: Goat Cheese and Smoked Onion Pizza

*Number of Servings: 4*
*Serving Size: 1/8 per serving*

*Prep Time: 20 minutes*
*Cook Time: 12 minutes*

Ingredients:
- 8 large egg whites
- 2 garlic cloves, minced
- 1 ½ cups crumbled goat cheese
- 1 cup chopped yellow onion
- ½ cup coconut milk
- ¼ cup coconut flour
- 4 Tbsp. organic barbecue sauce, no sugar added
- ¼ tsp. baking powder
- ½ tsp. onion powder
- ½ tsp. garlic powder'
- Freshly ground black pepper, to taste

Cooking Directions:
1. Set the oven to 425 degrees F to preheat.
2. Combine the coconut flour, baking powder, and garlic and onion powders in a large bowl.
3. Add the egg whites and coconut milk then stir until smooth.
4. Place a skillet over medium high flame and heat through. Once hot, add ¼ of the mixture and tilt until a flat "pizza crust" is formed.
5. Cook for 2 minutes per side, or until browned. Transfer to a baking sheet and repeat with the remaining batter.

6. Divide the barbecue sauce among the pizza crusts and top with onion, garlic, goat cheese, and a dash of black pepper.
7. Bake the pizzas for 5 minutes, or until the cheese is melted.
8. Transfer to a cooling rack and let cool. Then, wrap in aluminum foil and refrigerate for up to 3 days or freeze for up to 2 weeks. Reheat in the oven or microwave before serving.

*Nutritional Facts per Serving:*

| | | |
|---|---|---|
| Energy (calories) | 565 | kcal |
| Protein | 36 | g |
| Fat | 38 | g |
| Net Carbohydrates | 13 | g |
| Fiber | 4 | g |
| Sugars, total | 8 | g |

# Recipe #12: Savory Butternut Squash Soup

*Number of Servings: 4*
*Serving Size: ¾ cup*

*Prep Time: 15 minutes*
*Cook Time: 30 minutes*

Ingredients:
- ½ lb. butternut squash, peeled, seeded, and cubed
- 1 bay leaf
- 2 garlic cloves, peeled and minced
- 2 cups organic chicken broth
- ¼ cup 36 percent heavy cream
- 2 ½ Tbsp. olive oil
- ½ tsp. fine sea salt

Cooking Directions:
1. Place a saucepan over medium flame and heat through. Once hot, add ½ tablespoon of olive oil and swirl to coat.
2. Stir the butternut squash and garlic into the saucepan and sauté for about 5 minutes or until the garlic is lightly toasted.
3. Pour the chicken broth into the saucepan along with the remaining olive oil. Add the bay leaf, then bring to a boil. Once boiling, reduce to a simmer.
4. Simmer the mixture for about 20 minutes or until the butternut squash is completely tender.
5. Take out and discard the bay leaf, then turn off the heat and allow to cool slightly. Once cooled, blend using an immersion blender or high power blender until smooth.

6. Pour in the cream and blend again until smooth. Then, return to the saucepan and reheat over medium low flame.
7. Season the soup to taste with salt then divide into individual servings. Allow to cool slightly then seal tightly. Refrigerate for up to 3 days. Reheat before serving.

*Nutritional Facts per Serving:*

| | | |
|---|---|---|
| Energy (calories) | 136 | kcal |
| Protein | 2 | g |
| Fat | 12 | g |
| Net Carbohydrates | 8 | g |
| Fiber | 1 | g |
| Sugars, total | 2 | g |

# Chapter 6 – Keto Meal Prep Snack Recipes

## Recipe #1: Avocado, Cream Cheese and Cucumber Bites

*Number of Servings: 5*
*Serving Size: 2 pieces*

*Prep Time: 15 minutes*

Ingredients:
- 1 large cucumber, sliced into 10 1/3 inch rounds
- 1 large avocado
- 8 oz. cream cheese
- 4 oz. red salmon, flaked
- 1 Tbsp. freshly squeezed lemon juice
- ½ Tbsp. chopped green onion
- Tabasco sauce, to taste

Cooking Directions:
1. Halve the avocado then discard the stone. Scoop out the flesh then place in a large bowl.
2. Mash the avocado and cream cheese together until everything is smooth. Add the lemon juice and mix well, then season to taste with tabasco sauce.
3. Arrange the cucumber slices on a platter then divide the avocado cream cheese mixture among them.
4. Divide the flaked red salmon among the pieces then garnish with green onion. Serve right away, or store in an airtight container and refrigerate for up to 3 days.

*Nutritional Facts per Serving:*

| | | |
|---|---|---|
| Energy (calories) | 277 | kcal |
| Protein | 19 | g |
| Fat | 22 | g |
| Net Carbohydrates | 5 | g |
| Fiber | 3 | g |
| Sugars, total | 2 | g |

# Recipe #2: Ham 'n' Cheese Puffs

*Number of Servings: 9*
*Serving Size: 2 puffs*

*Prep Time: 15 minutes*
*Cook Time: 30 minutes*

Ingredients:
- 6 large eggs
- 10 oz. sliced deli ham, diced
- 1 ½ cups shredded cheddar cheese
- ¾ cup mayonnaise
- 1/3 cup coconut flour
- 1/3 cup coconut oil
- 1/3 tsp. baking powder
- 1/3 tsp. baking soda
- Nonstick cooking spray, as needed

Cooking Directions:
1. Set the oven to 350 degrees F to preheat. Lightly coat rimmed baking sheet with nonstick cooking spray and set aside.
2. In a bowl, mix together the eggs, coconut oil, and mayonnaise. Set aside.
3. In a separate bowl, combine the baking soda, baking powder, and coconut flour. Add the dry ingredients to the wet ingredients and mix well until smooth.
4. Fold the ham and cheddar cheese into the mixture and set aside.
5. Divide the dough into 18 small pieces and arrange on the prepared baking sheet.
6. Bake for 30 minutes, or until the puffs are golden brown and set.

7. Arrange the puffs on a cooling rack and allow to cool slightly.
8. Store into an airtight container for up to 5 days. If desired, reheat in the microwave before serving.

*Nutritional Facts per Serving:*

| | | |
|---|---|---|
| Energy (calories) | 249 | kcal |
| Protein | 15 | g |
| Fat | 20 | g |
| Net Carbohydrates | 3 | g |
| Fiber | 0.3 | g |
| Sugars, total | 0.5 | g |

# Recipe #3: Walnut Parmesan Bites

*Number of Servings: 10*
*Serving Size: 4 crackers*

*Prep Time: 10 minutes*
*Cook Time: 8 minutes*

Ingredients:
- 6 oz. freshly grated Parmesan cheese
- 2 Tbsp. chopped walnuts
- 1 Tbsp. unsalted butter
- ½ Tbsp. chopped fresh thyme

Cooking Directions:
1. Set the oven to 350 degrees F to preheat. Line two large rimmed baking sheets with baking paper and set aside.
2. In a food processor, combine the Parmesan cheese and butter. Blend until combined.
3. Pour in the walnuts and pulse until crushed and combined with the mixture.
4. Using a tablespoon, scoop the mixture onto the prepared baking sheets, then top with chopped thyme.
5. Bake for about 8 minutes, or until golden brown.
6. Transfer to a cooling rack and let set for about 30 minutes. Then, transfer to an airtight container and store for up to 5 days.

*Nutritional Facts per Serving:*

| | | |
|---|---|---|
| Energy (calories) | 80 | kcal |
| Protein | 7 | g |
| Fat | 3 | g |
| Net Carbohydrates | 7 | g |
| Fiber | 0.1 | g |
| Sugars, total | 0.2 | g |

# Recipe #4: Cream Cheese Bacon Stuffed Jalapenos

*Number of Servings: 4*
*Serving Size: 2*

*Prep Time: 15 minutes*
*Cook Time: 10 minutes*

Ingredients:
- 12 large jalapeno peppers
- 16 bacon strips
- 6 oz. full fat cream cheese
- 2 tsp. garlic powder
- 1 tsp. chili powder

Cooking Directions:
1. Set the oven to 350 degrees F to preheat. Place a wire rack over a roasting pan and set aside.
2. Put on a pair of plastic gloves.
3. Make a slit lengthways across the jalapeno peppers, taking care not to cut through. Scrape out and discard the seeds. Set aside.
4. Place a nonstick or cast iron skillet over high flame and heat through. Once hot, add half the bacon strips and cook until crispy. Transfer to a plate lined with paper towels and let drain.
5. Chop the cooked bacon strips and place in a large bowl. Add the cream cheese and mix well to combine.
6. Season the cream cheese and bacon mixture with garlic and chili powder, then mix well.
7. Stuff the jalapeno peppers with the cream cheese mixture, then wrap a raw bacon strip around each pepper.

8. Arrange the stuffed jalapeno peppers on the prepared wire rack, then roast for up to 10 minutes, or until tender.
9. Transfer the stuffed jalapeno peppers on a cooling rack and allow to cool slightly. Transfer to an airtight container and refrigerate for up to 5 days.

*Nutritional Facts per Serving:*

| | | |
|---|---|---|
| Energy (calories) | 209 | kcal |
| Protein | 9 | g |
| Fat | 13 | g |
| Net Carbohydrates | 19 | g |
| Fiber | 3 | g |
| Sugars, total | 10 | g |

# Recipe #5: Low Carb Guacamole

*Number of Servings: 6*
*Serving Size: 1/6 of the recipe*

*Prep Time: 15 minutes*

Ingredients:
- 3 large ripe avocados
- 1 large red onion, peeled and diced
- 4 Tbsp. freshly squeezed lime juice
- Sea salt, to taste
- Freshly ground black pepper, to taste
- Cayenne pepper, to taste

Cooking Directions:
1. Halve the avocados then discard the stone.
2. Scoop out the avocado flesh from 3 avocado halves and place in a large glass bowl. Mash well with a fork or potato masher.
3. Add 2 tablespoons of lime juice into the mashed avocado and mix well.
4. Dice the remaining avocado then place in a separate bowl. Add the remaining lime juice and toss gently to coat.
5. Combine the diced avocado with the mashed avocado, then add the chopped onion. Toss again to combine.
6. Season the guacamole with salt, pepper, and cayenne pepper then mix gently to combine.
7. Store in an airtight container for up to 3 days. Serve with carrot, celery, and cucumber sticks.

*Nutritional Facts per Serving:*

| | | |
|---|---|---|
| Energy (calories) | 172 | kcal |
| Protein | 2 | g |
| Fat | 15 | g |
| Net Carbohydrates | 11 | g |
| Fiber | 7 | g |
| Sugars, total | 2 | g |

# Recipe #6: Smoked Salmon and Dill Spread

*Number of Servings: 8*
*Serving Size: 2 tablespoons*

*Prep Time: 20 minutes*

Ingredients:
- 4 oz. smoked salmon
- 4 oz. full fat cream cheese, at room temperature
- 2 ½ Tbsp. mayonnaise
- 2 Tbsp. chopped fresh dill
- Sea salt, to taste
- Freshly ground black pepper, to taste

Cooking Directions:
1. Pour the smoked salmon, mayonnaise, and cream cheese into a food processor. Pulse until combined.
2. Pour the mixture into an airtight container and mix in the fresh dill. Season to taste with salt and pepper.
3. Cover and refrigerate for up to 3 days. Best served with carrot, celery, and cucumber sticks.

*Nutritional Facts per Serving:*

| | | |
|---|---|---|
| Energy (calories) | 70 | kcal |
| Protein | 5 | g |
| Fat | 5 | g |
| Net Carbohydrates | 2 | g |
| Fiber | 0.4 | g |
| Sugars, total | 0.8 | g |

## Recipe #7: Coco Lime Fat Bombs

*Number of Servings: 8*
*Serving Size: 1 fat bomb*

*Prep Time: 1 hour 15 minutes*

Ingredients:
- 1 oz. cream cheese
- 2 Tbsp. butter
- 2 Tbsp. coconut oil
- 2 Tbsp. heavy cream
- 1 Tbsp. freshly squeezed lime juice
- ½ tsp. lime extract
- ½ tsp. liquid stevia

Cooking Directions:
1. Combine the cream cheese, coconut oil, and butter in a microwaveable bowl. Microwave for 10 seconds three times until melted.
2. Stir the mixture then add the heavy cream. Mix well, then add the lime juice, lime extract, and liquid stevia. Stir well.
3. Pour the mixture into an ice cube tray with 8 compartments. Freeze for at least 1 hour. Store in the freezer for up to 2 weeks. Serve chilled.

*Nutritional Facts per Serving:*

| | | |
|---|---|---|
| Energy (calories) | 81 | kcal |
| Protein | 0.4 | g |
| Fat | 9 | g |
| Net Carbohydrates | 0.4 | g |
| Fiber | 0.4 | g |
| Sugars, total | 0.4 | g |

# Recipe #8: Coco Lemon Fat Bombs

*Number of Servings: 8*
*Serving Size: 1 fat bomb*

*Prep Time: 1 hour 15 minutes*

Ingredients:
- 1 oz. cream cheese
- 2 Tbsp. butter
- 2 Tbsp. coconut oil
- 2 Tbsp. heavy cream
- 1 Tbsp. freshly squeezed lemon juice
- ½ tsp. lemon extract
- ½ tsp. liquid stevia

Cooking Directions:
4. Combine the cream cheese, coconut oil, and butter in a microwaveable bowl. Microwave for 10 seconds three times until melted.
5. Stir the mixture then add the heavy cream. Mix well, then add the lemon juice, lemon extract, and liquid stevia. Stir well.
6. Pour the mixture into an ice cube tray with 8 compartments. Freeze for at least 1 hour. Store in the freezer for up to 2 weeks. Serve chilled.

*Nutritional Facts per Serving:*

| | | |
|---|---|---|
| Energy (calories) | 81 | kcal |
| Protein | 0.4 | g |
| Fat | 9 | g |
| Net Carbohydrates | 0.4 | g |
| Fiber | 0.4 | g |
| Sugars, total | 0.4 | g |

## Recipe #9: Choco Peanut Fat Bombs

*Number of Servings: 8*
*Serving Size: 1 fat bomb*

*Prep Time: 1 hour 15 minutes*

Ingredients:
- 2 Tbsp. butter
- 2 Tbsp. coconut oil
- 2 Tbsp. heavy cream
- 1 Tbsp. smooth peanut butter
- 1 Tbsp. unsweetened cocoa powder
- ½ tsp. pure vanilla extract
- ½ tsp. liquid stevia

Cooking Directions:
1. Combine the peanut butter, coconut oil, and butter in a microwaveable bowl. Microwave for 10 seconds three times until melted.
2. Stir the mixture then add the heavy cream. Mix well, then add the cocoa powder, vanilla extract, and liquid stevia. Stir well.
3. Pour the mixture into an ice cube tray with 8 compartments. Freeze for at least 1 hour. Store in the freezer for up to 2 weeks. Serve chilled.

*Nutritional Facts per Serving:*

| | | |
|---|---|---|
| Energy (calories) | 73 | kcal |
| Protein | 0.6 | g |
| Fat | 8 | g |
| Net Carbohydrates | 1 | g |
| Fiber | 0.5 | g |
| Sugars, total | 0.5 | g |

# Recipe #10: Almond Olive and Herb Tapenade

*Number of Servings: 8*
*Serving Size: 2 tablespoons*

*Prep Time: 15 minutes*

Ingredients:
- 2 garlic cloves, peeled and minced
- 1 cup pitted green olives
- ¼ cup slivered almonds
- ¼ cup packed fresh basil leaves
- ¼ cup extra virgin olive oil
- ½ Tbsp. freshly squeezed lemon juice
- ½ tsp. drained capers
- Sea salt, to taste

Cooking Directions:
1. Combine the almonds, garlic, olives, capers, and lemon juice in a food processor. Pulse until shredded.
2. Add the basil leaves into the food processor and pulse again until combined.
3. Pour in the olive oil and add a dash of salt. Pulse again until the mixture turns into a chunky paste.
4. Pour the mixture into an airtight container and refrigerate for up to 5 days. Best served with grilled chicken tenders or pan-seared white fish strips.

*Nutritional Facts per Serving:*

| | | |
|---|---|---|
| Energy (calories) | 28 | kcal |
| Protein | 0.1 | g |
| Fat | 3 | g |
| Net Carbohydrates | 0.36 | g |
| Fiber | 0.1 | g |
| Sugars, total | 0.04 | g |

# Recipe #11: Chocolate Coated Bacon

*Number of Servings: 6*
*Serving Size: 2 pieces*

*Prep Time: 15 minutes*
*Cook Time: 20 minutes*

Ingredients:
- 12 bacon slices
- 4 ½ Tbsp. unsweetened dark chocolate
- 2 ¼ Tbsp. coconut oil
- 1 ½ tsp. liquid stevia

Cooking Directions:
1. Set the oven to 425 degrees F to preheat.
2. Skewer the bacon in iron skewers, spreading the bacon out.
3. Arrange on a baking sheet. Bake for 15 minutes, or until crisp.
4. Transfer the bacon to a cooling rack and allow to cool completely.
5. Melt the coconut oil in a saucepan over low flame, then stir in the chocolate until melted. Add the stevia and stir well to combine.
6. Place the bacon on a sheet of parchment paper and coat in the chocolate mixture on both sides.
7. Allow the chocolate to dry on the bacon, then transfer the bacon to an airtight container and refrigerate for up to 5 days.

*Nutritional Facts per Serving:*

| | | |
|---|---|---|
| Energy (calories) | 258 | kcal |
| Protein | 7 | g |
| Fat | 26 | g |
| Net Carbohydrates | 0.5 | g |
| Fiber | 0 | g |
| Sugars, total | 0.4 | g |

# Recipe #12: Portobello Mushrooms Stuffed with Ricotta Cheese and Spinach

*Number of Servings: 6*
*Serving Size: 1 stuffed mushroom*

*Prep Time: 15 minutes*
*Cook Time: 45 minutes*

Ingredients:
- 6 large Portobello mushroom caps
- 3 garlic cloves, peeled and minced
- 2 small eggs
- 1 ¼ cups full fat ricotta cheese
- ¾ cup steamed spinach, drained
- ¾ cup freshly grated Parmesan cheese
- ½ cup extra virgin olive oil
- Sea salt, to taste
- Freshly ground black pepper, to taste

Cooking Directions:
1. Set the oven to 425 degrees F to preheat. Line a baking sheet with aluminum foil and set aside.
2. Rinse and clean the Portobello mushroom caps thoroughly until all the dirt is washed off. discard the gills and stems, then blot the mushroom caps with paper towels.
3. Season the inside of the mushroom caps with salt and pepper, then arrange on the prepared baking sheet.
4. Bake the mushroom caps for 15 minutes.
5. Meanwhile, combine the rest of the ingredients in a large bowl until completely combined. Set aside.
6. Remove the mushroom caps out of the oven and then divide the filling among them. Return to the oven and

bake for an additional 25 minutes, or until the mushrooms are browned and tender.
7. Place the stuffed mushroom caps on a cooling rack and allow to cool slightly. Serve warm.
8. Store in an airtight container and refrigerate for up to 3 days. Reheat in the microwave oven before serving.

*Nutritional Facts per Serving:*

| | | |
|---|---|---|
| Energy (calories) | 239 | kcal |
| Protein | 16 | g |
| Fat | 17 | g |
| Net Carbohydrates | 12 | g |
| Fiber | 3 | g |
| Sugars, total | 3 | g |

# Recipe #13: Cinnamon Butter

*Number of Servings: 8*
*Serving Size: 1 tablespoon*

*Prep Time:*
*Cook Time:*

Ingredients:
- ½ cup butter, at room temperature
- 5 drops liquid stevia
- ½ tsp. pure vanilla extract
- ½ tsp. ground cinnamon
- 1/8 tsp fine sea salt

Cooking Directions:
1. Combine the butter, vanilla, cinnamon, salt, and stevia in a large bowl. Mix well until smooth.
2. Line a baking sheet with wax paper then spread the cinnamon butter mixture on top. Roll the paper to seal the butter mixture, then seal the ends.
3. Refrigerate the butter for 1 hour before using. Store in the refrigerator for up to 2 weeks. Best served on the Keto Bread or with celery sticks.

*Nutritional Facts per Serving:*

| | | |
|---|---|---|
| Energy (calories) | 103 | kcal |
| Protein | 0.1 | g |
| Fat | 12 | g |
| Net Carbohydrates | 0.1 | g |
| Fiber | 0 | g |
| Sugars, total | 0.1 | g |

# Recipe #14: Roasted Eggplant Spread

*Number of Servings: 8*
*Serving Size: 2 tablespoons*

*Prep Time: 15 minutes*
*Cook Time: 1 hour*

Ingredients:
- 1 lb. eggplant
- 2 ½ Tbsp. chopped roasted red peppers
- 2 Tbsp. extra virgin olive oil
- 2 Tbsp. pine nuts
- 1 Tbsp. freshly squeezed lemon juice
- ½ Tbsp. crumbled feta cheese
- Sea salt, to taste
- Freshly ground black pepper, to taste
- Garlic powder, to taste

Cooking Directions:
1. Set the oven to 400 degrees F to preheat. Slice the eggplant lengthwise in half, then arrange on a baking sheet lined with baking powder.
2. Roast the eggplant for 1 hour, or until extra tender. Then, transfer to a cooling rack and allow to cool slightly.
3. Once cooled, scrape the eggplant flesh out of the skin and place in a food processor. Add the olive oil, red peppers, lemon juice, and pine nuts. Then, blend until smooth.
4. Transfer the eggplant mixture into a bowl and season to taste with salt, pepper, and garlic powder.
5. Sprinkle the crumbled feta cheese over the eggplant mixture and fold in well. Transfer to an airtight

container and refrigerate for up to 5 days. Serve with carrot, celery, and cucumber sticks.

*Nutritional Facts per Serving:*

| | | |
|---|---|---|
| Energy (calories) | 54 | kcal |
| Protein | 2 | g |
| Fat | 4 | g |
| Net Carbohydrates | 4 | g |
| Fiber | 2 | g |
| Sugars, total | 2.5 | g |

# Recipe #15: Cauli Cheddar Bites

*Number of Servings: 6*
*Serving Size: 6 pieces*

*Prep Time: 15 minutes*
*Cook Time: 1 hour and 30 minutes*

Ingredients:
- 1 large cauliflower, broken into small florets
- 4 large egg whites
- ½ cup freshly grated strong cheddar cheese
- 2 Tbsp. heavy cream
- 2 Tbsp. butter
- Sea salt, to taste
- Freshly ground black pepper, to taste
- Paprika, to taste
- Nonstick cooking spray

Cooking Directions:
1. Place the cauliflower florets into a pot and add just enough water to cover the base of the pot. Season with salt to taste.
2. Place the pot of cauliflower over high flame and bring to a high simmer. Cook until the cauliflower is tender.
3. Drain the cauliflower florets then transfer to a food processor. Add the heavy cream and butter then blend until the mixture becomes a thick mixture.
4. Season the mixture with salt and pepper, then set aside to cool.
5. Meanwhile, beat the egg whites until soft peaks form. Then, fold in the cauliflower mixture and mix until evenly combined.

6. Add the cheddar cheese to the mixture and fold well until combined.
7. Cover the bowl and refrigerate the mixture for 30 minutes, or until chilled.
8. Set the oven to 375 degrees F to preheat. Lightly coat two rimmed baking sheets with nonstick cooking spray and set aside.
9. Take the cauliflower mixture out of the refrigerator. Using a tablespoon, scoop the mixture onto the prepared baking sheets into bite-sized balls. Ensure there is about 1 ½ inches of space between them.
10. Bake for 30 minutes, or until the bites are golden brown and crisp. Then, transfer to a cooling rack and sprinkle with paprika.
11. Store in an airtight container and refrigerate for up to 5 days. If desired, reheat in a toaster oven before serving.

*Nutritional Facts per Serving:*

| | | |
|---|---|---|
| Energy (calories) | 142 | kcal |
| Protein | 8 | g |
| Fat | 10 | g |
| Net Carbohydrates | 7 | g |
| Fiber | 3 | g |
| Sugars, total | 3 | g |

# Recipe #16: Bacon Mozzarella Sticks

*Number of Servings: 4*
*Serving Size: 2 mozzarella sticks*

*Prep Time: 10 minutes*
*Cook Time: 5 minutes*

Ingredients:
- 8 bacon strips
- 4 mozzarella string cheese pieces
- Sunflower oil, as needed

Cooking Directions:
1. Place a heavy duty skillet over medium flame and add about 2 inches of oil. Heat to 350 degrees F.
2. Meanwhile, halve each string cheese to make 8 pieces.
3. Wrap each piece of string cheese with a strip of bacon and secure with a wooden toothpick.
4. Cook the mozzarella sticks in the preheated oil for 2 minutes, or until the bacon is browned and cooked through.
5. Place the sticks on a plate lined with paper towels and let drain. Transfer to an airtight container and store in the refrigerator for up to 3 days. Reheat before serving.

*Nutritional Facts per Serving:*

| | | |
|---|---|---|
| Energy (calories) | 278 | kcal |
| Protein | 32 | g |
| Fat | 15 | g |
| Net Carbohydrates | 3 | g |
| Fiber | 2 | g |
| Sugars, total | 2 | g |

# Chapter 7 – Keto Meal Prep Smoothie Recipes

## Recipe #1: Creamy Matcha Green Tea Smoothie

*Number of Servings: 2*
*Serving Size: ½ of the recipe*

*Prep Time: 10 minutes*

Ingredients:
- 1 cup crushed ice
- 1 cup unsweetened almond milk
- ¼ cup heavy cream
- 3 Tbsp. unsweetened vanilla protein powder
- 1 Tbsp. coconut oil
- 1 ½ tsp. green tea powder

Cooking Directions:
1. Combine all the ingredients inside a high powder blender.
2. Blend on low until all ingredients are combined. Then, increase to high speed and blend until smooth.
3. Add a few drops of liquid stevia to taste, then divide into three equal servings. Best served right away.
4. Store extra servings in airtight mason jars and refrigerate for up to 3 days.

*Nutritional Facts per Serving:*

| | | |
|---|---|---|
| Energy (calories) | 442 | kcal |
| Protein | 17 | g |
| Fat | 41 | g |
| Net Carbohydrates | 7 | g |
| Fiber | 3 | g |
| Sugars, total | 4 | g |

# Recipe #2: Peanut Butter Choco Smoothie

*Number of Servings: 3*
*Serving Size: 12 oz.*

*Prep Time: 5 minutes*

Ingredients:
- 84 grams whey protein powder
- 3 cups water
- ¾ cup full fat unsweetened coconut milk
- 3 Tbsp. and ¾ tsp. coconut oil
- 3 Tbsp. unsweetened organic peanut butter
- 3 Tbsp. cacao powder
- Liquid stevia, to taste

Cooking Directions:
5. Combine all the ingredients inside a high powder blender.
6. Blend on low until all ingredients are combined. Then, increase to high speed and blend until smooth.
7. Add a few drops of liquid stevia to taste, then divide into three equal servings. Best served right away.
8. Store extra servings in airtight mason jars and refrigerate for up to 3 days.

*Nutritional Facts per Serving:*

| | | |
|---|---|---|
| Energy (calories) | 371 | kcal |
| Protein | 22 | g |
| Fat | 25 | g |
| Net Carbohydrates | 18 | g |
| Fiber | 2 | g |
| Sugars, total | 4 | g |

# Recipe #3: Super Berry Almond Smoothie

*Number of Servings: 2*
*Serving Size: ½ of the recipe*

*Prep Time: 10 minutes*

Ingredients:
- 1 cup crushed ice
- ½ cup unsweetened almond milk
- ½ cup frozen raspberries
- ½ cup frozen blueberries
- ½ cup blackberries or strawberries
- 1 Tbsp. coconut oil
- ½ tsp. pure vanilla extract

Cooking Directions:
1. Combine all the ingredients inside a high powder blender.
2. Blend on low until all ingredients are combined. Then, increase to high speed and blend until smooth.
3. Add a few drops of liquid stevia to taste, then divide into three equal servings. Best served right away.
4. Store extra servings in airtight mason jars and refrigerate for up to 3 days.

*Nutritional Facts per Serving:*

| | | |
|---|---|---|
| Energy (calories) | 252 | kcal |
| Protein | 3 | g |
| Fat | 22 | g |
| Net Carbohydrates | 16 | g |
| Fiber | 6 | g |
| Sugars, total | 10 | g |

# Recipe #4: Strawberries and Cream Smoothie

*Number of Servings: 2*
*Serving Size: ½ of the recipe*

*Prep Time: 10 minutes*

Ingredients:
- 1 cup crushed ice
- ½ cup sliced and hulled strawberries
- ½ cup heavy cream
- ¼ cup unsweetened almond milk
- 1 Tbsp. coconut oil
- 1 tsp. pure vanilla extract

Cooking Directions:
1. Combine all the ingredients inside a high powder blender.
2. Blend on low until all ingredients are combined. Then, increase to high speed and blend until smooth.
3. Add a few drops of liquid stevia to taste, then divide into three equal servings. Best served right away.
4. Store extra servings in airtight mason jars and refrigerate for up to 3 days.

*Nutritional Facts per Serving:*

| | | |
|---|---|---|
| Energy (calories) | 249 | kcal |
| Protein | 2 | g |
| Fat | 25 | g |
| Net Carbohydrates | 6 | g |
| Fiber | 1 | g |
| Sugars, total | 4 | g |

# Recipe #5: Pumpkin Spice Smoothie

*Number of Servings: 2*
*Serving Size: 6 oz.*

*Prep Time: 10 minutes*

Ingredients:
- 2 scoops vanilla whey protein powder
- 1 cup ice cubes
- 1 cup pureed pumpkin
- 1 cup unsweetened vanilla almond milk
- 1 cup ice water
- 1 tsp. pumpkin pie spice
- ¼ tsp. ground cinnamon
- 2 oz. cream cheese
- Liquid stevia, to taste

Cooking Directions:
1. Combine all the ingredients inside a high powder blender.
2. Blend on low until all ingredients are combined. Then, increase to high speed and blend until smooth.
3. Add a few drops of liquid stevia to taste, then divide into three equal servings. Best served right away.
4. Store extra servings in airtight mason jars and refrigerate for up to 3 days.

*Nutritional Facts per Serving:*

| | | |
|---|---|---|
| Energy (calories) | 268 | kcal |
| Protein | 29 | g |
| Fat | 10.5 | g |
| Net Carbohydrates | 9.5 | g |
| Fiber | 3 | g |
| Sugars, total | 6 | g |

# Recipe #6: Zesty Green Smoothie

*Number of Servings: 3*
*Serving Size: 6 oz.*

*Prep Time: 10 minutes*

Ingredients:
- ½ avocado, pitted and peeled
- 7 oz. full fat unsweetened coconut milk
- 1 cup chopped baby kale
- ½ cup diced cucumber
- 2 Tbsp. freshly squeezed lemon juice
- 2 Tbsp. freshly squeezed orange juice
- Water, as needed

Cooking Directions:
1. Combine all the ingredients inside a high powder blender.
2. Blend on low until all ingredients are combined. Then, increase to high speed and blend until smooth.
3. Add a few drops of liquid stevia to taste, then divide into three equal servings. Best served right away.
4. Store extra servings in airtight mason jars and refrigerate for up to 3 days.

*Nutritional Facts per Serving:*

| | | |
|---|---|---|
| Energy (calories) | 218 | kcal |
| Protein | 3 | g |
| Fat | 21 | g |
| Net Carbohydrates | 9 | g |
| Fiber | 4 | g |
| Sugars, total | 4 | g |

# Recipe #7: Chia Seeds and Crisp Greens Smoothie

*Number of Servings: 2*
*Serving Size: ½ of the recipe*

*Prep Time: 10 minutes*

Ingredients:
- 1 ½ cups crushed ice
- 1 cup packed kale leaves, rinsed thoroughly
- ½ cup water
- ½ cup packed Swiss chard leaves, rinsed thoroughly
- ½ cup packed spinach leaves, rinsed thoroughly
- 2 Tbsp. chia seeds
- 2 Tbsp. coconut oil

Cooking Directions:
1. Combine all the ingredients inside a high powder blender.
2. Blend on low until all ingredients are combined. Then, increase to high speed and blend until smooth.
3. Add a few drops of liquid stevia to taste, then divide into three equal servings. Best served right away.
4. Store extra servings in airtight mason jars and refrigerate for up to 3 days.

*Nutritional Facts per Serving:*

| | | |
|---|---|---|
| Energy (calories) | 293 | kcal |
| Protein | 8 | g |
| Fat | 23 | g |
| Net Carbohydrates | 15 | g |
| Fiber | 11 | g |
| Sugars, total | 3 | g |

# Recipe #8: Buttered Coffee Smoothie

*Number of Servings: 2*
*Serving Size: ½ of the recipe*

*Prep Time: 10 minutes*

Ingredients:
- 2 cups crushed ice
- ½ cup iced coffee
- ½ cup heavy cream
- 3 Tbsp. coconut oil

Cooking Directions:
1. Combine all the ingredients inside a high powder blender.
2. Blend on low until all ingredients are combined. Then, increase to high speed and blend until smooth.
3. Add a few drops of liquid stevia to taste, then divide into three equal servings. Best served right away.
4. Store extra servings in airtight mason jars and refrigerate for up to 3 days.

*Nutritional Facts per Serving:*

| | | |
|---|---|---|
| Energy (calories) | 486 | kcal |
| Protein | 1 | g |
| Fat | 55 | g |
| Net Carbohydrates | 0.9 | g |
| Fiber | 0 | g |
| Sugars, total | 0.9 | g |

# Recipe #9: Smooth Vanilla Smoothie

*Number of Servings: 2*
*Serving Size: ½ of the recipe*

*Prep Time: 10 minutes*

Ingredients:
- 1 cup crushed ice
- 1 cup unsweetened almond milk
- ¼ cup heavy cream
- 3 Tbsp. unsweetened vanilla whey protein powder
- 1 Tbsp. coconut oil
- 1 tsp. pure vanilla extract

Cooking Directions:
1. Combine all the ingredients inside a high powder blender.
2. Blend on low until all ingredients are combined. Then, increase to high speed and blend until smooth.
3. Add a few drops of liquid stevia to taste, then divide into three equal servings. Best served right away.
4. Store extra servings in airtight mason jars and refrigerate for up to 3 days.

*Nutritional Facts per Serving:*

| | | |
|---|---|---|
| Energy (calories) | 448 | kcal |
| Protein | 17 | g |
| Fat | 41 | g |
| Net Carbohydrates | 8 | g |
| Fiber | 2 | g |
| Sugars, total | 5 | g |

# Recipe #10: Avocado Coco Smoothie

*Number of Servings: 2*
*Serving Size: ½ of the recipe*

*Prep Time: 10 minutes*
Ingredients:
- 1 avocado, peeled and pitted
- 1 cup crushed ice
- 1 cup unsweetened full fat coconut milk
- 2 Tbsp. freshly squeezed lime juice
- 1 Tbsp. coconut oil
- 1 Tbsp. unsweetened coconut flakes

Cooking Directions:
1. Combine all the ingredients inside a high powder blender.
2. Blend on low until all ingredients are combined. Then, increase to high speed and blend until smooth.
3. Add a few drops of liquid stevia to taste, then divide into three equal servings. Best served right away.
4. Store extra servings in airtight mason jars and refrigerate for up to 3 days.

*Nutritional Facts per Serving:*

| | | |
|---|---|---|
| Energy (calories) | 512 | kcal |
| Protein | 4 | g |
| Fat | 51 | g |
| Net Carbohydrates | 13 | g |
| Fiber | 7 | g |
| Sugars, total | 6 | g |

# Chapter 8 – Keto Meal Prep Dessert Recipes

## Recipe #1: Keto Choco Brownies

*Number of Servings: 12*
*Serving Size: 1 large or 2 small brownie squares*

*Prep Time: 15 minutes*
*Cook Time: 20 minutes*

Ingredients:
- 1 scoop chocolate flavored whey protein powder
- 3 medium eggs, beaten
- 6 oz. dark chocolate, 80 percent
- ¾ cup unsweetened cocoa powder
- ¾ cup almond flour
- 1/3 cup coconut flour
- 1/3 cup heavy cream
- 1/3 cup cold water
- 3 Tbsp. unsalted butter
- ¾ Tbsp. baking powder
- 1 ½ tsp. pure vanilla extract

Cooking Directions:
1. Set the oven to 325 degrees F to preheat. Line a 9 x 9 inch square baking pan with baking paper and set aside.
2. In a large bowl, mix together the almond and coconut flours, whey protein powder, and baking powder. Set aside.

3. In a glass bowl, combine the heavy cream, chocolate, water, cocoa powder, and butter. Place over a pot of simmering water and stir until melted and evenly combined.
4. Set the bowl of chocolate aside and allow to cool, then add the pure vanilla extract and mix well. Add the eggs and mix well again to combine.
5. Gradually mix the flour mixture into the chocolate mixture until smooth. Then, transfer to the prepared baking pan.
6. Bake the brownies for 20 minutes, or until the brownies are set, but still gooey and chewy.
7. Transfer the pan to a cooling rack and allow to set for about 15 minutes. Then, slice into 12 large squares or 24 small squares.
8. Store the brownies in an airtight container and refrigerate for up to 5 days. Warm in the oven before serving, if desired.

*Nutritional Facts per Serving:*

| | | |
|---|---|---|
| Energy (calories) | 156 | kcal |
| Protein | 4 | g |
| Fat | 12 | g |
| Net Carbohydrates | 12 | g |
| Fiber | 3 | g |
| Sugars, total | 4 | g |

## Recipe #2: No Bake Coconut Macaroons

*Number of Servings: 18*
*Serving Size: 2 maracoons*

*Prep Time: 2 hours and 20 minutes*

Ingredients:
- 1 ½ cups shredded unsweetened coconut
- ¾ cup full fat unsweetened coconut milk
- 2 ¼ tsp. stevia

Cooking Directions:
1. Combine all the ingredients in a bowl until thoroughly mixed.
2. Pack down on the mixture then cover with plastic wrap. Refrigerate for at least 2 hours.
3. Once chilled, scoop the coconut mixture into small balls and arrange in a large airtight container.
4. Cover and keep refrigerated for up to 3 days or freeze for up to 3 weeks. Serve chilled.

*Nutritional Facts per Serving:*

| | | |
|---|---|---|
| Energy (calories) | 47 | kcal |
| Protein | 0.4 | g |
| Fat | 5 | g |
| Net Carbohydrates | 2 | g |
| Fiber | 0.8 | g |
| Sugars, total | 0.7 | g |

# Recipe #3: Raspberry Cream Cheese Pops

*Number of Servings: 8*
*Serving Size: 2 pieces*

*Prep Time: 20 minutes*

Ingredients:
- ¼ cup cream cheese
- ¼ cup chopped fresh raspberries
- 4 Tbsp. coconut oil
- 4 Tbsp. heavy cream
- 4 Tbsp. butter
- 1 tsp. pure vanilla extract

Cooking Directions:
1. Mix together the cream cheese, coconut oil, and butter in a bowl. Microwave for three times for 10 seconds per interval, or until the mixture is melted.
2. Carefully remove the bowl from the microwave oven and stir well. Then, stir in the heavy cream and fold in the chopped raspberries.
3. Stir the vanilla extract into the mixture and mix well until evenly combined.
4. Pour the mixture into an ice cube tray with 16 sections. Place in the freezer and freeze for at least 2 hours. Serve chilled. Store in the refrigerator for up to 2 weeks for best flavor.

*Nutritional Facts per Serving:*

| | | |
|---|---|---|
| Energy (calories) | 166 | kcal |
| Protein | 0.8 | g |
| Fat | 17 | g |
| Net Carbohydrates | 2 | g |
| Fiber | 0.3 | g |
| Sugars, total | 2 | g |

## Recipe #4: Coco Peanut Butter Bites

*Number of Servings: 12*
*Serving Size: 2 pieces*

*Prep Time: 15 minutes*
*Cook Time: 12 minutes*

Ingredients:
- 2 medium eggs
- ¾ cup unsweetened peanut butter
- ¾ cup butter, at room temperature
- 4 ½ tsp. stevia
- 3 tsp. coconut flour

Cooking Directions:
1. Set the oven to 350 degrees F to preheat. Line a baking sheet with baking paper and set aside.
2. In a large bowl for an electric mixer, combine the peanut butter, butter, eggs, stevia, and coconut flour. Blend well until smooth with an electric mixer.
3. Using a tablespoon, scoop out 24 pieces of the cookie dough and arrange on the prepared baking sheet.
4. Bake for 12 minutes, or until crisp and golden brown.
5. Place the baking sheet of cookies on a cooling rack and allow to cool completely. Then, transfer to an airtight container and refrigerate for up to 5 days, or store for up to 3 weeks.

*Nutritional Facts per Serving:*

| | | |
|---|---|---|
| Energy (calories) | 159 | kcal |
| Protein | 2 | g |
| Fat | 15 | g |
| Net Carbohydrates | 4 | g |
| Fiber | 0.3 | g |
| Sugars, total | 3 | g |

## Recipe #5: Cocoa Nibbles with Cream Cheese

*Number of Servings: 6*
*Serving Size: 4 small pieces*

*Prep Time: 15 minutes*
*Cook Time: 10 minutes*

Ingredients:
- 2 medium eggs
- 4 oz. melted butter
- 2 oz. full fat cream cheese
- 1 oz. coconut flour
- ½ tsp. baking soda
- ½ tsp. baking powder
- ½ tsp. xanthan gum
- ½ tsp. pure vanilla extract
- ¼ tsp. liquid stevia

Cooking Directions:
1. Set the oven to 350 degrees F to preheat. Line a rimmed baking sheet with baking paper and set aside.
2. In a large bowl, beat the cream cheese and butter until smooth. Set aside.
3. In another bowl, combine the coconut flour, baking soda, baking powder, and xanthan gum. Set aside.
4. In a small bowl, combine the vanilla extract, liquid stevia, and egg, then beat well until smooth.
5. Gradually stir the flour mixture into the cream cheese mixture until well combined. Add the egg mixture and mix well.
6. Using a tablespoon, scoop the mixture onto the prepared baking sheet, making sure there is at least 1 ½ inches between each piece.

7. Bake for 10 minutes, or until the pieces are golden brown around the edges.
8. Transfer to a cooling rack and allow to set for about 10 minutes. Transfer to an airtight container and refrigerate for up to 5 days.

*Nutritional Facts per Serving:*

| | | |
|---|---|---|
| Energy (calories) | 178 | kcal |
| Protein | 3 | g |
| Fat | 18 | g |
| Net Carbohydrates | 1 | g |
| Fiber | 0.1 | g |
| Sugars, total | 0.8 | g |

# Recipe #6: Creamy Vanilla Pudding

*Number of Servings: 4*
*Serving Size: ¼ cup*

*Prep Time: 5 minutes*
*Cook Time: 12 minutes*

Ingredients:
- 2 large egg yolks
- 1 cup 36 percent heavy cream
- 1 ½ tsp. stevia
- 1 tsp. arrowroot flour
- ½ tsp. pure vanilla extract
- Fine sea salt, to taste

Cooking Directions:
1. Combine the egg yolks in a heavy duty saucepan then whisk in the heavy cream, stevia, arrowroot flour, and pure vanilla extract. Mix well.
2. Add a dash of salt and whisk to combine. Then, place over medium flame and stir until the mixture starts to steam.
3. Reduce to low flame and continue to stir for about 10 minutes.
4. After 10 minutes, pour the pudding through a mesh sieve into 4 heatproof containers.
5. Place a sheet of plastic wrap directly on top of the pudding and refrigerate for up to 3 days. Serve chilled.

*Nutritional Facts per Serving:*

| | | |
|---|---|---|
| Energy (calories) | 135 | kcal |
| Protein | 2 | g |
| Fat | 13 | g |
| Net Carbohydrates | 2 | g |
| Fiber | 0 | g |
| Sugars, total | 0.9 | g |

# Recipe #7: Lemon Poppy Seed Cupcakes

*Number of Servings: 12*
*Serving Size: 1 cupcake*

*Prep Time: 15 minutes*
*Cook Time: 30 minutes*

Ingredients:
- 7 large eggs
- 10 oz. full fat plain Greek yogurt
- 4 oz. melted butter
- 3 oz. coconut flour
- 2 ½ Tbsp. freshly squeezed lemon juice
- 2 Tbsp. poppy seeds
- 2 ½ tsp. freshly grated lemon zest
- 2 tsp. baking powder
- 1 tsp. liquid stevia

Cooking Directions:
1. Set the oven to 375 degrees F to preheat. Line 12 cupcake tins with paper liners and set aside.
2. In a large bowl, whisk together the eggs, yogurt, and liquid stevia. Then, add the melted butter and mix well. Set aside.
3. Combine the coconut flour with the baking powder in a separate bowl, then mix into the egg mixture. Stir until smooth.
4. Stir the lemon juice and zest into the batter, followed by the poppy seeds. Stir well until evenly combined.
5. Pour the batter into the prepared cupcake tins, then bake for up to 30 minutes, or until the cupcakes are done. To check for readiness, insert a toothpick into

the center of one cupcake; if it comes out done, they are ready.
6. Transfer the cupcakes onto a cooling rack and allow to cool slightly. Transfer to an airtight container and refrigerate for up to 5 days. Reheat in the oven before serving, if desired.

*Nutritional Facts per Serving:*

| | | |
|---|---|---|
| Energy (calories) | 214 | kcal |
| Protein | 10 | g |
| Fat | 16 | g |
| Net Carbohydrates | 10 | g |
| Fiber | 3 | g |
| Sugars, total | 2 | g |

# Conclusion

Since you have reached the end of this book, it is safe to assume that you have tried many, if not all, of the recipes in this book and you are probably wondering what to have next. Of course, you can always make modifications to these recipes to give your taste buds variety, and at the same time, make the most out of seasonal ingredients.

You can also continue to add more recipes to this collection so that you would never run out of ideas on what to meal prep in the next 30 days. But with over 70 recipes to choose from, you probably never will!

# Intermittent Fasting

A Simple, Proven Approach to the Intermittent Fasting Lifestyle - Burn Fat, Build Muscle, Eat What You Want

# Introduction

If you are an avid searcher for methods and techniques that you hopefully think would help you achieve your desired body figure and health, you might have already run into several terms associated with diet and workout like Atkins diet, ketogenic diet, water therapy, and strength training.

There are actually a lot more terms and each of them probably had become a top searched figure at least once. But, there is this one method that is becoming more and more prominent these days, as it continues to prove its effectiveness not only to weight loss but also to the overall health of an individual—the intermittent fasting.

What if I told you that losing weight is not necessarily a matter of "what you eat," but instead a matter of "when you eat?" In this book, you'll find out what intermittent fasting is, and why people who relied on several diet methods before are gradually moving into this method.

This book will guide you throughout your journey; from learning everything about intermittent fasting up to applying the method to your lifestyle. You'll discover the benefits of the method not only as a way to lose fat but also as a means to improve certain functions in your health. There is also a step-by-step, comprehensive guide that will provide all the help you need so you could start on your new weight-loss program.

Get ready for the huge changes in your lifestyle and be prepared for the massive results that await you, as you take your very first step in this life-changing journey to a healthy weight loss!

# Part I – Everything You Need to Know About Intermittent Fasting

# Chapter 1: The Practice of Fasting

Fasting has been one of the most prominent methods of weight loss ever since it was introduced to our history. Up until today, there are a lot of people who prefer using the fasting method to shed some pounds, as they believe it's the best way to lose weight. Some of those who have proven the effectiveness of fasting even call it a "life cheat" or a "life hack" as it provides the result they desire without any cost at all.

There are, however, several claims that discredit the method and prove contrary to what is said to be its effect. Some nutritionists say that fasting is unhealthy and should not be promoted to the public as it can cause nutrition deficiencies and other health-related problems. In spite of this, there are still people who find fasting a great and easy way to lose weight. But, is fasting really just a matter of not eating to reduce body weight?

Fasting, in its purest definition, is the abstinence from consuming foods, drinks, or both for a certain period of time. During the early ages when different religions were still fighting over lands, people, and beliefs, it was not considered a form of diet; but instead, a practice to prove one's faith to the god of whatever religion a man believed. It was more of an obedience rather than a health-related practice.

Nowadays, fasting is still associated with existing religions and is still regarded as a part of religious practices. In Buddhism, monks and nuns strictly abide by the Vinaya rules. They do not eat after the noon meal and they stick to this practice every day. Under Christianity, the practice of fasting is linked to the passages expressly written in the biblical Book of Isaiah. In there, fasting is said to be not only a mere abstinence from food or water but also a decision to fully obey the god's commands. And in Islam, Muslims believe that aside from food abstinence, the practice of "fasting" also entails avoidance of acting and speaking of falsehood.

In the context of physiology and health, fasting refers simply to a person's metabolic status when he has not eaten overnight. It's the metabolic state after a person achieves full digestion and absorption of meal. It usually happens during sleep as this is the phase when the body doesn't receive anything and thus, is focused only on full digestion. From this very description, we can say that fasting is not just one of the thousands of methods of losing weight. It's actually a normal phenomenon that happens to every person, every day.

Just like those of any other practice related to health improvement and diet, the effects of fasting differ from person to person, depending on a variety of factors such as a person's age, current medication he is currently taking, his existing health issues if there are any, and his body's response to hunger. Nonetheless, fasting still has proven its own importance in the field of medicine and medical research.

There are distinguished types into which different ways of fasting are usually categorized namely dry fasting, water fasting, diagnostic fast, and intermittent fasting. All of these types use abstinence from either food or water but vary on their purposes.

## Absolute Fast

An absolute fast (also known as dry fasting) is the complete abstinence of food and liquid that lasts commonly for 24 hours. This type of fasting can further be extended up to a couple of days. This is usually a practice done for religious purposes.

## Water Fast

This type of fasting is almost like an absolute fasting except that it allows the consumption of drinking water during fasting period; but aside from drinking water, all other liquids are prohibited. This type is believed to be practiced by some people in order to "cleanse" their bodies. The most common diet method associated with this type is the water therapy which has been proven effective in weight-loss procedures.

## Diagnostic Fast

Diagnostic fast is a fasting supported by medical practitioners. It is technically a part of medical procedure performed as a pre-observation measure. It is a fasting advised to, and done by people who undergo or will undergo a medical investigation with regard to certain health problems like hypoglycemia. Some procedures also require diagnostic fasting before the actual check-up such as in a colonoscopy.

## Intermittent Fast

Intermittent fasting is the type of fasting that is neither absolute nor done for diagnostic purposes. It is seen as an aid in diet and is proven effective for burning fats, building muscle, and controlling nutritional intake. This will be elaborately discussed in the proceeding chapters. There is also a section that will guide you on how to perform intermittent fasting properly and the supplemental things that will help you achieve better results. So, what are you waiting for? Let's proceed to the next chapter!

# Chapter 2: Intermittent Fasting

They say an apple a day keeps the doctor away, but consuming like seven or more apples each day is not anymore covered by this golden saying.

Eating a lot of healthy foods can surely provide dramatic changes to your overall health. However, "a lot" of these foods could sometimes be "too much" for your body that it wouldn't be able to respond properly anymore; yes, even those foods which are worshipped as the healthiest. This is when intermittent fasting comes in—promoting nutrition regulation and diet control.

But, what exactly is intermittent fasting? Intermittent fasting is an eating or diet schedule which follows a cycle of alternating eating and no-eating periods. A person who practices intermittent fasting basically abides by a schedule that divides the day or the week into fasting and eating periods which are patterned at regular intervals. For example, on a week-based intermittent fasting schedule, a person might assign his Mondays, Wednesdays, and Saturdays as fasting periods, which means he should not eat on those days; and then his Sundays, Tuesdays, Thursdays, and Fridays as his eating periods.

Assigning schedules for intermittent fasting can be as simple as every other day, or as complex as a combination of week-based and day-based fasting—in a day-based fasting, a person splits his daily time frame into eating and fasting periods. In any case, intermittent fasting isn't really that much of a new idea to the body.

As once mentioned in the preceding chapter, the time when a person sleeps can already be considered as fasting time. This is because the body's digestive properties do not have any new substance to digest during sleep; thus, they stop right after fully completing the digestion. The idea of intermittent fasting is simply to extend this portion of time and retain the "empty" state of stomach until the next scheduled eating time. It's almost just like sleeping for a longer period.

**How Intermittent Fasting Is Done**

Let's say for example, you are planning to start practicing a day-based intermittent fasting. The first thing you want to know is how long your fasting period should be in each day. Ideally, the proper fasting period should be 15 to 16 hours a day; this leaves you nine to eight hours for your eating period. The remaining eight- or nine-hour eating window should strictly be the only time when you are allowed to eat. Majority of those who practice intermittent fasting usually set two meals for this length.

Now that you know both your eating period and fasting period, you need to choose which time should each period start and end. If you are familiar with weight-loss diet plans and protocols, you probably know that the best time at which you can set your dinner is as early as seven or eight in the evening. Let's say that you set your dinner at seven in the evening, counting back eight hours from 7 pm you'll have 11 am. This means that your eating period should start at 11 in the morning and should end at seven in the evening. The rest of the hours that are not covered by your eating window should be a no-eating or -drinking period. If you normally wake up at 8 am then you should skip the breakfast, take your lunch at 11 am, have your dinner at 7 pm and sleep at whatever time you usually go to bed.

## Science and Medical Research

Several studies were already done to examine the effectiveness and safety of intermittent fasting. Most of the results of these research studies showed remarks that were close to each other although the proponents and other scientists have not yet come up with a hard and fast conclusion. This is because each result had its own distinct negative impact to the samples; from minor issues to major health problems. Scientists believe that these issues were brought by a lot of factors such as the differences in the health of participants, and the foods, themselves which are offered during eating time. Nevertheless, the positive effects of most of these studies were found to be more dominant than the negative ones. This induces the scientists and researchers to further conduct studies to support this type of fasting.

One of the most prominent and current research done concerning the effects of scheduled or intermittent fasting was a research in endocrinology conducted by proponents from the United States of America. The study called the fasting schedule as intermittent energy restriction or IER. The IER's counterpart was the ad libitum feeding or free feeding. The IER followed the intermittent fasting schedule while the ad libitum feeding simply based the feeding on the sample's own biological hunger phase.

Like in the usual setting of laboratory tests, the first testing was done on rodents. The mice were divided into two groups—the IER group and the free-feeding group. After five months of feeding, both groups were observed and examined.

It was found out that among the mice used for testing, those under the IER group showed dramatic reduction from their initial glucose and insulin levels—the examination was a part of a study about type 2 diabetes. Those under the free-feeding group, on the other hand, either retained their original glucose and insulin levels or developed slight changes from their original levels. Either way, it was found out that the glucose and insulin levels of mice in the IER group were significantly lower than those of the mice in the other group.

It was further found out from the same research study that despite having lower glucose and insulin levels, the mice under the IER group were surprisingly not suffering from energy deficiency. The proponents believe that it was because the mice of IER group had already adapted to their new eating setting and they therefore would require only less levels of glucose and insulin intake to suffice their energy needs.

There was also a study that found intermittent fasting as a huge contributory factor when it comes to weight loss. Such study also involved rodents as its subjects. In the first phase of the test, all of the rats had ad libitum access to standard food; they were able to consume meals whenever they felt hungry. The first phase lasted for four weeks. After the fourth week, the rats were then divided into two groups. The first group of rats continued with the ad libitum feeding while the second group underwent strict diet schedule which consisted eating and fasting days, similar to the IER group from the previously mentioned study.

The rats from each group were then further tested for another 10 weeks. After the 10th week, each of the group was examined—it was discovered that there were huge reductions in the body weights of those rats under the second group or the IER group. The differences between the body weights of the rats belonging to the IER group after the first phase of the study and after the second phase, were comparable to those of the rats which belonged to the first group. The results were further examined and brought to an analysis of the IER's efficacy in relation to the development of insulin resistance due to high fat diet.

## Intermittent Fasting Effects on Humans

Of course, the previously mentioned pieces of evidence won't be enough to back up even just half of the claimed efficacy of intermittent fasting for these only involved rodents as their subjects. But in the usual research laboratory environment, such tests are relevant and reasonable enough to consider the study as applicable to an upper level form of subject—humans.

One research study featured on an article entitled, Nutrition & Diabetes, suggested that intermittent fasting—coupled with low-energy diet—resulted to improvements on both glucose metabolism and cardiovascular health. The study involved both overweight and obese people. It used IER trial as well and the observation period lasted three months. After the third month of strict diet implementation, the subjects were examined to identify the presence of cardiovascular risk markers and to assess the glucose levels of individuals.

Majority of the subjects showed positive changes on both aspects. There were less risk markers on their cardiovascular health which could lead to serious heart diseases if left maintained at a high level. Plus, their glucose metabolism has improved. The subjects' levels of blood pressure were also examined in the same study although there were minimal inconsistencies when such results are compared to the results of other studies which also focused on the effects of intermittent fasting. Thus, only the IER's effect on cardiovascular health and glucose properties of humans was considered safe to conclude, at least as of the current state.

There was also an intermittent fasting trial performed on non-obese, healthy individuals. In a matter of three weeks, effects became evident on the individuals who took part in the trial. On men participants, triglyceride levels were lowered to a healthier state. Triglyceride is an organic compound which can be found in a human body. The presence of high levels of triglyceride compounds in the body is a sign that an individual is prone to or has diabetes or kidney disease.

With regard to the women participants, the researchers found a post-treatment increase in high-density lipoprotein or HDL cholesterol. HDL cholesterol functions as an important substance in the body as it removes excess cholesterol from the blood, the cells, and the walls of blood vessels; hence, called the good cholesterol. The variation of the effects based on gender is believed to be caused by the level of fasting each gender group naturally possesses; men participants tended to have higher fasting levels than women participants. Though the results of the study were found to be gender-specific, they were considered a helpful tool to demonstrate the positive effects of intermittent fasting.

There are more studies to back up the effects of intermittent fasting but enumerating each would take a lifetime to be thoroughly explained. Besides, the concept of intermittent fasting, being widely accepted as a major topic on health and diet, has just yet begun on getting attention in the field of medical research. That is why the studies related to it are not as numerous and as conclusive as those which have focused on well-known, broader health topics such as diabetes, skin care, or workout trainings.

# Chapter 3: Benefits of Intermittent Fasting

Even if intermittent fasting sounds like a common practice that has been naturally existing for centuries, the conceptualization of the practice is actually not that old. A number of research studies are still on the line and medical researchers are still either planning or conducting several trials in pursuit of developing a solid conclusion to close the case—which would be more likely to take years or decades to happen.

But as of the studies that are currently on record, intermittent fasting already holds quite a decent impression when it comes to human health. Majority of the past trials ended up with a positive conclusion regarding the beneficial effects of the diet concept to people. These benefits include induced cell repair processes, reduced oxidative stress, lowered insulin resistance, increased brain function and protection, weight loss and muscle growth, as well as increased protection against certain diseases.

**Induced Repair Processes on Cells**

Fasting prompts the cells in your body to perform autophagy which is the process through which cells undergo self-destruction. Autophagy is a normal physiological phenomenon which is meant to maintain normal cellular functioning. Destroyed cell organelles are turned over for the generation of new cells. This helps the body maintain a healthy set of cells and get rid of unnecessary or damaged organelles which could cause serious diseases such as cancer, when not destroyed.

When an individual does not consume food or water for a prolonged span of time, the stress level in his body increases. A healthily elevated stress level induces autophagy to take place; and this is the exact reason that fasting is considered a biological stressor which brings a healthy amount of positive effects in the body including autophagy.

**Reduced Oxidative Stress**

Oxidative stress happens when the production of free radicals is not countered by the body's ability to detoxify their negative effects to health. This happens either because there is an abnormally excessive production of free radicals that the body's natural ability, even at a normal state, cannot battle the free radicals' harmful effects; or because the body's antioxidant activity became too weak that it couldn't keep pace even with the normal production of free radicals.

The ability of the body to deter harmful effects of free radicals is called neutralization which is brought by the body's antioxidants. Antioxidants are molecules that safely interact with free radicals, as well as counteract and detoxify their harmful effects, to maintain a healthy set of cells. An imbalance between antioxidant activity and free radical production brings oxidative stress to place; and therefore, damages the components of the cell.

Short-period fasting works by ironically causing a slight increase in free radical production. This triggers the cells in the body to respond on a more secure level by increasing the level of anti-oxidant activity. When this happens, the antioxidants will be able to detoxify all the free radicals and will lessen the oxidative stress.

## Lowered Insulin Resistance

Insulin is a hormone produced by the pancreas which extracts glucose from carbohydrates and converts them into energy. It can also store glucose in the body for future use. However, when the body receives too much insulin, it tries to counter this excessive level until it eventually fails to respond properly to the hormone.

Insulin resistance is a serious complication that entails some of the known major health problems. This is because insulin helps keep the body's blood sugar level in regulation. Thus, when the body resists insulin, it also loses its control over blood sugar level; making the body prone to both hyperglycemia or the surge in blood sugar level, or hypoglycemia or the abnormal drop in blood sugar level.

In a certain study involving humans as subjects, intermittent fasting was attributed to a 3-6% decrease in blood sugar and 20-31% drop in insulin level. The figures showed good indications of insulin level improvement. A decrease in insulin level is technically helpful since in the first place, insulin resistance is brought by excessive insulin level. The study also showed that intermittent fasting protected the subjects from kidney damage.

## Increased Brain Function and Protection

As of the currently existing studies, though only involving animal samples, intermittent fasting has proven a number of benefits to the brain. One of these studies discovered that the growth of nerve cells on those mice which underwent intermittent fasting, accelerated after the intervention period. Another study showed that intermittent fasting could prevent brain damage that could further lead to stroke.

An increase in brain-derived neurotrophic factor or BDNF was also found evident on the samples involved in a study about dietary restriction and its effects on the brain. Deficiency in BDNF hormones are implicated in various mental health issues including depression.

**Weight Loss and Muscle Growth**

Among the effects of intermittent fasting, weight loss is what people sought after the most. This type of diet pattern has been used and incorporated in several fitness plans and is becoming more and more trendy among health-conscious people because of its huge impact to the body. Plus, it comes with a bonus—studies show that intermittent fasting helps retain lean mass and promote muscle growth. All of these will be elaborately discussed in the next chapter.

**Increased Protection Against Certain Diseases**

Due to the previously mentioned benefits, it is apparent that intermittent fasting can safely be attributed to lowered risks of certain types of diseases. The improved cell repair processing can help the body get rid of cancer. The decrease in oxidative stress may battle brain-health issues such as depression and Alzheimer's disease. Improvements in insulin level, on the other hand, are directly connected to insulin resistance and are therefore helpful to combat diabetes as well. Above all, intermittent fasting is an effective tool for a healthier way of losing weight, making it both a preventive and a corrective measure against obesity.

# Chapter 4: Intermittent Fasting – Key to a Healthy Weight Loss and Muscle Growth

The most probable reason a person follows an intermittent fasting schedule is weight loss. Fortunately, weight loss is among one of the evidence-supported benefits that intermittent fasting promotes. Well, fasting in general promotes weight loss; so, what makes intermittent fasting a different and better option?

When you fast, you basically do not allow your body to receive calories from foods. This means you are not prone to storing excess calories as fats in your body. Therefore, if your body continues to fast, there are only two things that can happen to your body weight—remain as is or decrease. Among the two, it is the latter which is more likely to happen since fats are naturally burned during activities regardless if they are eventually replaced or not.

Although the idea is scientifically true, not all people who tried fasting succeeded in losing weight. As a matter of fact, some of them even ended up gaining more. This is because the general term "fasting" simply means abstaining from foods, drinks, or both. It does not define how much to abstain, for how long one should abstain, nor what happens next after someone starved himself for an unusual length of time—it often ends up being misinterpreted as an unregulated way of skipping at least one full meal.

Most of the people "fast" by skipping breakfast. But when the lunch time comes, they tend to eat more than usual to satisfy the prolonged hunger they endured before the meal. This is the common mistake people do when they fast; they do not pair it with discipline. If you fast for 48 hours, you'll most probably eat a lot on your next meal as your body needs to gain what it didn't during the fasting period; regardless if you try to control it or not. This is why fasting for straight long periods is not recommended by nutritionists and health experts.

Intermittent fasting, on the other hand, follows a uniform cycle of periods; hence, regulated. It gradually lets the body adjust into a new setup until it becomes used to it. It does not abuse hunger too much as it still includes the three main meals of the day, or two at the least. So, there is nothing to worry about not being able to control food intake. The diet concept actually just expands the span of time when your body is not consuming anything and narrows your eating-window. This is considerably a healthy setup if you want to shed some pounds. In here, you are giving your body enough time to fully digest meals so as to absorb the nutrients properly instead of merely storing them as fats.

**Accelerated Fat-Burning Process**

Moreover, short-period fasting also accelerates your metabolism which means your body can burn more calories when you follow intermittent fasting. In a certain study published by the National Center for Biotechnology Information or NCBI in the US National Library of Medicine, short-term starvation led to an average of 3.6% increase in the metabolic rate of the subjects.

11 healthy young individuals took part in the said study, all of whom are normal-weight. They were not allowed to eat meals for 48 hours. After the intervention period, the metabolic rate of each individual increased in varied rates with a mean of 3.6%. Such number was considered as a large increase in metabolism level and was entirely attributed to the starvation or fasting period.

## Intermittent Fasting vs. Daily Calorie Restriction

There exists a traditional diet regimen called daily calorie restriction or CR through which an individual limits his daily calorie intake to a fixed measure. If you adopt this kind of diet technique, you need to be conscious on the quantity of the food you consume and make sure that you do not exceed your calorie limit. So, if let's say, you are only allowed to take 1500 calories per day, your total calorie consumption should not be 1600 or 1700 calories but 1400 calories or below are allowed. This technique has proven favorable results to individuals who practice the CR method but there's one downside to this—it's hard to maintain such kind of diet.

First of all, the meals an individual takes every day usually do not have a readily available calorie measure. And in such case, the individual must rely heavily on estimation which is not a good thing, considering that the very purpose of the CR method is to quantify the exact calorie intake of a person in order to regulate consumption. Unfortunately, approximation is not ideal most especially when you need to implement the diet method in the strictest terms.

Secondly, even if an individual consumes foods and products in boxes or cartons (which most probably have a calorie amount indicator on their nutrition facts sections), it will be hard for an individual to guarantee that what he had just consumed would be equal to the calorie amount that was written on the packaging; say, what if he did not consume all the content? Besides, packed foods are not really the healthiest option for an individual who claims to be "on a diet."

Lastly, it's not always safe to say that a person can control his food intake every day based on a fixed calorie limit. It should not be forgotten that calories are also energy providers and not just "potential" fats. There might come a day which would demand more energy from an individual and choosing to stick with the limited-calorie food intake clearly would not be efficient.

In contrast to the quantified restriction of CR method, intermittent fasting allows free intake of food during eating-windows. This diet schedule is after the lengthening of fasting period and shortening the eating period without necessarily limiting the calorie intake; while the CR method does not restrict consumption based on time but on the size of food, itself. To be honest, both are equally effective in reducing weight but there are recent studies which can back up the claim that intermittent fasting is better than calorie restriction method in some aspects other than mere fat mass reduction.

According to an article published by the Department of Kinesiology and Nutrition of the University of Illinois in Chicago, the intermittent diet schedule may be more effective in retaining the lean mass in the body while reducing weight. The study used obese individuals as subjects. The review focused on examining weight loss as well as the corresponding fat mass loss and lean mass retention. Under the daily CR diet, the average weight loss was 5-8% while the average fat mass loss was 10-20%. On the other hand, the intermittent diet resulted into 4-8% average weight loss and 11-16% fat mass loss.

The figures were evidently near to each type. However, the researchers further identified that although both were effective for weight reduction, the intermittent fasting resulted to a greater retention of lean mass than CR diet. Lean mass, in a nutshell, is the portion in your weight that isn't fat. This portion includes the weight of your bones, your muscles, the water in your body, and technically, all of your organs. This is the reason that a lot of nutritionists advise body builders to go after either retaining or gaining lean mass while reducing fat mass.

**Muscle Mass Retention and Growth**

An unregulated fasting might be helpful in losing weight but the problem with it is that along the process of shedding fat mass, you might also lose some of your lean mass. This is a crucial matter as a lot of people mistake losing weight as synonymous to being healthy. Unless all the weight you lost is composed of fat mass, it is not safe to say that your body did get healthier.

It is only important to understand that fat loss is different from muscle loss although the tricky part is that, both can happen in a single weight loss activity. If you focus too much on losing weight without keeping track of your muscle health, chances are you'll end up degrading your muscle strength. Since intermittent fasting helps retain lean mass amid weight reduction, it can therefore also help retain muscle mass for body builders.

Retaining muscle mass is just as hard as gaining it. Even if you gained much, it won't make any noticeable change if you also lost much of it at the same time. Let's say for example, you weigh 170 pounds and that you constantly gain two pounds of muscle mass per month because of consistent training. In a span of one year, we can say that you'll gain 24 pounds of lean muscle mass turning your initial 170-pound weight into 194 pounds. That is a huge muscle improvement considering you didn't gain any significant fat mass the whole year. But what if during the year, due to unregulated fasting, you also lost a total of 23 pounds of lean mass? Your weight at the end of the year will then only be 171 pounds—a frustratingly one-pound gain for a whole year of training.

Consistency in growth is the key to build stronger muscles—and to look more ripped in case appearance is a factor. This is why muscle gainers must follow diet patterns which support retention of lean muscle mass. And such rule shall also apply to those who want to lose weight and gain muscle at the same time.

**Getting Rid of Belly Fat**

If you are one of those people who are overly conscious with their fat tummies and how they keep on showing a bump under your otherwise gorgeous clothes, then there's a good news for you—intermittent fasting is also associated with belly fat reduction.

There was a study regarding the effect of intermittent fasting on type 2 diabetes, which tested individuals with "fat tummies." These individuals underwent intermittent fasting and after 24 weeks, the fasting alone provided the individuals 4-7% waist circumference reduction. This is largely connected to the previously tested efficacy of intermittent fasting when it comes to overall weight loss.

# Chapter 5: Types of Intermittent Fasting

Several variations of intermittent fasting have already been made even before the diet pattern became popular to the world. And as it gets more and more attention from health enthusiasts and nutritional experts, the list becomes longer. All of the types that exist to date are created out of varying needs so it cannot really be identified which among these "best" fits all. In fact, majority of those who largely benefited from intermittent fasting are using a mixture of two or more of these types.

There are, however, a few types of intermittent fasting that have established a decent impression to both nutritionists and diet experts. These intermittent fasting variants have made it to the list mainly because a number of people found these diet patterns appropriate for them and for their needs.

**5:2 Diet**

Popularized by British journalist and producer Michael Mosley, this is by far the most prominent kind of intermittent fasting. 5:2 diet is a week-based fasting schedule meaning; a cycle lasts for a week and every cycle or week is split into fasting and eating days. This is a simple schedule that can be followed by anyone and is also among one of the most flexible diet patterns.

5:2 basically means five whole days of free-eating for two full days of fasting. Since a week is composed of seven days, you can just set two of these days as your fasting days and freely consume foods for the rest of the week. On every fasting day, you can only consume a total of not more than 25% of your average daily calorie consumption. Yes, "fasting" here refers to a period of limited intake and not an absolutely no-food nor -drink period; thus, you can still eat but with limitation.

To provide a clearer picture of how 5:2 diet is followed, let's say you designated your Wednesdays and Thursdays as your fasting days. On your Fridays up to your Tuesdays, you can eat your meals the way you normally do; you can eat breakfast, lunch, dinner and even snacks. There are no limits on eating days. On the other hand, your Wednesdays and Thursdays are a little stricter when it comes to your consumption. If your average calorie consumption per day is let's say 2000, your calorie limit would be 500 (2000 multiplied by 25%). This means you should not eat more than 500 calories on your Wednesdays and neither on your Thursdays. Fasting days in 5:2 diet aren't that strict though. You can still have three meals during these days except that the meals would be relatively smaller.

Do your fasting days have to be consecutive days? Well, as stated earlier, 5:2 diet is known for being one of the most flexible diet patterns; so nope, those days do not necessarily have to be consecutive. Majority of the 5:2 diet users find hunger easier to sustain when the two fasting days are apart from each other like Mondays and Wednesdays or Tuesdays and Fridays. It is even highly recommended for beginners to set these periods on non-consecutive days, considering a 75% decrease in one's normal calorie intake is a huge, sudden drop. So, if you want to overcome your first few weeks under 5:2 diet, better refrain from picking two consecutive days. Consecutive days are more convenient though and as long as the fasting won't exceed 48 hours, they are believed to provide equally healthy but slightly faster results.

Another thing that makes it a flexible diet pattern is that each cycle does not have to follow a uniform pattern. This means you can fast on the Thursday and Friday of the current week and switch these fasting days into the Tuesday and Wednesday of the following week. Of course, uniform cycles are better so your body could adapt to consistency but it's much better to stick to reality and consider the possibilities that you can't always be free to fast on the same days of every week. Nonetheless, it is still up to you how you would like to apply this type of intermittent fasting to each of your weeks.

Further, some of the other types of intermittent fasting were actually just variations of the 5:2 diet. There is also a 4:3 diet which sets three fasting days for every week; and 6:1 diet which only involves one fasting day in a week. If you don't find yourself fit to practice fasting for two days every week, then you can try some of these variations. As long as you stick to cutting your calorie intake into 25% during fasting periods, there shouldn't be any problem.

**Eat-Stop-Eat Diet Plan**

The eat-stop-eat diet plan was created by weight-loss expert Brad Pilon based on the concept of intermittent fasting. Pilon has a background in sports nutrition and supplements that is why this specific diet plan, according to diet experts, is more suitable for people who are usually involved in physical activities or sports.

In an eat-stop-eat diet plan, you fast for full 24 hours once or twice a week; thus, it is also called the 24-hour fast plan.

Similar to 5:2 diet, you may eat normally during your non-fasting days. However, if both the consecutive and non-consecutive fast days are acceptable in 5:2 diet, in eat-stop-eat diet plan, only the non-consecutive days are deemed appropriate. In fact, Pilon even expressly emphasized that one should not fast for consecutive days and neither should one fast for more than 48 hours in a single week.

There are no quantified calorie limits during fast days in this type of intermittent fasting; as you should aim for a complete abstinence from food if you are following eat-stop-eat diet. You can, however, take diet soda, sparkling water, tea, or coffee during such period. If you felt the need to break the full fast, Pilon says that you can eat whatever you want to eat but he also suggests that you moderate your consumption. Also, if you cannot fast for 24 hours straight, shorter periods will also work as long as it is not less than 20 hours.

After the 24-hour fast, it is advised that appropriate amount of calorie intake per day should be taken—approximately 2000 calories for women and 2500 calories for men. Also, high-quality protein is highly recommended in this diet. You may take 20 to 30 grams of it every four to five hours for a total of 100 grams per day. This is to ensure that lean muscle mass is retained during intermittent fasting.

Say, if you started your fast at 8 am on Tuesday, you can resume eating normally at 8 am on Wednesday. During the fasting period, starting at 8 am on Tuesday, you may drink coffee or diet soda and consume a total of 100 grams of high-quality protein. If you still find it hard to go through the day without eating meals, you may eat a little but make sure to limit it otherwise it cannot be considered as a fasting period. You can have your breakfast exactly at 8 am in the next morning as the fasting period ends at that time. You can go back to eating normally and after several non-fasting days, you can then repeat the 24-hour fast.

Remember, your fasting days should not be near to each other for this kind of plan not only is after weight loss but is also aiming to maintain lean muscle mass. Pilon also does not recommend pairing this diet schedule with low-carb meals as this will only result into energy deficiency. Individuals who adopt this type of intermittent fasting need appropriate levels of energy; hence, appropriate amount of glucose. This is also the reason that Pilon recommends taking the right amount of calorie intake per non-fasting day. The results of this diet plan are enhanced by consumption of fruits and vegetables.

**16:8 Protocol**

This intermittent fasting variant was originated by personal trainer and nutritional expert Martin Berkhan. Unlike the first two mentioned diet plans, this is a day-based fasting; which means that a cycle takes only a day to repeat and that each day is split into fasting and eating hours. 16:8 simply means a day should be composed of 16 hours of fasting and 8 hours of free-eating. The diet plan is known for its effectiveness not only to weight loss but also to lean mass gain, that's why Berkhan calls it the "leangains" method. You'll find out more about this type of intermittent fasting on the part II of this book.

**The Warrior Diet**

Ever imagined a Viking devouring a whole table of foods? What about a Spartan gulping a big barrel of wine? Well, one of these days, you might find yourself looking like these men as you take your meal under the Warrior Diet plan.

The Warrior Diet is one of the most popular diet plans that incorporate intermittent fasting. There is actually a whole book discussing about this and it was written by nutritional and fitness expert Ori Hofmekler, who apparently started this kind of diet philosophy. Hofmekler is the founder of Defense Nutrition. He has already authored a number of books to date, all of which tackle health and fitness.

So, how is Warrior Diet done? The diet plan essentially follows a day-based intermittent fasting schedule. On each day, you have to fast for 20 hours straight and eat at least once during the remaining four hours. The fasting period of 20 hours might sound like an uphill battle to some, considering it must be applied every—single—day; but don't worry, the fasting period in this diet protocol allows consumption of minimal servings of raw fruits and veggies, or a glass of fresh juice. You may also take small servings of protein if you want. Just don't eat a full-course meal during fast.

Fasting and eating periods under this diet pattern are more appropriately termed as "undereating" and "overeating" periods, respectively. So, we can say that the undereating phase is really intended for you to still be able to consume foods although such consumption must strictly be observed and limited. Overeating phase, on the other hand, is the four-hour period where you can eat tons of foods covering as many nutrients as possible. It is also important to set the overeating phase at night time.

For example, if you choose to set your overeating phase at six o'clock to ten o'clock in the evening, you must limit your food intake from 10 pm of the same night to 6 pm of the next day. During your 20-hour undereating phase you may take a small plate of pure vegetable salad or drink freshly extracted fruit or vegetable juice. You can also add a bit of protein to your salad by putting a few strips of lean chicken meat to it. Once the clock turns to 6 pm, you can now "overeat" as pointedly instructed by the diet plan. You may eat a large meal composed of a bowl of Caesar salad, a plate of steak and seared salmon, as well as a dish of carbonara or a clubhouse sandwich if you want to. Yes, this diet plan does mean it when it says to eat "tons" of foods. Besides, it isn't called Warrior Diet for nothing.

Speaking of being a "warrior" in this diet plan, you also need to discipline yourself like one. The diet protocol does not just instruct eating a lot during the four-hour overeating phase, it also highly recommends proper sequence of food intake once you start with your free-eating period. The order of food intake from first to last should be: vegetables, protein, fat, and carbohydrates. The first three should as much as possible be strictly taken in order. You may omit the carbohydrates if you want but you'd most likely need to eat some, considering this comes after a long period of fasting. The carbs are neither limited anyway so you can take as much as you want as long as they come after the veggies, protein, and fat.

The science behind this diet plan is a bit complex to explain. Contrary to the common diet rule that one should not eat late at night, as such will only result to weight gain, the philosophy that backs up this diet plan is linked to a different theory—humans are inherently nocturnal eaters. But despite holding on to a different view, nutrition experts are convinced with the protocol's effects in the body.

To explain, the undereating phase is meant to maximize "fight or flight" response of the sympathetic nervous system. Fight-or-flight response is a reaction made by the body in response to a perceived threat. Threat includes harmful events, imminent danger, or even survival threats like hunger. And since the body struggles with hunger during the 20-hour fast, the fight-or-flight responds by making the body more alert and boosting the energy which would eventually result to stimulating the fat burning process.

The overeating phase, on the other hand, is supposed to utilize the ability of the Parasympathetic Nervous System to promote digestion, as well as relaxation within the body. This allows the body to absorb the consumed nutrients and use it for repair and growth. It also helps the body burn fats during the day.

The benefits of Warrior Diet to the body will only be maximized if one follows the plan accordingly. Majority of those who tried this diet plan claim that this is a tough job to take. But at the end of the day, being able to witness the progress in your body is what matters the most. After all, it's a diet plan for the devoted and disciplined individuals—for the warriors-in-training.

**Alternate-Day Fasting**

Alternate-day fasting or up-day-down-day diet is a fasting protocol that follows a two-day cycle. It originated from the book UpDayDownDay Diet™ which was authored by plastic surgeon Dr. James Johnson. Doctor Johnson also struggled with weight loss himself, which led him to the discovery of an eating plan effective for weight loss.

The diet plan is fairly plain; you eat minimal servings of meals one day and you eat your usual servings the next day. In here, the days when you eat small or limited servings are called "down days" while those which allow you to consume normal servings are called "up days." The process simply repeats every two days and since it's a two-day cycle, there are really no particular days which can be set as either up days or down days (if your Monday this week is a down day then your Monday next week won't be the same assuming you followed the fasting schedule throughout the week).

The plan also entails a quantified limit of calorie intake that should be followed on down days as much as possible. It instructs that you only consume one fifth of your usual calorie intake during your down days. Therefore, if your normal consumption is approximately 2000 calories per day, then you should only take approximately 400 calories on your down days. Your down days would typically comprise regular or normal meals although those must come in smaller servings.

According to Doctor Johnson, if you find it hard to stick to your down days, you may opt for protein and calorie shakes or meal replacement shakes. These shakes are packed with essential nutrients and can safely substitute meals. However, these shakes are merely a help for you to survive down days especially when you are a beginner to this. They should only be taken on your first two weeks under this diet schedule and should not be a regular substitute for your meals every down day. After at most, two weeks, you should go back to eating "real" foods or meals so your body won't get used to depending on liquids and shakes.

If you are a gym rat, you might want to consider hitting the gym only on your up days, as these are the days on which you can surely sustain endurance on physical activities without breaking the diet plan. Lifting weights and engaging to other strenuous activities require quite a pack of energy and you can only have a decent amount of it on days when you eat "normal" or "enough" servings. Besides, alternate-day fasting is designed solely to promote weight loss. Trying to gain lean muscle mass while under this diet plan would entail additional efforts and those include disciplining your gym-enthusiast-self to rest on down days (and probably to eat more protein-rich servings).

**Fat Loss Forever**

If you're torn between the flexibility of eat-stop-eat diet and the free-eating feature of Warrior Diet, Fat Loss Forever diet might be the one that you're looking for. The diet plan was conceptualized by fitness expert John Romaniello and was made for gym-goers who want a flexible diet schedule that also includes the most important day of the week—cheat day.

The name "Fat Loss Forever" is actually a fancy title for a diet plan with a complicated mixture of different fasting protocols in one schedule. Unless you pull off the diet schedule properly, the "fat loss" is not going to come and the possibility that the fat will be lost "forever" won't be guaranteed. Nevertheless, it's still labeled as one of the most effective diet plans anchored to the concept of intermittent fasting.

The diet plan is essentially a week-based intermittent fasting and each week should include two primary periods: the cheat day and the 36-hour fast. The 36-hour fast should always come after the cheat day. After that, you should incorporate one or more intermittent fasting protocols for the rest of the week. Romaniello suggests that you save your 36-hour fast for the busiest days of your week so you'd be focused on more important things (e.g. work) other than your hunger.

Let's say, if you started your cheat day on Thursday at 8 am and ate your last "cheat" meal for the day at 9 pm, your 36-hour fast should start at 9 pm on the same day. Counting 36 hours from 9 pm, your next "normal meal" should be on Saturday at 9 am. That is indeed a long period of fast but of course, you can consume small servings of protein, carbs, fruits, and vegetables during the 36-hour period; just make sure you are not taking any full-course meal. Afterwards, if you decided to adopt alternate-day fasting for the rest of the week, then the day after your 36-hour fast (Saturday in this case) should be an up day as your body needs to recover enough nutrients after the fast. The next day which is Sunday, should then be a down day. The remaining days before the next Thursday should just be an alternating series of up and down days.

It is important to apply the corresponding rules under the different fasting protocols that you use for the rest of the week, after the cheat day and 36-hour fast. From the illustration above, your down days should only comprise one fifth of your average calorie consumption. If you happen to consume an average of approximately 2500 calories a day, you should limit your Sunday and Tuesday meals at 500 calories (one fifth of 2500) for the whole day.

For another example, let's say you started your cheat day on Sunday from 9 am to 10 pm. This sets your 36-hour fasting period at 10 pm on Sunday and from that, the period should end at 10 am on Tuesday. If you use the Warrior Diet for the rest of the week, then that forces you to extend the 36-hour fasting period to 44 to 48 hours. This is because the Warrior Diet follows a night-time eating schedule; and since your 36-hour fasting period ends at morning, you'll need to wait for another couple of hours before you can eat. Therefore, your next large meal should be on Tuesday around 6 or 8 pm. For Wednesday up to Saturday, the night-time eating rule shall also be applied accordingly. You can have your cheat day once again when the next Sunday arrives.

With regard to cheat days, it is crucial that you know what to eat when you are given such heavenly freedom. On these days, cakes, ice cream, sodas, fast foods, junk foods, or charred meats might be enticing but are they really worth it? Well, considering that you sacrificed probably the majority of your week in the name of fasting, those are more or less fine to eat (it's a cheat day anyway). You deserve them!

However, it will be a lot better if you focus on eating the healthier foods which offer all the nutrients that you were deprived of during the past few days of struggle. You fasted, so you technically did not just lose fats; some essential nutrients were also lost along the way. At least try to eat a lot of vegetables, fruits, lean meats, and healthy amount of fats and carbs first before taking the not-so-healthy second options. Also, do not forget the fact that anything taken excessively has corresponding undesirable effects.

The diet might seem so complicated at first but once you and your body get used to it, you'll find out that it's actually a rewarding diet plan. Plus, your body will also be able to flexibly adapt to changes as you switch from one diet protocol to another in order to fit in with your ever-changing personal schedule. Just stick to the two important parts of the week namely, the cheat day and the 36-hour fasting period; and let the rest of the week adapt to whatever intermittent fasting plans you decide to use.

# Part II – Comprehensive Guide to Intermittent Fasting

# Chapter 6: Taking the Action

If you already feel, by now, that you're ready to take the action and start implementing intermittent fasting to your daily life, you might want to consider to take it easy. Not that being excited is bad, though. It's just that, this is one of those points in your life when you should stop your happily excited spirit from rushing things out. Why?

A lot of people fail to realize that just because you have already learned the basics and foundational concepts of intermittent fasting, doesn't mean you are fully ready to apply it in your life. Those who failed with their diet plans most probably overlooked something that could've otherwise made their weight-loss journey successful—preparation.

Reading about fasting is different from actually doing it. It's easier said than done. Therefore, preparation must come in between reading and practicing. And to help you with your preparation, you may consider the following order of guidelines: self-assessment, choosing a diet plan, understanding the importance of exercise, and learning about the fasting foods and liquids.

**Assessing Yourself**

First things first—are you ready? In intermittent fasting, being ready doesn't just refer to your body's capability to undergo sets of fasting periods; it also refers to your mental state of readiness. Being physically ready to intermittent fasting is generally easy. The human body can inherently last even up to two weeks without food. So, the real question would be, are you mentally ready?

You need to assess yourself as early as now because if you are not mentally ready, chances are you'll end up breaking your fasting rules, ditching your fasting periods, disregarding your diet, giving in to temptations, or worse, losing your motivation halfway. The reason you need to assess yourself is that you'll be sacrificing time and effort for this matter, and you probably wouldn't want to spend significant amounts of these two precious things just to find out that you don't want to continue with your diet plan anymore.

If you are, however, sure that you are ready for a change in your lifestyle and that you can take or endure whatever it may bring, then you can expect that everything else that follows after this first stage of preparation would be easy for you.

**Choosing a Diet Plan**

The worst part about choosing a diet plan, most especially if you are a beginner, is that you are not sure whether your chosen plan will be successful or not; and that it takes at least a month before you can say if you made the right choice or not. The truth is, each and every type of intermittent fasting diet plan entails a risk of failure and that there's no such thing as a "perfect" diet plan that can absolutely guarantee either weight loss or muscle mass gain, not even among the most prominent ones listed in the previous chapter.

There is, however, a measure that can help you minimize the risk of failing with a diet program; we'll call it personal filtering. Personal filtering simply means that you filter out, among the options you have, the one which best suits your preferences. It's a pre-implementation analysis that identifies which among the option, prior to its implementation, could provide the most positive outcome by examining the features of each available option. The main idea is to remove as many options as possible from the choices you have until you come up with, most preferably, one option which will then be deemed as fit for you.

To demonstrate, let's try to use the types of intermittent fasting given in the previous chapter (except for the 16:8 protocol since it was not yet discussed thoroughly). The first eliminating question should be, "what is your goal?" Are you after weight loss? Muscle gain? Or both? Assuming you are after both, then that already removes Fat Loss Forever Diet from the list since it's designed solely for weight loss. Next question would be, "how much fasting can you endure?" The question can be answered as a number of hours per day or a number of days per week. Suppose that your work schedule only permits fasting for a maximum of two days a week. This cancels out The Warrior Diet and the Alternate-day fasting from your choices as both require more than two days of fasting in a single week.

You now have narrowed down your choices into two: the 5:2 diet and the Eat-Stop-Eat diet. The deciding factor should now be based on the differences between the two. The 5:2 diet is a more flexible than Eat-Stop-Eat as you can fast for either two straight consecutive days or two non-consecutive days. It is also good if you only want to limit your consumption during fasting days rather than to completely abstain from it. Plus, it goes with a quantified limit (25% of your average daily calorie intake) so in case you feel like you're going beyond limit you can just check it through computation.

Eat-stop-eat on the other hand, best suits the sports and gym enthusiasts as such diet plan is specifically made for them. If you are seriously devoted to fasting, this is also a better choice since the goal in each fasting day is full abstinence. Now, assuming you are a sports enthusiast whose desire to lose weight and gain muscle mass is at peak, then your final choice would obviously be the Eat-stop-eat Diet.

It is important to remember that personal filtering is merely a guide to help you choose the most appropriate diet plan for you. It does not guarantee success although it can be inferred that it somehow increases your chance to succeed since through it, you'll be able to choose the diet program which can be implemented in accordance to your schedule and needs.

## Recognizing Exercise as an Important Factor to Weight Loss

If your ultimate goal for using intermittent fasting is to shed pounds, then from now on, you must see weight-loss exercises as your biggest friend. It is true that intermittent fasting alone can burn your fats and provide evident results; but pairing it with proper exercise, you'll cut the progress time almost into half. Yes, with proper guidance and consistent dedication, these rather exhausting activities could accelerate the results.

Of course, if you are new to diet plans and intermittent fasting, you do not have to engage immediately on physical exercise. Let your body adapt to the changes first and when you feel like it already has, you can start by choosing which set of exercises is suitable for your physique, for your endurance, and most importantly, for your diet program.

## Learning About Fasting Foods and Liquids

Pre-familiarizing yourself with the foods and drinks you can take during partially restricted fasting periods is also important. It's because most of the diet plans under intermittent fasting allow consumption of minimal servings of foods during fast hours or days. In general, foods that are considered safe during fasts include vegetables and fruits, whole grains, low-fat and low-sodium foods.

Liquids on the other hand are usually more available and safer during fasts. Water and fresh juices are typically recommended when you are under intermittent fasting. Protein or meal replacement shakes are also used in some techniques. Smoothies, juices, and shakes that are made up of nutrients-rich ingredients are also advised to be taken.

If you want to know the particular options you have, there is a list provided on the latter part of the book that enumerates specific fasting foods and liquids you can take during partially restricted fasting periods.

It must be emphasized that the measures above are mere guidelines for you to maximize the potential results of any weight-loss program that you decide to implement in your lifestyle. They do not guarantee perfect outcomes. The only key to make sure that a diet plan is going to provide desirable results is strict adherence. Honestly, all of these diet plans are programmed to work but unless you follow them correctly, you can never achieve optimum results. Temptations and frustrations already await you the moment you take your first step to your weight-loss journey. So, let me ask you the question once again—are you ready?

# Chapter 7: The Beginner's Protocol

By now you should have assessed yourself and have also decided that you are going to openly welcome intermittent fasting to your life—that's the spirit! And assuming you are indeed done with the self-assessment process, let's now proceed to the second step which is choosing the best type of intermittent fasting-based diet plan.

Whether you are new exclusively to intermittent fasting or completely new to diet plans in general, there's one type of intermittent fasting that would likely fit your current lifestyle, and would only incur little changes in your daily life once implemented. If you are, however, neither of the two, don't worry because this diet plan is also suitable to everyone else, even if you are a healthy person of normal weight. The diet plan is called the 16:8 method.

**16:8 Method - How It Is Done**

As once explained in chapter 5, this diet plan was introduced by personal trainer and nutritional expert Martin Berkhan. It's a daily intermittent fasting which divides each day into 16 hours of fasting period and 8 hours of normal- or free-eating period. The original term for this method was "Leangains method" as referred to by Berkhan but the term "16:8 method" is kind of getting more and more popular than the former. In this book, we'll also refer to it as the beginner's protocol.

The first thing to consider in 16:8 protocol is on which part of the day should both the fasting and eating periods be set. Fortunately, there exists a "standard" setting for both periods so you might want to just adopt it since it has already been tested and proven by the majority of 16:8 diet plan followers. Under the said setting, the 16-hour fasting period runs from 8 pm one day to 12 pm or 12 noon the next day. This means that, in a single day, you can only eat from 12 pm to 8 pm.

Such standardized setting is not really that hard to implement. Come to think of it, a dinner at let's say, 7:30 pm is quite an appropriate time considering that you are most probably in a fat-loss diet. It's not too early which means your body can sustain hunger before sleeping time; and neither is it too late which means proper digestion can still be expected.

There are no restrictions with regard to the meals that you can take during the eight-hour eating window; thus, you can eat normal meals at normal servings. Most of the people who practice the 16:8 method, however, cuts the number of meals they take into two. They usually skip breakfast since the eating window starts at lunch time anyway. Nonetheless, you can still stick to taking three regular-sized meals a day if you want to, as long as you take all three within the eating window.

The schedule simply repeats every day. You can expect your first few days or weeks to be burdensome but once your body adapts to the cycle, you'll get used to it and most importantly, you'll start to notice the progress.

**Benefits of 16:8 Method**

- Increased Chances of Fat Loss

Since your body's metabolism becomes slower as it enters the sleeping state, it naturally functions slower at night.

Therefore, anything that is consumed beyond 8 pm to 9 pm, or at any time near bed time, won't likely be burned properly. This is the reason 16:8 method is a top choice when it comes to weight loss. It limits the chances of calories getting stored as fats by setting the dinner or last meal for the day, at an earlier and safer hour. And because the body is most probably secured from obtaining unwanted increase in fat mass, it'll be easier to lose weight.

- Lean Mass Retention

The body weight comprises two major composition namely, fat mass and lean mass. Therefore, when we say "weight loss," it can refer to the loss of either fat mass or lean mass; but most of the time, both. The ideal result, however, is to lose fat mass but not lean mass. Lean mass is important as it includes muscle mass which certainly needs to be maintained as much as possible, to keep your muscle strength at an optimal level. Fortunately, 16:8 method promotes retention of much of the lean mass in the body amid significant reduction in fat mass.

- Controlled Hunger

In 16:8 diet plan, your eating window is narrowed down to an eight-hour period. This eventually leads to changes in your body's natural cravings. Of course, you won't notice the effect on your first few weeks under the diet plan; but if you continue to commit yourself to the plan, your body will start to "reprogram" itself and get used to not feeling much of the usual, stubbornly constant hunger. Plus, it'll also be easier for you to get satisfied with meals.

- Improved Insulin Response

An improved insulin response is a contributory factor to both the lean mass retention and the controlled hunger mentioned above. But aside from that, it also makes insulin levels more stable that's why some of the people who are at risk of diabetes type 2 devotedly follow 16:8 method.

- Enhanced Brain Function

If you're stressing about not being able to think properly while fasted, then let 16:8 method cut your worries. On your first few days under 16:8 method, your brain will probably not function well as it's still trying to adapt to certain changes. But once it has, you'll notice that your mentality can function just as normally as it could before intermittent fasting—or even better. This is because your body is not forced to pump large amount of blood to your digestive system when you are fasted. Thus, it's able to deliver more oxygen to other parts including your brain.

**Constructing Your Own 16:8 Schedule**

For most people, especially to beginners, it's highly advised to implement 16:8 diet using the standard, 12 pm to 8 pm eating-window schedule. However, if your personal schedule does not permit such setting or you simply don't want to follow the norm, then you can schedule your own plan to fit your lifestyle.

The first question to ask here is which among the three major meals is going to be eliminated? The answer will either be based on your schedule or be coming from your own preference although you should also consider the importance of each meal to your weight-loss goal. Putting that in mind, it would be best for you to skip dinner. If it's impossible, however, your second-best choice would be eliminating breakfast so as to make sure that any excess on your dinner intake still has time to be burned in the morning. Lunch is the most unlikely to be eliminated since the meals that you consume on your lunch time are more or less burned properly regardless if you are under a diet plan or not.

Say, for example, your work starts at 8 am and ends at 3 pm, your best option would be skipping dinner, as it is the time of the day when much, if not all, of your work is probably done; hence, no hunger-triggering activity. Skipping breakfast might be dangerous when you are a complete beginner to fasting. So, for such situation, you may start your eating window at 7:30 am to 3:30 pm. Within such window, you can eat your breakfast at 7:30 am or 7:45 am, before you go to work; and have your last meal right exactly at 3 pm, after work or a little later at 3:30 pm. Addition of an in-between meal is not much of an issue here so you can have lunch at 11 am or 12 pm and still eat some more after work as long as it's covered by the eating window.

If you can, however, endure a no-breakfast morning even at work, you can move the beginning of your eating window to 11 am to 12 pm or exactly to your lunch break. If your lunch break starts at 11 am, then you can eat your lunch at 11 am and adjust your last meal time to 7 pm, or to any time earlier than that. If you get used to this setting, you'll find out that it's actually easier and better to skip breakfast as you can expect an increase in focus and other brain functions as previously explained in the benefits of 16:8 method.

Your eating-window also does not necessarily have to be a full eight-hour period. You may further narrow it down into seven or four hours. However, such is only advisable if you have been using intermittent fasting for a long period of time. If you are still beginning to adapt to the lifestyle, then sticking to an eight-hour eating window is strongly recommended.

## Cheat Days - to Cheat or Not to Cheat?

16:8 method is not a religious devotion so you can start celebrating because apparently, cheat day is allowed under this diet schedule. Some of the followers of the diet plan claimed that they've still succeeded losing significant weight even if they admittedly cheated for a couple of days in some of the weeks. The safest number of cheat days you can have per week is one; but it's not a hard and fast rule so you can have your cheat days for two or three days a week. Just make sure that majority of the days in your week still follow the 16:8 plan, especially if you really are into achieving weight loss.

Also, it would be better not to overeat on your cheat days. A cheat day only means that you can extend your eating-window for more than eight hours or you can simply break the fasting period; but it does not mean that you should eat a lot of sweets and fatty foods every hour. Always eat in moderation whether it involves a healthy or unhealthy food. The result of 16:8 diet plan largely depends on you so always consider that.

## Famous People with 16/8-Diet-Bodies

Actor Hugh Jackman, majorly known for playing the role of Wolverine in the X-men movies, is one of the most prominent Hollywood figures to date. The actor has always been a center of interest to diet experts and fitness magazines for his ripped, Wolverine physique which Jackman proudly claims to be the result of his 16:8 diet schedule. At least now you know that the secret to Wolverine's size and strength is not found on his mutant genes—but to 16:8 diet.

Another popular actor who uses 16:8 diet plan is Terry Crews. He explained that his eating-window goes from 2 pm to 10 pm and he fasts for the rest of the day. He also does not eat foods, even minimal amounts of it during fasts, although he drinks coffee or tea during such periods. According to Crews, the only problem with 16:8 method is that you don't want a "bad meal" for your eating period because no one waits for 16 hours just to end up eating a bad meal.

David Kingsburry, trainer of some celebrities including Chris Hemsworth, Michael Fassbender, and Jennifer Lawrence, also promotes the 16:8 diet plan because aside from its effectiveness, the schedule, as Kingsburry said, can easily fit in an individual's lifestyle.

# Chapter 8: The Complementary Guide

After choosing the intermittent fasting diet plan, the guidelines state that the next two things to consider would be: learning about exercise and getting familiar with fasting foods and liquids. The first thing you need to know about these two is that they are both supplemental factors to intermittent fasting and are meant to help you maximize results.

**Guide to Exercises**

What's better than acquiring the weight-loss benefit of the beginner's protocol is maximizing the lean mass retention it features. It would be easier to gain muscle mass while under the diet plan since, as once mentioned earlier, much of the lean mass is retained despite weight loss. But if you are only after the weight loss, then that's equally fine. In any case, it's important that you utilize your 16-hour fasting window for many positive things can happen within that period of time.

The ideal time to apply weight-loss exercises while under intermittent fasting would be during the fasted period, most preferably in the morning. Considering you skip breakfasts during your 16-hour fasts, a complete exercise in the morning can burn significant amount of fats in your body. Provided below is a list of some of the well-known exercises that you may do every morning, to help accelerate the fat burning process and maintain your weight-loss progress:

- Squats
- Lunges (including explosive lunges)
- Kettlebell Swings

- Tabata Drill
- Double Jump
- Body-Weight Exercises
- Burpees
- Mountain Climbers
- Jump Rope

**Guide to Training and Workout**

Guidelines for strength training and muscle workouts are essentially stricter than weight-loss exercises. This is because in the latter, the only goal is to lose weight while in the former, the objective is to gain muscle mass while losing weight at the same time.

Training or workout may be done either during a fasted period or within an eating window. If you cannot commit to a fasted training, then it would be more appropriate if you train or work out in the middle of your eating window. In such case, you have to secure three meals within your eating window to support your system.

To illustrate, assume for example that you adopted the standard 16:8 schedule. This means that your workout shall be within the eating window, 12 pm to 8 pm. Your 12-noon lunch shall serve as your pre-workout meal. It must comprise 20-25% of your daily calorie intake. After that, your training should be set around 3:30 to 4:00 pm (it is important that the training is set at least an hour after pre-workout meal). Assuming the training takes an hour, your post-workout meal should be around 4:30 to 5:00 pm. Your post-workout meal should always be the largest meal. You should then take your dinner or the last meal of the day at either 7:00 pm or 8:00 pm to help you sustain the following fasting period.

It is also possible that you take two pre-workout meals before working out. Let's use one of the examples we had last chapter (eating window at 7:30 am to 3:30 pm) for demonstration. Your breakfast at 7:30 am should serve as your first pre-workout meal. Your next meal, let's say at 11:30 am, should then be your second pre-workout meal. Each of your pre-workout meals should consist 20-25% of your daily calorie consumption. Counting a few hours from your second pre-workout meal, you may start your training at 2:30 pm. Assuming again that your training takes only an hour, your post-workout, and last meal for the day should be taken exactly at 3:30 pm.

Now for the fasted training, you should first familiarize yourself with the branched-chain amino acids or BCAAs. These are amino acids usually taken, in the form of tablets or powder, to stimulate protein synthesis especially during trainings or workouts. Protein synthesis is essential for muscle growth and stimulating it serves as a defense against protein breakdown.

For a workout day, it is strongly recommended that you ready three 10-gram BCAA tablets or a 30-gram BCAA powder. The BCAA supplements will be used throughout a portion your fasted period. You should take one 10-gram BCAA tablet after your pre-workout. Afterward, you can proceed to your workout. Take another tablet an hour after your workout and take the last one two hours after your last intake. If you are going to use the powder, simply mix it in a shake or in a drink and divide the whole drink into three equal servings.

To demonstrate using the standard schedule, if you wake up at 6 am, your first tablet shall be taken after a five- to fifteen-minute pre-workout. Your training shall then start at 7 am and end at 8 am assuming it's a one-hour training. You shall take the second tablet around 8 am, right after the training. The last tablet shall then be taken at 10 am, two hours after the last intake.

Your lunch at 12 pm should serve as your post-workout meal; hence, the largest meal of the day. Your dinner or last meal should normally be taken at 8 pm. It's up to you if you want to consume in-between meals. If you commit to this strategy, your body will gain more muscle strength and will only lose fat mass in the process.

## Guide to 16:8 Diet-Specific Fasting Foods and Liquids

There are no fasting foods that are labeled safe to be consumed during the 16-hour period. To be honest, the fasting period in beginner's protocol is not much of a burden if you compare it to other fasting periods; like the 20-hour fast in Warrior Diet or the two-day fast under 5:2 Diet. Therefore, fasting foods aren't really an ultimate necessity. And the only means available to ease your 16-hour struggle are gums and fasting liquids.

Gums are good for people who often confuse boredom with hunger. If you're bored and you feel like the only answer to it is food, then try chewing a gum. Sometimes, you're not really craving for a food but instead, you just want to chew something in your mouth. The gum, however, that is referred to in this guide is a sugar-free gum. Sweeteners on regular chewing gums will only break your fast so you should avoid them.

In terms of fasting liquids, you can drink water if you want. As a matter of fact, you should drink a lot of it during fast. It does not only improve your metabolism but it also helps suppress hunger. Detox water, is also counted and is actually more preferable. Try adding a mint leaf or a slice of lemon to each glass to obtain better and more refreshing effects.

Black coffee and green tea can also save you from your fasting struggles most especially during the morning. They can help increase fat burning process and delay hunger. These beverages, however, should not come with large amounts of milk and sugar.

Take note that all of these are specifically applicable only to 16:8 diet protocol. Some diet plans do not allow most or all of the foods and drinks stated above, while some allow a wider range of options. If you want to learn more about the general fasting foods and liquids that are allowed under most of intermittent fasting-based diet plans, you can check the list provided in the next chapter.

# Part III – Supplemental Section

# Chapter 9: Fasting Foods and Liquids

Contrary to the traditional fasting that refers to absolute abstinence from foods and liquids, intermittent fasting refers to a period where one's consumption is limited only to some fasting specifications. The limits among diet plans slightly vary depending on which type of intermittent fasting you opted to follow. Nevertheless, there are specific foods and liquids that are generally present and allowed in almost any type of diet plan.

**Fruits and Vegetables**

The tandem always tops almost any list of ideal foods that must be eaten for a healthier life. This is obviously because fruits and vegetables are legitimate sources of vitamins and minerals. Plus, they are naturally high in antioxidants. You can eat a serving or two of either a fruit salad or vegetable salad during your partially restricted fasting period. Or you can just directly eat a raw fruit or veggie for convenience. Below is a list of the most recommended fruits that you may consume during fasted periods:

- Green Apples
- Strawberries
- Oranges
- Blackberries
- Cranberries
- Grapefruit
- Papaya
- Cantaloupes

- Raisins
- Apricots
- Guava

Roughly speaking, any vegetable, as long as it's not canned, is fairly good during fasted periods. However, there are vegetables which pack a particular combination of nutrients fit for an empty stomach; hence, perfect for fasting periods. Some of these vegetables are:

- Spinach
- Mustard Greens
- Cauliflower
- Brussels Sprouts
- Tomatoes
- Kale
- Lettuce
- Broccoli
- Cabbage
- Bok Choy
- Swiss Chard

Take note that the available fruits and vegetables appropriate for your fasting periods are not limited to the lists given above. Those just list the most recommended ones as they contain the vitamins and minerals that your body specially needs during fasted state. You have several more choices beyond those included in the list.

**Nuts**

In some intermittent fasting variants, foods which contain fats are allowed, and even suggested, to be consumed during fasted periods. So, to ensure that you are getting only the healthy fats, you can opt to go with nuts. Nuts contain both monounsaturated and polyunsaturated fats. These fats are also known as the good fats.

Good fats are "good" because they help lower your risk of stroke and other heart diseases and they also help lower cholesterol levels. Furthermore, they also contain omega-3 fatty acids, fiber, L-arginine, and vitamin E, all of which are known for being heart-friendly substances. The healthiest nuts that you can eat during fasting period are listed below:

- Brazil Nuts
- Macadamia Nuts
- Cashews
- Pecans
- Pine Nuts
- Walnuts
- Almonds
- Chestnuts
- Pistachios

Of course, nuts during fasting periods should be limited accordingly to what your specific diet plan allows. The main reason they are fine to eat during fasted state is that they satisfy the body almost the same way as meats do. Therefore, they can somehow extend your body's endurance to hunger. Their benefits, especially to the heart, are also considered as a contributory factor.

## Soups

If you want to spend your fasted period eating something with a meaty taste but your diet plan only allows liquid, then the best option you have is a soup. Soups are easily digested by the body so it can be safely taken without worrying about breaking the fast. The ideal number of servings for a soup during a fasted period is one; but taking two bowls of it won't hurt your fasting. Try to limit soup intake only up to two servings per fasting period. To name a few diet-friendly soups, we have:

- Vegetable Broth
- Spinach-Artichoke Soup
- Moroccan Stew
- Corn Chowder
- Black Bean Minestrone
- Lentil-Vegetable Soup
- Carrot and Ginger Soup

## Protein and Meal Replacement Shakes

First on the list of fasting liquids are the protein and meal replacement shakes. Protein shakes are flavored shakes which contain large amounts of protein good for working out and training. Meal replacement shakes, on the other hand, contain almost similar substances except that they have lower protein content, but higher calorie content than protein shakes.

If the fasting periods under your specific diet plan limit meals into a certain number of calories per day, it will be best for you to substitute your meal with a meal replacement shake. Meal replacement shakes have quantifiable calorie amounts (e.g. 400 calories per glass) so it will be easier for you to track your calorie intake during fasted periods.

If you are more into training during your fasted days, going for protein shakes is a wise idea. A protein shake, with its massive protein content, can help support your muscle strength throughout and after training. Plus, measuring calorie intake with protein shakes is easy as well.

## Detox Water

You can safely drink a detox water under any intermittent fasting plan. Detox water is simply a plain water with a bit of "detoxifying" agents in it, like mint leaves, orange slices, or cinnamon sticks. And since it combines the cleansing-benefit of water and the fat-burning, detoxifying properties of herbs or fruits, into one glass, it's pretty much a better option to drink than plain drinking water. You get to be cleansed and detoxified at the same time.

## Fresh Juices and Smoothies

Making a smoothie or juice out of fruits or vegetables is a common practice among people who couldn't stand a fasting period without sipping a refreshing flavored drink. There are no specifications about which flavors of juices and smoothies must be drunk. As long as a juice or smoothie is made from fresh, raw, and organic fruits and vegetables, a glass or two of the drink is perfectly fine.

## Coffees and Teas

Teas are more flexible in fasting than coffees. You can drink a cup of jasmine tea, green tea, or any tea during fasted periods.

Teas contain few calories and they won't derail your fasting protocol. They can also be served either hot or cold but a hot tea is more preferred by most.

On the other hand, only black coffees are allowed during fasted periods. It is also advised not buy coffees from coffee shops, as they roughly contain excessive amount of artificial sweetener, and high-fat creamers. If you want to add some sugar to your tea or coffee, you may do so as long as you limit such at regulated amounts.

# Chapter 10: Recipes for the Hungry

You, and everyone else who follow any type of intermittent fasting will always have something in common—you're all at your hungriest a few minutes before the eating window starts. And you know what's better than being able to eat after a long period of starvation? The foods, themselves.

Your first and last meals (or perhaps any meal within the eating window) are considerably precious to you that's why there's really no space for—as Terry Crews calls it—a "bad meal." So, consider rewarding yourself every time you survive a fasting period and serve some of the best recipes that you'll discover in this section.

# Fresh Mexican Tuna Salad

It's a Pico de Gallo-inspired tuna recipe which combines protein-packed tuna with fresh veggies. It's low in fat and carbohydrates so you can eat more servings of this recipe during your eating window. It's a good post-workout meal too!

Ingredients:

- 2 large tomatoes (chopped)
- 1 large red onion (chopped)
- 1 bunch of Chinese parsley (chopped)
- 1 400-gram can of Tuna (flakes, preferably)
- 1 pc. of lime

Number of Servings:
2 bowls

Directions:

To get rid of the onions' aftertaste, place the chopped onion in a bowl and liberally sprinkle salt on it. Pour a cup of water into the bowl or until the salted onions are all covered with water. Let them sit for half an hour or until the onions have soaked. Afterwards, drain the onions and rinse with running water to remove any excess salt.

In a large bowl, mix the chopped tomatoes, Chinese parsley, and the onion. Squeeze a piece of lime over the mixture. Drain the can of tuna and combine the flakes with the vegetables. Gently toss the ingredients and serve.

## Grilled BBQ Chicken Flatbreads

Eating pizza while under a diet plan might sound like an unforgivable sin—but if it's a pizza in the form of grilled flatbreads then it's totally fine. The recipe is an ideal snack to pack your calorie-deprived body with some calories and protein after a fasting period. Plus, this provides portion-controlled servings so there is nothing to worry about overeating.

Ingredients:
- 2 flatbreads
- 12 ounces chicken breast (boneless and skinless)
- 2 slices chopped Canadian bacon
- 1 cup of sliced red onions
- 1 cup of sliced bell pepper (yellow or red)
- 1 tbsp. fresh pineapple juice
- 1/4 cup chopped pineapple tidbits
- 1/4 cup barbeque sauce*
- 1/4 cup grated cheese
- a pinch of black pepper

Number of Servings:
4 slices

Directions:

Preheat the grill at 500 °F. On a grill tray, place the sliced onions and bell peppers then sprinkle on some pepper. Coat the chicken breast with cooking spray. Bring the chicken and the onions and bell peppers to grill. Cook each side of the chicken for three to four minutes or until the inside reaches

165 °F. Remove the veggies and chicken from the grill and then reduce the heat to 400 °F.

Transfer the chicken on to a cutting board and cut into strips or bite-sized pieces. In a blender, add the pineapple juice and barbecue sauce and pulse until the combination forms a thick sauce.

Place the flatbreads on a pizza stone or screen. Spread half a cup of the sauce on each flatbread, and top with the chicken cuts, Canadian bacon, grated cheese, grilled onions and bell peppers, and pineapple tidbits; then place on the grill. Close the lid and wait for around 10 minutes to cook, or until the cheese has melted.

Remove from heat. Let the flatbread cool for a while before slicing; then serve.

# Low-fat Chicken Spaghetti Carbonara

If you're a pasta lover then here's a simple recipe for you. This is specially made for people who devote themselves so much in a diet plan that they thought they are prohibited from indulging in dishes like Spaghetti Carbonara. But more importantly, this is made to complement low-fat diet plans.

Ingredients:

- 150 grams of pasta
- 1 skinless chicken breast (chopped)
- 4 short-cut lean bacon slices
- 2 cloves garlic (crushed)
- 1/2 onion (sliced)
- 2 spring onions (sliced)
- 1 tbsp. olive oil
- cracked pepper
- 3/4 cup light evaporative milk

Number of Servings:
2 plates

Directions:

Cook pasta as per instructions; then drain and set aside.

Preheat a non-stick fry-pan at medium heat. Add a little olive oil on the pan and cook bacon until crispy. Once the bacon becomes crispy, set it aside. Add a little olive oil again on the same pan then cook the onion on low heat until soft. Set the onion aside along with the bacon.

Add the remaining olive oil on the pan, turn to medium heat, and cook the chicken breast for around four to five minutes, until semi-cooked. Afterwards, slightly lower the heat and add the bacon and onion to the chicken, and then add garlic. Pour the evaporated milk then season with pepper to taste.

Stir the sauce occasionally while heating. Once the sauce bubbles, further lower the heat and add the cooked pasta. When the sauce turns into a slightly thick consistency, turn off the heat. Add the sliced spring onions then serve.

# Green Tea Powerhouse Smoothie

There's no way that you won't look for a refreshing break after a heated struggle with your fasting period. And one of the best refreshments available for a conscious, weight-watcher is this antioxidant-rich smoothie recipe. Combine all the vitamins that your body would surely need after a fasting window and add a pack of protein to that—voila! A green tea powerhouse smoothie.

Ingredients:

- 1 bag of green tea
- ½ medium banana
- 1½ frozen blueberries
- ¾ light vanilla soy milk
- 3 tbsp. water
- 2 tsp. honey

Number of Servings:
1 glass


Directions:

Steam or microwave water in small bowl. Once steaming hot, add tea bag and let it brew for three to five minutes. Remove tea bag afterwards. Add honey and stir the mixture. In a blender, combine tea mixture, banana, blueberries, and soy milk. Blend on the highest setting. Transfer the smoothie into a glass and serve.

# Protein-Packed Dark Choco-Almond Cookies

Dessert time is always more fun when you're not anxious about your weight and health. These cookies are going to bring your protein-diet gaming to the next level. Imagine being able to enjoy a delicious cookie while also gaining a dose of protein in every bite. It's a win-win situation, isn't it?

Ingredients:

- 1/4 cup unflavored protein powder
- 2 squares chopped dark chocolate (20 grams)
- 1/4 cup almonds (ground)
- 3 tbsp. almond butter
- 1/4 cup almond milk
- 1 tsp. coconut oil
- 2 tsp. coconut sugar

Number of Servings:
5 cookies

Directions:

Preheat oven to 350 °F. Mix protein powder, almonds, coconut sugar, almond butter, almond milk, and coconut oil together to make a dough. Once mixed, add dark chocolate. Roll dough into small-sized balls and place onto a tray lined with parchment paper. Flatten the balls with a spoon or with your fingers.

Place in the oven and bake for around 10 to 12 minutes or until baked. Remove from oven. Let the cookies rest to stiffen (and to prevent crumbling). Serve once completely cooled.

# Conclusion

Perhaps, for the past centuries, people haven't found the ideal method of losing weight because we focused solely on the idea that what makes a person unhealthy or over-weight, is the kind of foods that he eats. Although it's legitimately true to some extent, it's not enough that we should focus only on a single idea and stop putting efforts to discover more from a different perspective.

Fortunately, intermittent fasting has been discovered right on the period when almost all of us are already giving up with our unsuccessful diet plans, brought by our desperate decisions—lots of thanks to the founders of the method!

And after reading all the chapters in this book, you have probably learned the important points about intermittent fasting. You discovered the method and learned about the science that, although is still being further proven by researchers across the globe, backs up much of the concept of the diet technique.

You also learned about the benefits of intermittent fasting not only to your weight but also to your overall health; from your insulin levels to your brain function. And above all, the method serves as a safer and even a better substitute to other diet plans as it has proven its purpose as a healthier way of losing weight and a bigger help to gaining muscle mass and strength.

You also know by now that there is a pool of options from which you can choose the type of intermittent fasting that best suits your lifestyle and needs. And if you can't decide on which among the options to choose, you can always go back to the book's comprehensive guide for beginners.

At this point, you already have everything you need to learn so you'd be able start your own journey to a healthy weight loss. Always remember that—regardless of the kind of diet plan that you implement, the outcome will always depend on your effort and most importantly, on your dedication. So, don't just do the process, commit yourself to it!

# Fat Bombs

## 60 Best, Delicious Fat Bomb Recipes You Absolutely Have to Try!

# Introduction

I want to thank you and congratulate you for purchasing the book, *"Fat Bombs: Sub- 60 Best, Delicious Fat Bomb Recipes You Absolutely Have to Try!"*

This is not your ordinary recipe book. Aside from the 60 healthy and delicious fat bomb recipes, it explains the basics about the low-carb diet. It aims to educate you on what you need to know about the diet while you learn how to prepare a variety of fat bomb recipes. These fat bombs are an essential part of any low-carb diet. They help you in reaching your daily required macros without going overboard.

This book explains the following aspects of a low-carb diet:

- The importance of fat bombs in the diet. It explains the most common ingredients used in making fat bombs and their health benefits.
- The right foods to eat when following this kind of diet. Each chapter gives you an idea of the ingredients to use in preparing your meals, including the fat bombs.
- What is the state of ketosis and what can you do to stay at it for a longer period. It also has a dedicated chapter of fat bomb recipes that you can eat to maintain this state.
- The health benefits and common side effects of a low-carb diet.

The fat bomb recipes contain nutrition information that you can use as a guide. It also offers the following details:

- The idea behind these treats.
- The basic ingredients needed to make them.

- The fats and sweeteners that you can use in making fat bombs.

Thanks again for purchasing this book, I hope you enjoy it!

# Chapter 1 – The Essence of a Low-Carb Diet and Fat Bombs

It is easy to make fat bombs. After you have tried certain recipes, you can make your own combinations and come up with even more variety of these healthy treats.

What is a fat bomb? It is a small treat, usually in size of a small ball, but can also be served in squares or in other shapes, depending on the molds that you use. The treat is low in carbs and high in concentrated and healthy fat. The recipes typically contain more than 85 percent of fat. Flavoring and specific fats are used in the process, such as butter, mascarpone cheese, Neufchatel cheese, cream cheese, coconut oil, and coconut butter.

You can eat this whenever your body needs to get recharged, as a snack, breakfast, or after doing a tedious activity. Fat bombs are suited for any low-carb diet, such as ketogenic and paleo. They have the healthy fat that your body needs to stay in ketosis. The best thing about these treats is that they taste good and won't make you feel that you are being deprived.

Here are some of the important things that you need to remember about fat bombs:

1. They contain a huge percentage of healthy fats, most of which solidifies fast when chilled or refrigerated. This is the reason the treats are not messy to prepare and consume despite the fats that they contain.

2. They are served in small sizes. This makes it easier to pop them into your mouth whenever you need a healthy fix. This

also allows you to control the nutrients, specifically the carb content of each piece.

3. Due to the fat content, these fat bombs will melt when kept at a room temperature for a long time. To keep them for up to 2 weeks, store leftovers in an airtight container and keep it in the fridge or freezer. If chilled, thaw them first at a room temperature for several minutes before serving.

4. You can tweak the taste of the fat bombs depending on your preference and the availability of ingredients. You can use zero-carb and low-calorie sweeteners to make sweet treats. You can add spices and herbs. You can also make savory bombs by incorporating ingredients, such as avocado and bacon, in the recipes.

5. If you are using nuts, make sure that you choose the types that don't contain too much carbs. If you are on a ketogenic diet, take note that you cannot use peanut butter. You can replace this with suitable nut butter, such as almond butter.

The basic fat bombs contain these three ingredients:

- Fat base. These are the healthy fats used as ingredients. They include coconut oil, coconut butter, cacao butter, coconut milk, and almond butter. You can also use coconut cream, which is the solid part of a can of coconut milk when refrigerated. It is safe to use butter if you can tolerate dairy. The other fats used are avocado oil, bacon fat, and ghee. For the latter, it is best to choose cultured ghee that is free of casein and lactose.
- Sweetener or flavoring. You can use various flavored syrups, cacao powder, spices, peppermint extract, sugar-free vanilla extract, salt, and dark chocolate.

- Mix-in ingredients. They give texture to the fat bombs. Some samples include shredded coconut, cacao nibs, nuts, low-carb fruit, seeds, and sugar-free crumbled bacon.

Coconut Oil

Among the fats used in making these treats, the healthiest choice is coconut oil. This is the healthiest ingredient used in making fat bombs. It makes the fat burning process faster. That fats that this oil contains do not get stored in your system. Instead, your body immediately utilizes the fats for energy. Aside from being healthy, it also gives a buttery and rich flavor to your food.

This can be used in many baking and cooking recipes. Shelf life is up to 2 years. For a healthier option, you can look for the organic type that is non-GMO and gluten-free.

Coconut oil is an essential part of any low-carb diet. It helps you lose weight by boosting your energy expenditure and reducing your hunger cravings. It is also effective in reducing the fat in the abdominal area or the visceral fat that is known as the dangerous (unhealthy) fat.

This ingredient alone has the following effects on your system:

- It lowers the risk of a heart disease by improving your cholesterol levels.
- It reduces inflammation and improves the health of your thyroid.
- It also has positive effects on your hair and skin.
- Coconut oil helps you get into the state of ketosis.

How does coconut oil help you get into ketosis? It has MCTs or medium-chain triglycerides that work by boosting your ketones. Coconut oil can supply your body with an immediate form of energy when taken orally. This is something usually done by keto-dieters who eliminate all forms of carbs from their diet.

Your body converts the MCTs in the liver into ketones. They replace glycogen as the source of your body's fuel. MCT oil is also used as a supplement that aids in ketosis.

Sweeteners

Not all sweeteners are created equal, especially when you are on a low-carb diet and you are intent on losing weight. You must teach yourself how to lessen your cravings for sweets. Use sugar alternatives occasionally. You can skip adding them to your regular meals and use them solely for treats, such as your healthy fat bomb recipes.

If you are on a very low-carb diet, stick to sweeteners with zero-carb content. As for the rest, make sure that the sweeteners are healthy and qualify for your net carb limit.

1. Stevia. The extract from this herb is used as a sugar substitute or sweetener. It is grouped in the non-nutritive sweeteners on the USDA database. It is devoid of any nutrients, vitamins and it doesn't have calories. Most of the stevia products are triple times sweeter than sugar when used in moderation. These products vary in taste. There are some that said to leave a bitter aftertaste. You should try different stevia products to test which suits your taste.

2. Inulin-based sweeteners. The most popular among this type is the chicory root inulin, which is commercially sold as

Just Like Sugar that contains orange peel, calcium, and vitamin C. The other natural sources of inulin include yacon, jicama, onion, banana, Jerusalem artichoke.

If you are using any of these ingredients, be sure to avoid adding other sweeteners. Inulin is beneficial not only to people on a low-carb diet but also for diabetics because of its beneficial effect on blood sugar. Unlike stevia, inulin has certain side effects because it feeds both the good and bad bacteria. This can cause digestive issues when you consume more than the daily dose of 20 grams.

3. Erythritol. This is a sugar alcohol naturally found in fermented foods, vegetables, and fruits. It has no calories and does not have any effects on your blood glucose. Take a daily dose of 1 gram of Erythritol per kilogram of your weight to avoid side effects, such as stomach ache.

4. Xylitol. This sugar alcohol has a similar taste to sugar but contains a lower number of calories. It naturally occurs in the fibers of some veggies and fruits. It contains low nutrients and must be used as a sweetener in moderation. Keep this out of reach of dogs because it can be toxic for your pets.

5. Dark chocolate. For your fat bombs, use the type that is made of 75 percent cacao or more with no unnecessary additives. This is a versatile ingredient. You can add this on your yogurt, baked treats, cereals, and more.

**The Benefits**

Fat bombs give you an instant energy boost and help you in reaching your daily nutritional requirement without going overboard. They are easy to make. You can bring them anywhere with you and pop a piece whenever hunger strikes.

They are an essential part of any low-carb diet, which requires you to eat real food and offers the following benefits:

1. Weight loss

The diet causes a decrease in your insulin levels. As a result, your kidneys will work in getting rid of the excess sodium in your system, which will lead to rapid weight loss for the first two weeks of the diet. If you do it right, you will continue to lose weight for the next 6 months. After this period, you will need to focus your attention on maintaining the weight that you have already lost. You can allow yourself to indulge on the foods that you have missed more often but always keep your carb intake in moderation.

2. Increases your good cholesterol levels

It boosts the levels of your HDL or good cholesterol and decreases the levels of your LDL or bad cholesterol. This is due to the limited amount of sugar and high amount of saturated fat that your system is getting. To ensure the health of your heart, you need to maintain above 39 mg HDL over your LDL. This will prevent arterial blockage and reduce your risk of inflammation.

3. Suppressed appetite

The ketone bodies and your intake of fat will make you feel full most of the time. They will take your mind away from eating. A low-carb diet effectively reduces your food cravings. It is important that you eat even though you are not hungry. Your body needs to work on something to give your body sufficient energy. You still need to eat to meet your daily required macros.

4. Lower blood pressure

This is effective in keeping your blood pressure at a normal rate but a low-carb diet is not advisable for those who are already taking medications for this condition. Talk to your doctor first if you want to proceed with the diet. People who are taking medications for high blood pressure often experience dizziness as a side effect of the diet.

5. Instant energy boost

The diet improves your sleeping patterns, which will make you feel energized at the start of the day. At times when you are feeling drained, you simply need to eat or pop a piece or two of fat bombs and you will instantly have an energy boost. The diet can also help in improving chronic fatigue. It prohibits eating grains and grain-based foods, which result to the relief of joint and muscle pain and stiffness.

6. Clearer mind

The first few days of the diet are the hardest. Your body is still getting used to the scheme of things – how you eat and what you are eating. After you have gotten used to it, your body will get keto-adapted. This will result to a better way of thinking.

7. Other health benefits

The diet is said to improve gut health and digestion. It also prevents epileptic seizures. It improves the health of your brain and gives you a better mood most of the time. There are certain studies, which proved that a low-carb diet can help in improving brain-related cases, such as ALS, Alzheimer's, and Parkinson's.

# Chapter 2 – Easy-to-Do Healthy Fat Bomb Recipes

Fat bombs are easy to make as long as you have the complete ingredients and you are equipped with the right tools. Some recipes will require the use of a food processor or blender. An electric hand mixer will also come in handy. Most fat bombs are refrigerated or frozen, and there are only a few that needs to be baked in an oven.

You can opt to use your hands to form your dough into small balls. You can also use baking pans or trays lined with wax or parchment paper, or lightly greased, as molds. After the fat bomb has firmed, you can cut them into squares or rectangular pieces. You can also get creative and use molds intended for candies or cupcakes. You can also turn your fat bombs into cake pops by placing them on sticks and dipping them in melted dark chocolate before adding texture and decorations.

Fat bombs are usually made by following these three steps:

1. Put all the ingredients in a bowl, blender, or a food processor. Process until you have attained the required consistency. If you are using solid fat, melt it on low heat or microwave for a few seconds.

2. Transfer the mixture into molds or put them in any container and cover with plastic before you freeze or refrigerate the mixture for several hours or overnight.

3. Slice the fat bombs or use your hands to shape them into small balls.

Now put what you have learned into practice. Begin with the following easy-to-make recipes that you can snack on any time of the day.

# Cocoa Almond Delight Fat Bombs

Servings: 24 pieces

Nutrition facts per piece: Calories 145 kcal, Fats 14.7 g, Protein 1.53 g, Net carb 1.1 g

Ingredients:

- 3 tablespoons cocoa
- 9 1/2 tablespoons almond butter
- 3/8 teaspoon (60 drops) liquid stevia
- 3/4 cup melted coconut oil
- 9 tablespoons melted salted butter

Directions:

1. Mix all the ingredients in a bowl until combined.

2. Prepare lightly greased mini muffin molds with 24 holes. Pour 2 tablespoons of the mixture into each hole. Freeze for half an hour or until set.

3. Carefully pop out the fat bombs from the molds and transfer to an airtight container. Serve immediately. Put back any leftover in the fridge.

# Toffee and Peanut Butter Fat Bombs

Servings: 24 pieces

Nutrition facts per piece: Calories 142 kcal, Fats 15 g, Protein 2 g, Net carb 0.9 g

Ingredients:

- 4 ounces cream cheese
- 1 cup coconut oil
- 3/4 tablespoons cocoa butter
- 2 tablespoons butter
- 3 tablespoons unsweetened toffee syrup
- 1/2 cup natural peanut butter

Directions:

1. Put all the ingredients in a pan over medium-low heat. Stir until melted and combined.

2. Transfer the mixture into greased molds like a mini muffin pan. Freeze for 30 minutes. Pop and serve.

3. Put any leftovers in an airtight container and refrigerate until ready to serve.

## Creamy Almond Fat Bombs

Servings: 8 pieces

Nutrition facts per piece: Calories 214 kcal, Fats 22 g, Protein 5 g, Net carb 2 g

Ingredients:

- 2 teaspoons cocoa powder
- 4 tablespoons coconut oil
- 10 tablespoons almond butter
- 1/4 teaspoon allspice
- 6 drops of liquid stevia (adjust according to taste)
- 5 tablespoons heavy cream

Directions:

1. Put the almond butter into the mold that you are using. Add the rest of the ingredients. Mix thoroughly until combined. Freeze for a couple of hours.

2. Remove from the mold. Slice and serve. You can sprinkle chopped almonds on top if preferred.

# Chocolatey Coconut Fat Bombs

Servings: 12 squares

Nutrition facts per piece: Calories 237 kcal, Fats 31 g, Protein 4 g, Net carb 1.3 g

Ingredients:

- 2 tablespoons cocoa powder
- 2 tablespoons honey
- A pinch of sea salt
- 2 cups of unsweetened shredded coconut
- 4 ounces cream cheese
- 1 cup coconut oil
- 1/4 teaspoon cinnamon
- Sugar substitute to taste

Directions:

1. Heat coconut oil in a pan over medium flame. Stir in the rest of the ingredients except for the cocoa powder and cream cheese. Mix until combined.

2. Pour the mixture into a pan lined with wax paper. Spread out and press to make an even layer. Cover the pan and freeze for an hour.

3. Put the cream cheese and cocoa powder in a pan over low heat. Mix until melted and combined. Pour the mixture on top of the solid layer of your fat bombs. Freeze for 15 minutes.

4. Slice and serve.

# Very Mocha Fat Bombs

Servings: 6 pieces

Nutrition facts per piece: Calories 167 kcal, Fats 19 g, Protein 0.1 g, Net carb 0.9 g

Ingredients:

- 12 teaspoons Splenda
- 4 tablespoons coconut oil
- 4 tablespoons grass-fed butter
- 1 tablespoon cocoa powder
- 2 tablespoons heavy cream
- 1/2 teaspoon coffee extract

Directions:

1. Put the butter in a heatproof bowl. Microwave until soft. Add the heavy cream and mix until combined. Leave to cool.

2. In another bowl, combine the coffee extract, cocoa powder, sweetener, and coconut oil.

3. Spread out the butter and cream mixture at the bottom of a greased pan. Refrigerate for 15 minutes to set. Pour the mocha mixture on top. Freeze for half an hour.

4. Remove from the pan. Slice and serve.

# Creamy White Bombs

Servings: 2 slices

Nutrition facts per piece: Calories 170 kcal, Fats g, Protein g, Net carb 1.5 g

Ingredients:

- 1/8 teaspoon cinnamon
- 1/2 cup creamed coconut (sliced into squares)

For the first icing

- 1 tablespoon almond butter
- 1 tablespoon extra-virgin coconut oil

For the second icing

- 1/2 teaspoon cinnamon
- 1 tablespoon almond butter

Directions:

1. Combine the cinnamon and coconut cream in a bowl. Transfer to a baking pan lined with wax paper. Press to make an even layer.

2. In a bowl, mix the ingredients for the first icing. Pour this over the first layer. Freeze for 10 minutes.

3. Whisk all the ingredients for the second icing in a bowl. Drizzle this over the frozen fat bomb. Freeze for at least 5 minutes. Slice and serve.

# Dark Choco Truffles

Servings: 2 dozens

Nutrition facts per 3 pieces: Calories 292 kcal, Fats 31 g, Protein 2.2 g, Net carb 1.3 g

Ingredients:

For the chocolate coating

- 1 tablespoon Swerve confectioners powder
- 2 ounces unsweetened baking chocolate
- 1/4 teaspoon sugar-free vanilla extract
- 1/2 ounce of cocoa butter
- 1/8 teaspoon of artificial sweetener

For the ganache filling

- 5 ounces of low-carb chocolate
- 1/2 teaspoon chocolate extract
- 1 1/4 teaspoons of chocolate extract
- 2 tablespoons plus 2 teaspoons of heavy cream

Directions:

1. To make the ganache, melt the chocolate in a double boiler.

2. Put the cream and vanilla in a heatproof bowl. Microwave for 2 minutes. Add the melted chocolate. Mix until combined. Leave for 5 minutes. Cover the bowl with a plastic wrap. Freeze for 5 hours or overnight.

3. Form the ganache into balls using your hands. Arrange them on a tray lined with wax paper. Refrigerate to set.

4. Mix the chocolate and butter in a double boiler over low heat. Add the sweeteners and vanilla. Dip each ball into the

melted coating. You can hold the ball with a fork or toothpick. Allow the coating to set before serving.

# Lemon Squares Keto Bombs

Servings: 16 squares

Nutrition facts per piece: Calories 112 kcal, Fats 11.9 g, Protein 0.76 g, Net carb 0.8 g

Ingredients:

- 7.1 ounces of coconut butter (softened)
- 1/4 cup extra virgin coconut oil (softened)
- A pinch of salt
- 2 teaspoons of lemon extract
- 20 drops of sweetener

Directions:

1. Mix all the ingredients in a bowl until combined. Pour into a pan lined with parchment paper. Refrigerate for 2 hours. Slice and serve.

Note: Instead of lemon, you can tweak the flavor of this recipe by using other extracts, such as herbs, fruits, and vanilla.

# Vanilla and Nutmeg Keto Treats

Servings: 12 pieces

Nutrition facts per piece: Calories 57 kcal, Fats 5.3 g, Protein 0.55 g, Net carb 0.8 g

Ingredients:

- 1 cup shredded coconut
- 1 cup full-fat coconut milk
- 1 teaspoon artificial sweetener
- 1/2 teaspoon cinnamon
- 1/2 teaspoon nutmeg
- 1 teaspoon vanilla extract
- 1 cup coconut butter

Directions:

1. Put all the ingredients except for the shredded coconut in a bowl. Put the bowl in a double boiler over low heat. Gradually mix the ingredients until combined and melted. Remove from heat and leave to cool. Cover the bowl and freeze for 2 hours.

2. Form balls from the mixture. Roll them in the shredded coconut. Arrange in a tray and put in the fridge for an hour or two.

3. Serve and enjoy.

# Spiced Pumpkin Fat Bombs

Servings: 6 pieces

Nutrition facts per piece: Calories 216 kcal, Fats 24 g, Protein 0.1 g, Net carb 1 g

Ingredients:

- ½ cup pumpkin
- 4 tablespoons coconut oil
- 8 tablespoons unsalted butter
- Liquid stevia to taste
- Ginger, cinnamon, nutmeg, and clove to taste

Directions:

1. Put the coconut oil in a heatproof bowl. Microwave until melted and hot. Add butter and mix until combined. Continue mixing as you gradually add the pumpkin. Add the spices and stevia. Mix until smooth and creamy.

2. Transfer the mixture to a pan lined with parchment paper. Refrigerate until set. Roll into 1-inch balls and arrange on a tray. Refrigerate for an hour before serving.

# Choco Coconut Flakes Fat Bombs

Servings: 6 pieces

Nutrition facts per piece: Calories 372 kcal, Fats 40 g, Protein 2 g, Net carb 6 g

Ingredients:

- 3 ounces unsweetened baking chocolate
- 5 ounces coconut oil
- ¼ teaspoon salt
- 3 ounces unsalted butter
- Liquid stevia to taste
- 1 ½ tablespoons cocoa powder
- 3 tablespoons unsweetened coconut flakes (big flakes)

Directions:

1. Preheat oven to 350 degrees. Spread out the coconut flakes on a baking sheet and toast. Check often to make sure they don't get burned or overcooked.

2. Put the unsalted butter, unsweetened dark chocolate, and coconut oil in a heatproof bowl. Microwave for 2 minutes. Stir in the salt, stevia, and cocoa. Pour into your preferred mold. Press the coconut flakes on top. Freeze until set.

3. Immediately store any leftovers in the fridge to prevent them from melting.

# Peanut Butter Keto Bombs

Servings: 10 pieces

Nutrition facts per piece: Calories 184 kcal, Fats 20 g, Protein 2 g, Net carb 1 g

Ingredients:

- 1/4 cup peanut butter
- 1/4 cup cocoa powder
- Liquid stevia to taste
- 3/4 cup coconut oil

Directions:

1. Put coconut oil in a heatproof bowl. Microwave for a few seconds until melted. Divide this into 3 bowls.

2. Add peanut butter to the first bowl with coconut oil. Mix until blended. Add stevia to taste. Combine the oil with cocoa powder on the next bowl. Add stevia to taste and mix well. Add stevia to the last bowl and mix until combined.

3. Transfer the mixtures into your molds. Spread out the chocolate flavored oil at the bottom. Put in the fridge for at least 10 minutes. Top it with the peanut butter layer and refrigerate until firm. Remove from the molds and pour the clear coconut oil over the fat bombs. You can opt to sprinkle them with chopped nuts or shredded coconut. Freeze until ready to serve.

# Spiced Cheesy Keto Treats

Servings: 6 pieces

Nutrition facts per piece: Calories 367 kcal, Fats 61 g, Protein 14 g, Net carb 1 g

Ingredients:

- 1 teaspoon liquid stevia
- 8 ounces Neufchatel cheese (softened)
- 1/2 teaspoon nutmeg
- 1/2 teaspoon ground cloves
- 1 tablespoon cinnamon
- 1 teaspoon ginger
- 3/4 cup coconut oil

Directions:

1. Put everything in a food processor, except the coconut oil. Process at low speed. Gradually add the oil as you continue to process the mixture.

2. Divide into 6 and roll into balls. Arrange in a tray, cover, and put in the fridge for 15 minutes. As an option, you can drizzle melted dark chocolate on top of the balls. Refrigerate until ready to serve.

# Coco-Vanilla Bombs

Servings: 6 pieces

Nutrition facts per piece: Calories 138 kcal, Fats 13 g, Protein 1 g, Net carb 2 g

Ingredients:

- 2 tablespoons coconut oil
- 1 cup unsweetened shredded coconut
- 1/8 teaspoon salt
- Liquid stevia to taste
- 1/2 teaspoon vanilla extract
- 1/4 cup water

Directions:

1. Put all the ingredients in a food processor. Process until combined. Transfer to your mold and press until firm. Refrigerate for 15 minutes. Slice and serve.

# Baked Cheesy Jell-O Flat Bomb Cookies

Servings: 12 pieces

Nutrition facts per piece: Calories 147 kcal, Fats 24 g, Protein 3 g, Net carb 1 g

Ingredients:

- 1 pack sugar-free Jell-O (any flavor)
- 6 ounces cream cheese
- 1/8 teaspoon sea salt
- 1 egg
- 1/2 teaspoon vanilla extract
- 1/2 teaspoon baking powder
- 1 cup almond flour
- 4 tablespoons unsalted butter (softened)
- 1/4 teaspoon almond extract
- 8 drops liquid stevia

Directions:

1. Put the softened butter and cream cheese in a bowl. Beat to combine. Add the extracts and sweetener.

2. In another bowl, combine the Jell-O powder and salt. Add the almond flour and baking powder. Mix well. Gradually add this to the cream cheese mixture. Blend using a fork. Roll the dough into a ball. Cover with a plastic wrap and refrigerate for 1 to 12 hours.

3. Form 1-inch balls from the dough. Arrange them on a baking sheet. Flatten the top of the cookies using the bottom of a glass. Bake in a preheated oven at 325 degrees for 6 minutes.

4. Allow to cool completely before serving. Avoid touching before cookies are completely cooled because they might crumble.

# Minty Layered Fat Bombs

Servings: 12 pieces

Nutrition facts per piece: Calories 155 kcal, Fats 18 g, Protein 0.1 g, Net carb 1 g

Ingredients:

- 1/3 cup coconut shreds
- 3/4 cup coconut butter
- 1/2 teaspoon peppermint extract
- Liquid stevia to taste
- 3 tablespoons coconut oil
- 2 teaspoons unsweetened cocoa powder

Directions:

1. In a bowl, put the shredded coconut, peppermint extract, a tablespoon of coconut oil, and coconut butter. Mix until combined. Pour at the bottom of your molds. Refrigerate for 15 minutes.

2. Combine the cocoa powder and coconut oil in a bowl. Pour this on top of the firm layer. Refrigerate until set. Leave at room temperature for 5 minutes before slicing and serving.

# Cheesy Bacon Bombs

Servings: 12 pieces

Nutrition facts per piece: Calories 201 kcal, Fats 32 g, Protein 8 g, Net carb 1 g

Ingredients:

- 8 bacon slices (fried and crumbled)
- 4 teaspoons bacon fat
- 8 ounces Neufchatel cheese (softened)
- 1/4 cup sugar-free maple syrup
- 4 tablespoons coconut oil
- 1/2 cup unsalted butter

Directions:

1. Set aside a little of the crumbled bacon.

2. Put the remaining ingredients in a heatproof bowl. Microwave until melted. Stir the mixture every now and then to make sure that everything is combined. Pour into a pan and freeze for at least 15 minutes. Sprinkle the crumbled bacon on top. Slice and serve.

# No-Bake Red Cheesecake Bombs

Servings: 48 pieces

Nutrition facts per piece: Calories 81 kcal, Fats 8.6 g, Protein 1 g, Net carb 1 g

Ingredients:

- A few drops of red food color
- 3 teaspoons raspberry extract
- 8 ounces cream cheese (softened)
- 2 tablespoons heavy cream
- 1 1/2 cups sugar-free chocolate chips
- 1/2 cup of sugar substitute
- 1/4 cup coconut oil (melted)
- A pinch of salt
- 1 teaspoon vanilla stevia

Directions:

1. Combine the cream cheese and sugar substitute in a blender. Process until smooth. Add the cream, salt, stevia, food coloring, and raspberry extract. Process until combined. Slowly add the coconut oil. Scrape the sides to make sure that the oil is distributed evenly to the mixture. Transfer to a bowl and cover with plastic. Put in the fridge for an hour or until set.

2. Use a cookie scoop to measure 1 1/4-inch size balls. Arrange in a tray. Freeze until ready to serve.

3. As an option, you can coat the balls with melted dark chocolate. Refrigerate until set.

# Mediterranean-Inspired Fat Bombs

Servings: 5 pieces

Nutrition facts per piece: Calories 164 kcal, Fats 17.1 g, Protein 3.7 g, Net carb 1.7 g

Ingredients:

- 1/4 cup of softened butter
- 1/2 cup full-fat cream cheese
- 5 tablespoons grated Parmesan cheese
- 2 garlic cloves (crushed)
- 4 sun-dried tomatoes (drained)
- 4 pitted olives
- 3 tablespoons of fresh herbs (or 2 teaspoons of dried herbs)
- Freshly ground black pepper and sea salt to taste

Directions:

1. In a bowl, mash the softened butter and cream cheese using a fork until combined. Add the herbs, tomatoes, garlic, and olives. Season with salt and pepper. Mix well. Cover the bowl and put in the fridge for at least 30 minutes.

2. Use your hands to create fat bomb balls from the dough. Roll each ball in cheese until completely covered. Arrange the balls on a tray. Refrigerate for 15 minutes before serving.

Note: For the herbs, you can use basil, oregano, or thyme.

# Lemon Keto Bombs

Servings: 16 pieces

Nutrition facts per piece: Calories 112 kcal, Fats 11.9 g, Protein 0.76 g, Net carb 0.8 g

Ingredients:

- 2 tablespoons fresh lemon zest
- 7.1 ounces coconut butter (softened)
- A pinch of salt
- 15 drops of liquid stevia
- 1/4 cup extra virgin coconut oil (softened)

Directions:

1. Combine all the ingredients in a bowl. Adjust the salt and sweetener according to taste. Transfer into molds and freeze for an hour before serving.

# Double Chocolate Keto Bombs

Servings: 2 dozens

Nutrition facts per 3 pieces: Calories 292 kcal, Fats 31 g, Protein 2.2 g, Net carb 1.3 g

Ingredients:

For the ganache filling

- 1 1/4 teaspoon chocolate extract
- 2 tablespoons, plus 2 teaspoons of heavy cream
- 5 ounces of low-carb chocolate
- 1/2 teaspoon sugar-free vanilla extract

For the chocolate coating

- 2 ounces of unsweetened baking chocolate
- 1 tablespoon sugar substitute
- 3 teaspoons cocoa butter
- 1/8 teaspoon stevia extract
- 1/4 teaspoon of sugar-free vanilla extract

Directions:

1. Put the chocolate in a double boiler and stir until melted.

2. Put the vanilla and cream in a heatproof bowl. Microwave for 2 minutes. Add the melted chocolate and chocolate extract. Mix well and leave for 5 minutes. Cover the bowl with a plastic wrap. Freeze for 12 hours or overnight.

3. Leave the chilled ganache at a room temperature for a couple of minutes. Divide and mold them into balls. Arrange the balls on a plate lined with wax paper. Refrigerate while you are working on the coating.

4. Melt the cocoa butter and chocolate in a double boiler. Add the sweeteners and vanilla. Mix well.

5. Dip each ball into the chocolate coating. Arrange them on a plate lined with wax paper and refrigerate until ready to serve.

# Guacamole Healthy Treats

Servings: 6 pieces

Nutrition facts per piece: Calories 156 kcal, Fats 15.2 g, Protein 3.4 g, Net carb 1.4 g

Ingredients:

- 1/2 large avocado
- 2 garlic cloves (crushed)
- 1/2 white onion (diced)
- 1/4 cup butter or ghee (room temperature)
- 4 large bacon slices
- 1 chili pepper (minced)
- Sea salt and freshly ground black to taste
- 1 tablespoon fresh lime juice
- 2 tablespoons freshly chopped cilantro

Directions:

1. Put the bacon slices on a baking tray lined with wax paper. Cook in a preheated oven at 375 degrees for 15 minutes or until golden brown. Transfer to a wire rack and allow to cool. Reserve the drippings and crumble the bacon to be used as breading.

2. Scoop out the meat of the avocado into a bowl. Add the chili pepper, butter, lime juice, cilantro, and crushed garlic. Season with salt and pepper. Mash and mix using a fork until everything is combined. Add the onion and mix thoroughly. Add the bacon drippings from the tray. Mix until combined.

3. Cover the bowl with foil and refrigerate for 30 minutes.

4. Divide the dough into 6 and form them into balls. Roll them in the crumbled bacon and arrange on a tray. Refrigerate for 15 minutes before serving.

Store the leftovers in an airtight container. They will last for a week when refrigerated.

## Pecan and Bacon Keto Treats

Servings: 3 pieces

Nutrition facts per 3 pieces: Calories 158 kcal, Fats 17 g, Protein 2 g, Net carb 1 g

Ingredients:

- 1 tablespoon unsalted butter
- 1 slice of bacon
- 2 pecan halves (toasted and chopped)
- A pinch of granulated garlic

Directions:

1. Cut the bacon into 3 slices. Spread butter on each side of the bacon and place it into a pecan. Sprinkle with a little salt and enjoy your treat.

# Coco-Choco Candy Cups

Servings: 20 mini cups

Nutrition facts per 2 pieces: Calories 240 kcal, Fats 25 g, Protein 2 g, Net carb 1 g

Ingredients:

- 1/2 cup coconut oil
- 1/2 cup coconut butter
- 3 tablespoons sweetener
- 1/2 cup unsweetened shredded coconut

For the chocolate topping

- 1-ounce unsweetened chocolate
- 1 1/2 ounces cocoa butter
- 1/4 cup cocoa powder
- 1/4 teaspoon vanilla extract
- 1/4 cup powdered sweetener

Directions:

1. Work on the candies first. Arrange 20 mini paper liners in a mini muffin pan. Set aside.

2. Put the coconut oil and coconut butter in a saucepan over low heat. Mix until melted and combined. Add the sweetener and shredded coconut. Mix well. Remove from heat. Divide among the prepared molds. Freeze for an hour.

3. Put the unsweetened chocolate and cocoa butter in a bowl. Put the bowl on top of a pan with simmering water over low heat. Mix until combined and melted. Sift the sweetener into the bowl. Add the cocoa powder. Mix until smooth. Turn off the heat. Add the vanilla extract and mix well.

4. Spoon the melted chocolate mixture on top of the candies. Freeze for 15 minutes before serving.

Put any excess in an airtight container. They will last for a week at a room temperature.

# Egg-Free Mini Lemony Tarts

Servings: 24 tarts

Nutrition facts per piece: Calories 101 kcal, Fats 10.3 g, Protein 1.3 g, Net carb 1.08 g

Ingredients:

For the crust

- 3/4 cup dried coconut (finely grated)
- 1 cup almond flour
- 2 tablespoons sugar substitute
- 1 1/2 teaspoons vanilla extract
- 3 tablespoons lemon juice
- A pinch of salt
- 4 1/2 tablespoons butter or ghee (melted)

For the filling

- 1/3 cup fresh lemon juice
- 1/2 cup butter or ghee (room temperature)
- 2 teaspoons lemon extract
- 1/3 cup full-fat coconut milk
- Grated zest of 2 lemons
- 1 teaspoon vanilla extract (sugar-free)
- 1/2 cup sugar substitute
- 1/4 teaspoon salt

Directions:

1. Lightly grease 2 mini muffin pans. Set aside.

2. Put all the ingredients for the crust in a bowl. Mix until combined. Transfer the dough on a wax paper and roll into a log. Slice into 24 parts. Form each part into a ball. Put each

ball in the hole of the muffin pan and press at the bottom. Cover with a plastic wrap and chill as you work on the filling.

3. Put the butter in a bowl. Beat using an electric mixer until smooth. Add the sweetener, salt, milk, extracts, lemon juice, and zest. Beat until everything is combined. Taste the mixture and add more sweetener or lemon juice according to preference.

4. Lay the muffin pans on the table. Spoon the filling on top of each crust. Top each with a bit of lemon zest. Put in the fridge for 15 minutes or until ready to serve.

You can serve the excess filling as a pudding. You can also put them into molds, freeze, and turn them into lemon-flavored fat bombs.

# Choco Candies with Coconut

Servings: 30 candies

Nutrition facts per piece: Calories 76 kcal, Fats 7.7 g, Protein 0.92 g, Net carb 1 g

Ingredients:

- 1 cup raw cocoa powder
- 1 cup extra virgin coconut oil
- 1/4 cup powdered Erythritol
- A pinch salt
- 1 teaspoon vanilla bean powder
- 1/4 cup coconut and pecan butter (chilled)
- 15 drops stevia extract

Directions:

1. Put the extra virgin coconut oil in a heatproof bowl. Microwave for a minute on a low setting. Stir in the stevia, Erythritol, cocoa powder, and vanilla extract. Take note that it is important to mix the Erythritol with the oil while it is still hot, otherwise, you'll find it hard to dissolve. Mix thoroughly until there are no lumps.

2. Fill the 1/3 portion of a silicone mold with the chocolate mixture. Once you are done with all the molds, put them in the fridge for 15 minutes.

3. Put half a teaspoon of the coconut and pecan butter on top of the chocolate in each mold. Pour over the rest of the chocolate mixture on top and refrigerate for an hour before serving.

Keep the candies refrigerated. Remove them from the molds when you are ready to eat them. The base is coconut oil, which easily gets soft at a room temperature.

# Yummy Keto Rolo

Servings: 12 pieces

Nutrition facts per piece: Calories 118 kcal, Fats 13.2 g, Protein 0.8 g, Net carb 0.8 g

Ingredients:

For the dark chocolate bar

- 1.5 ounces unsweetened baking chocolate (melted)

For the milk chocolate bar

- 1/4-ounce unsweetened baking chocolate (melted)

For the white chocolate bar

- 1 teaspoon toffee extract
- 2 ounces cocoa butter
- Sea salt to taste
- 1/3 cup Swerve confectioners

For the caramel filling

- 6 tablespoons organic butter
- 1/2 cup heavy whipping cream (organic)
- 1 cup Swerve confectioners

Directions:

1. Put the cocoa butter in a heatproof bowl. Microwave for a minute on a high setting. Stir and check every 30 seconds to make sure that it is fully melted. This fat takes a longer time to melt than the traditional kinds. Add the sweetener and mix well. Add the salt and extracts, and stir until combined. Transfer the white chocolate mixture into your molds. Refrigerate for an hour or until set.

2. Gather all the ingredients for the filling before working on it. You have to work fast so that the ingredients won't burn. Heat butter in a saucepan over low heat. Once it boils, immediately add the cream and confectioners. Whisk and scrape the sides to combine everything. Continue whisking until smooth. Turn off the heat.

3. Lay the molds with the chilled white chocolate layer on the table. Scoop the filling into each mold. Top each piece with melted chocolate. Refrigerate until set.

# Frozen Cocoa Bombs

Servings: 20 pieces

Nutrition facts per 2 pieces: Calories 48.8 kcal, Fats 5 g, Protein 0.7 g, Net carb 1.1 g

Ingredients:

- 2 tablespoons unsweetened cocoa powder
- 1/4 teaspoon cayenne pepper
- 1 cup coconut milk
- 1 teaspoon cinnamon
- 20 drops stevia extract
- 1 teaspoon unsweetened vanilla extract
- 2 tablespoons powdered Erythritol

Directions:

1. Put the coconut milk in a heatproof bowl. Microwave for several seconds or until slightly warm. This will make it easier for the other ingredients to dissolve. Add the rest of the ingredients. Mix well.

2. Scoop a tablespoon of the mixture into each hole of an ice cube tray. Chill for 2 hours.

# Fudgy White Choco Bombs

Servings: 24 pieces

Nutrition facts per piece: Calories 175 kcal, Fats 17.8 g, Protein 2.2 g, Net carb 1.2 g

Ingredients:

- 1/2 cup vanilla protein powder
- 1 15-ounce can coconut milk
- 4 ounces cacao butter
- A pinch salt
- 1/2 cup coconut oil
- 1 teaspoon coconut liquid stevia
- 1 cup coconut butter
- 1 teaspoon vanilla extract
- Unsweetened coconut flakes as toppings

Directions:

1. Put the cacao butter in a sauce pan over low flame. Stir until melted. Add the coconut oil, coconut milk, and coconut butter. Mix well until combined and free of lumps. Remove from the stove. Stir in the vanilla extract, salt, stevia, and protein powder. Mix until everything is incorporated.

2. Transfer the mixture to a square baking pan lined with parchment paper. Sprinkle coconut flakes on top. Cover and refrigerate overnight.

3. Slice and serve.

You can keep the leftovers at a room temperature.

# Spiced Keto Candies

Servings: 6 pieces

Nutrition facts per piece: Calories 372 kcal, Fats 36.98 g, Protein 2.32 g, Net carb 1.7 g

Ingredients:

- 1/2 cup of sweetener
- 8 ounces full-fat cream cheese (room temperature)
- 3/4 cup coconut oil (melted)
- 1 teaspoon ground cinnamon
- 1 teaspoon freshly grated ginger
- 1/2 teaspoon ground nutmeg
- 1/2 teaspoon ground cloves

Directions:

1. Put everything, except the coconut oil, in a food processor. Process until smooth. Gradually add the oil while the machine is running. Continue mixing until the mixture resembles the consistency of a mayonnaise.

2. Transfer the mixture into 6 small molds with lids. Lock the lids and refrigerate until ready to serve.

# Low-Carb Chocolate Bars

Servings: 12 pieces

Nutrition facts per piece: Calories 216 kcal, Fats 22 g, Protein 2 g, Net carb 2 g

Ingredients:

For the coconut layer

- 1/3 cup virgin coconut oil (melted)
- 2 cups shredded coconut (unsweetened)
- 2 drops liquid stevia

For the chocolate layer

- 1 tablespoon coconut oil
- 3 ounces unsweetened baking chocolate
- 2 drops liquid stevia

Directions:

1. Attach the S blade on your food processor. Put all the ingredients for the coco layer. Process until combined. Scrape the sides and process until the dough is formed.

2. Transfer the dough into a silicone loaf pan. Press it at the bottom. Freeze until set.

3. Put the chocolate and coconut oil in a heatproof bowl. Microwave on a high until melted. Add the sweetener. Mix well.

4. Pour the melted chocolate on top of the chilled coconut layer. Put back in the freezer for half an hour.

5. Remove from the mold and slice into 12 bars. Keep the leftovers in a Ziploc bag and store in the freezer.

# Double Chocolate Truffles

Servings: 2 dozens

Nutrition facts per 3 pieces: Calories 292 kcal, Fats 2.8 g, Protein 2.2 g, Net carb 1.3 g

Ingredients:

For the ganache filling

- 2 tablespoons, plus 2 teaspoons heavy cream
- 5 ounces low-carb dark chocolate
- 1 1/4 teaspoon chocolate extract
- 1/2 teaspoon vanilla extract

For the chocolate coating

- ½ ounce cocoa butter
- 2 ounces unsweetened baking chocolate
- 1/4 teaspoon vanilla extract
- 1 tablespoon Swerve confectioners
- 1/8 teaspoon stevia extract

Directions:

1. Prepare the ganache. Melt the chocolate in a double boiler.

2. Put the vanilla and cream in a heatproof bowl. Microwave until the mixture is in the bubbling stage. This means that it is near to boiling point. Add the mixture to the melted chocolate. Stir in the chocolate extract. Leave to temper for 5 minutes. Transfer the hot mixture into a bowl. Put a plastic wrap on top. The plastic must touch the surface of the mixture. Freeze for 6 hours or overnight.

3. Scoop small balls from the chilled ganache. Arrange them on a tray lined with wax paper. Refrigerate while you work on the coating.

4. Melt the chocolate in a double boiler over low heat. Add the cocoa butter. Mix until melted and combined. Remove from heat. Add the vanilla and sweeteners. Mix well.

5. Dip each ball into the melted chocolate mixture. Allow to set and dip one more time for a thicker coating.

You can also opt to roll the ganache in chopped nuts or sprinkle them with a bit of sea salt before dipping into the melted chocolate.

# Cheesy Almond Keto Bombs

Servings: 12 pieces

Nutrition facts per piece: Calories 86 kcal, Fats 7 g, Protein 2 g, Net carb 2 g

Ingredients:

- 1 ounce cream cheese
- 4 tablespoons coconut butter
- 1 tablespoon cocoa powder
- 16 grams dark chocolate
- 4 tablespoons almond butter
- 2 tablespoons sugar-free syrup

Directions:

1. Put all the ingredients except for the coconut butter in a heatproof bowl. Microwave until melted while stirring the mixture every 15 seconds to check. Once everything is combined, add the coconut butter, and mix well.

2. Pour the mixture into your molds. Freeze for an hour. Remove from the molds when ready to serve. Keep the leftovers in the fridge because they will easily melt when left at a room temperature.

# Chapter 3 – Low-Carb Fat Bomb Recipes with Berries

It is important that you are aware of the right ingredients to use when following a low-carb diet. After trying out the recipes from this book and when you already know the right techniques in creating fat bombs, you can come up with recipes of your own. You can use any ingredient that you want as long as they contain a low amount of carbs.

Vegetables and fruits are quite common in any low-carb diet. Stick with the dark and leafy kinds when choosing veggies because they are low in carbs and high in nutrients. Most green cruciferous veggies that are grown above the ground are suitable for the diet. Anything that grows underground has to be consumed in moderation.

Here's a list of the vegetables that you can eat anytime:

- Leafy greens (contain 0.5 to 5 grams net carbs for every cup) – Kale, beet greens, dandelion, chard, mustard, fennel, endive, chicory, turnip, romaine
- Cruciferous vegetables (contain 3 to 6 grams net carb for every cup) – Cabbage, cauliflower, broccoli, Brussels sprouts
- Fresh herbs (almost no carbs for every 1 to 2 tablespoons)
- Cucumber, chives, celery, leeks, zucchini (contain 2 to 4 grams net carbs for every 1 cup)

The following vegetables have slightly higher carb content at around 3 to 7 grams net carbs for every 1 cup but are still safe to eat on a low-carb diet:

- Green beans
- Asparagus
- Tomatoes
- Bamboo shoots
- Water chestnuts
- Jicama
- Radish
- Mushroom
- Bean sprouts
- Sugar snap peas

Fruits

Berries are among the safest fruits to eat when you are on a low-carb diet. They can help you in sticking to your 30 grams or less carb limit per day. Here's a list of the fruits that you can include in your diet and how much carbs they have for every 100 grams and their average serving sizes.

- Avocado – 1.84 grams (1/2 of the fruit)
- Starfruits – 3.93 grams (1 medium piece)
- Tomato – 2.69 grams (1 piece of small vine type)
- Honeydew melon – 5.68 grams (8 honeydew balls)
- Cantaloupe – 7.26 grams (7 cantaloupe balls)
- Watermelon – 7.15 grams (8 watermelon balls)
- Rhubarb – 2.74 grams (2 stalks)
- Apricot – 9.12 grams (3 pitted fruits)
- Clementine – 10.32 (1 medium piece)
- Coconut meat – 6.23 grams (1 cup of shredded coconut)
- Lemon – 6.52 grams (2 pieces)
- Kiwi – 11.66 grams (1 1/2 pieces)
- Granny Smith apple – 10.81 grams (3/5 of a medium piece)

- Peach – 8.05 grams (3/4 of a small fruit)
- Plum – 10.02 grams (1 1/2 pieces)

Berries

This chapter features recipes that include berries in the ingredients. Here are some of the berries used in the recipes, including their carb content and health benefits:

1. Blackberries

These berries have been used since the ancient times in treating gout and other illnesses. They contain high amounts of nutrients, such as manganese, and vitamins C and K. They reduce inflammation, boost the motor, and brain function, and improve the health of your skin. The fruit is also loaded with anthocyanin and ellagic acid that can help in slowing down the growth of cancer by suppressing the mutation of the cell. One cup of raspberries contains 7 grams of net carbs and 8 grams of fiber.

2. Raspberries

They are high in nutrients and low in carbs. Aside from fat bombs, you can also use raspberries in other sweet and savory dishes and treats. They have antioxidant properties that help in fighting inflammation and in protecting your body from harmful free radicals. Raspberries have a high content of polyphenol that helps in preventing the buildup of platelet in the arteries and lowers the blood pressure. A serving of 1/2 cup of the fruit contains 3.5 grams net carbs.

3. Strawberries

The fruit has slightly higher carb content than raspberries and blackberries. You'll get about 5 grams net carbs for every 3/4 cup serving. Always remember to eat them in moderation. Aside from being refreshing, strawberries help in improving your blood sugar and insulin levels.

4. Blueberries

They are rich in vitamin C and antioxidants that are good for the skin. They must also be consumed in moderation because the fruit contains higher amount of carbs than strawberries. They have about 17.4 grams net carbs for every serving of 1 cup. They also have a higher fructose content than the other berries that is why it is important that you limit its intake.

Here are some samples of the fat bomb recipes with different berries as part of the ingredients:

# Coconut and Berries Fat Bombs

Servings: 16 small squares

Nutrition facts per 1 square: Calories 170 kcal, Fats 18.7 g, Protein 1.1 g, Net carb 0.8 g

Ingredients:

- 1/2 cup fresh or frozen berries of your choice (raspberries, blackberries, or strawberries)
- 1 cup coconut oil
- 1 tablespoon lemon juice
- 1 cup coconut butter
- 1/2 teaspoon vanilla extract
- 1/2 teaspoon stevia drops

Directions:

1. Heat coconut oil and coconut butter in a pan over medium heat. Stir in the berries if frozen. Mix until combined and the oils are melted.

2. Allow the oil mixture to lightly cool before transferring to a food processor. Add the rest of the ingredients and process until smooth.

3. Pour the mixture into a square pan lined with parchment paper. Put in the fridge for at least an hour. Slice into squares and serve.

# Chocolatey Strawberry Swirl Bombs

Servings: 12

Nutrition facts per piece: Calories 99 kcal, Fats 11 g, Protein 0.1 g, Net carb 1 g

Ingredients:

- 2 tablespoons cocoa powder
- 1/4 teaspoon liquid stevia
- 4 tablespoons coconut oil
- 4 tablespoons unsalted butter

For the strawberry swirl

- 1/4 cup strawberries
- 1/4 teaspoon liquid stevia
- 1 tablespoon coconut oil
- 1 tablespoon unsalted butter
- 1 tablespoon heavy cream

Directions:

1. Put the butter in a heatproof bowl. Microwave until soft. Allow to cool a little before adding the cocoa powder, stevia, and coconut oil. Mix well and set aside.

2. Prepare the strawberry swirl. Put the heavy cream and strawberries in a heatproof bowl. Mash the berries as you mix. Microwave for 10 seconds and set aside.

3. Melt butter in another bowl. Gradually add the warm strawberry mixture, stevia, and coconut oil. Mix using a stick blender until combined.

4. To assemble, pour the chocolate mixture first into your molds. Add the strawberry mixture at the center and swirl using a toothpick. Freeze the fat bombs for 20 minutes before

removing from the molds. Put any leftover in an airtight container and store in the freezer.

# Blackberries and Cheese Fat Bombs

Servings: 12

Nutrition facts per piece: Calories 392 kcal, Fats 50 g, Protein 4 g, Net carb 1.3 g

Ingredients:

- 1 cup blackberries
- 3 tablespoons mascarpone cheese
- 4 ounces cream cheese (softened)
- Stevia to taste
- 2 ounces macadamia nuts (crushed)
- 1/2 teaspoon lemon juice
- 1/2 teaspoon vanilla extract
- 1 cup coconut butter
- 1 cup coconut oil

Directions:

1. Put the macadamia nuts in the food processor and process until crushed. Transfer to a baking dish and press at the bottom. Bake for 7 minutes at 325 degrees or until golden brown. Leave until slightly cool.

2. Spread the softened cream cheese on top of the macadamia layer.

3. In a bowl, put the mascarpone cheese, sweetener, vanilla, blackberries, lemon juice, coconut butter, and coconut oil. Mix until smooth. Pour this over the cream cheese layer and spread using a spatula.

4. Cover and freeze for an hour. Slice and serve.

# Blueberry and Cheese Fat Bombs

Servings: 16 pieces

Nutrition facts per piece: Calories 231 kcal, Fats 29 g, Protein 3 g, Net carb 2 g

Ingredients:

- 4 ounces Neufchatel cheese (softened)
- 1 cup blueberries
- Liquid stevia to taste
- 1/4 cup coconut cream
- 8 ounces unsalted butter
- 3/4 cup coconut oil

Directions

1. Put the blueberries in a pan and crush them at the bottom.

2. Melt butter in a saucepan over low heat. Stir in the oil. Remove from heat and leave for 5 minutes. Add the rest of the ingredients. Use a hand blender to whisk well. Gradually add stevia to taste. Pour this on top of the crushed berries. Chill for an hour.

3. Slice and top with whole blueberries before serving.

Note: You can also opt to use pureed berries. To get it done, put the berries, cream cheese, and coconut cream in a blender. Process until pureed. Melt the coconut oil and butter in a saucepan over low heat. Cool for 5 minutes and add stevia to taste. Put the mixture in the blender. Process until everything is combined. Transfer into your molds and freeze for an hour.

# Raspberry and Choco Treats

Servings: 14 pieces

Nutrition facts per piece: Calories 164 kcal, Fats 17.1 g, Protein 2.2 g, Net carb 2.6 g

Ingredients:

You have 2 options for the chocolate.

For milder taste, use the quick keto chocolate:

- 100 grams cocoa butter
- 1 teaspoon unsweetened vanilla extract
- 2 tablespoons extra virgin coconut oil
- 300 grams dark chocolate (at least 85 percent)
- Sweetener to taste

Your other option is to make homemade chocolate:

- 4.2 ounces unsweetened dark chocolate (100 percent cacao)
- 1/2 cup cocoa butter
- 1 teaspoon unsweetened vanilla extract
- 3 tablespoons extra virgin coconut oil
- 25 drops stevia extract
- 1/3 cup unsweetened cacao powder
- Powdered Erythritol to taste

For the toppings

- 30 grams almonds (around 25 pieces)
- 1 1/2 cups fresh or frozen raspberries

Directions:

1. Roast the almonds in a pan for 5 minutes. Put each nut into a raspberry. Arrange them on a tray and chill for an hour.

2. If you are using the quick keto chocolate, put all the ingredients in a double boiler. Mix until melted and combined.

3. For the other option, put the coconut oil, cocoa butter, and unsweetened chocolate in a bowl. Put the bowl on top of a pot with boiling water over low heat. Stir the mixture until melted. Remove from heat. Add the unsweetened cacao, vanilla extract, stevia, and powdered Erythritol. Mix thoroughly.

4. Lay mini muffin paper cups on a tray. Scoop a tablespoon of the chocolate mixture into each cup. Put 2 chilled raspberries in every cup. Scoop another tablespoon of chocolate on top. Refrigerate for 30 minutes or until ready to serve.

These treats will last up to 3 days when stored in the fridge and up to a week when chilled.

# Low-Carb Strawberry Cheesecake Delights

Servings: 14 pieces

Nutrition facts per piece: Calories 67 kcal, Fats 7.4 g, Protein 0.96 g, Net carb 0.85 g

Ingredients:

- 1/2 cup strawberries (fresh or frozen)
- 1/4 cup butter or coconut oil (softened)
- 1 tablespoon vanilla extract
- 5.3 ounces cream cheese (room temperature)
- 15 drops liquid stevia

Directions:

1. Cut the butter and cream cheese into small pieces and put them in a bowl. Leave at a room temperature for an hour.

2. Remove the green parts and rinse the strawberries. Put them in a blender and process until smooth. Add the vanilla extract and stevia. Pulse until combined.

3. Add the strawberry mixture to the bowl of softened cream cheese and butter. Whisk using a hand mixer. You can also use a food processor to make sure that everything is combined.

4. Scoop the mixture into candy or small silicon molds. Freeze for 2 hours. Remove from the molds when ready to serve.

# Chapter 4 – Low-Carb Fat Bomb Recipes with Nuts

Nuts are technically fruits but the main difference is that they are not that sweet and soft. They are found inside hard outer shells that you need to crack open to get them. Nuts are generally rich in monounsaturated fatty acids or MUFAs that are good for the heart, except for walnuts.

Nuts and seeds contain a low amount of carbs and are rich in vitamins, minerals, and fiber, which make these 2 ingredients suitable for a low-carb diet. It is easy to over eat these foods since they are easy to consume. You only need to get a handful and pop them into your mouth.

If you want to snack on nuts and seeds, divide them into portions and limit your serving to once or twice a day. They are also used in a variety of low-carb recipes, including fat bombs.

Here are some of the healthiest nuts that you can include in your diet, including the amount of carbohydrates that they contain for every 28 grams serving:

1. Macadamia nuts (1.5 g net carbs, 2.4 g fiber, 3.9 g total carbs)

These nuts have the highest amount of fat among the other kinds of nuts. Around 78 percent of the fats in these nuts are MUFA, which is among the highest as compared to other nuts. They are effective in increasing the levels of your good cholesterol and in decreasing the levels of the bad cholesterol.

2. Almonds (2.6 g net carbs, 3.5 g fiber, 6.1 g total carbs)

You can get 37 percent of the Recommended Dietary Allowance for vitamin E from almonds. It helps in decreasing the levels of your bad cholesterol. It also works by improving the condition of your heart. They contain the highest amount of protein among all nuts and seeds. You'll get 6 grams of protein for every serving of almonds.

3. Pecans (1.2 g net carbs, 2.7 g fiber, 3.9 g total carbs)

They contain the lowest amount of carbs among all nuts. They are also a good source of zinc. Pecans help in lowering your blood pressure and they also have antioxidant properties.

4. Walnuts (2 g net carbs, 1.9 g fiber, 3.9 g total carbs)

They are rich in omega-3 fatty acids. Walnuts lower your LDL particles and reduce your LDL cholesterol. It also helps in improving the function of your artery.

5. Brazil nuts (1.4 g net carbs, 2.1 g fiber, 3.5 g total carbs)

These nuts contain a high amount of selenium that helps in keeping your thyroid function healthy. It is important that you don't get too much selenium in your system so make sure that you limit your intake of Brazil nuts. When taken in moderation, the nuts can help in protecting your cells from free radicals and decrease your risk of inflammation.

6. Pistachios (5 g net carbs, 2.9 g fiber, 7.9 g total carbs)

You will get 24 percent of your daily vitamin B6 requirement from a serving of these nuts. They help in improving the values of your lipid and blood sugar. Pistachios are also beneficial to people with diabetes because they can lower the levels of your blood sugar, triglyceride, and cholesterol.

7. Hazelnuts (2 g net carbs, 2.7 g fiber, 4.7 g total carbs)

They help in improving your lipid profile by giving sufficient amount of vitamin E. They boost the levels of your good cholesterol and decrease the levels of the bad type.

Here are the recipes that you can try with nuts as one of the main ingredients. You can try using other nuts to tweak each recipe, but make sure that you adjust the nutritional information accordingly.

# Chewy Bombs with Macadamia

Servings: 6 pieces

Nutrition facts per piece: Calories 267 kcal, Fats 28 g, Protein 3 g, Net carb 3 g

Ingredients:

- 2 tablespoons unsweetened cocoa powder
- 1/4 cup heavy cream (if you want a dairy-free recipe, use coconut oil)
- 2 tablespoons sugar substitute
- 2 ounces cocoa butter
- 4 ounces macadamia nuts (chopped)

Directions:

1. Put the cocoa butter in a saucepan over low heat. Stir until melted. Add the cocoa butter. Mix well. Stir in the sugar substitute. Mix until everything in melted and combined. Stir in the chopped nuts.

2. Remove from heat. Add the cream and mix well. Leave to cool.

3. Pour the mixture into molds. Refrigerate until set or until ready to serve.

# Walnut Keto Delights

Servings: 36 squares

Nutrition facts per piece: Calories 170 kcal, Fats 17.4 g, Protein 2.2 g, Net carb 1 g

Ingredients:

- 1 cup all-natural roasted almond butter
- 1/2 cup ghee (melted)
- 1/2 cup full-fat coconut milk (frozen overnight)
- 1 cup creamy coconut butter
- 1 tablespoon pure almond extract
- 1 cup coconut oil
- 2 teaspoons chai spice
- 1/4 cup ghee
- 1/4 teaspoons sea salt
- 1/4 cup walnuts (chopped)

Directions:

1. Line a greased square baking pan with parchment paper. Set aside.

2. Put the ghee in a saucepan over low flame. Stir until melted. Set aside.

3. In a bowl, put all the ingredients, except for the walnuts and melted ghee. Mix using an electric mixer on a low speed setting. Gradually add the speed to a high until the mixture becomes fluffy and light. Set the mixer's speed back on a low. Add the melted ghee and mix until everything is combined.

4. Pour the mixture and spread evenly in the prepared pan. Sprinkle with the chopped nuts. Put in the refrigerator overnight.

5. Slice into 36 squares. Serve and enjoy.

# Orange and Nuts Low-Carb Delights

Servings: 25 pieces

Nutrition facts per piece: Calories 86.4 kcal, Fats 8.4 g, Protein 1.5 g, Net carb 1.5 g

Ingredients:

- 125 grams of dark chocolate (85 percent cocoa)
- 1 tablespoon of orange peel and fresh orange extract
- 1 teaspoon cinnamon
- 15 drops of liquid stevia
- 150 grams walnuts (chopped)
- 1/4 cup of extra virgin coconut oil

Directions:

1. Put the chocolate in a heatproof bowl. Microwave until melted. Gradually add the coconut oil and cinnamon. Add the remaining ingredients. Mix until well combined. Transfer into molds and refrigerate for an hour or until set.

# Choco-Macadamia Treats

Servings: 6 pieces

Nutrition facts per piece: Calories 267 kcal, Fats 28 g, Protein 6 g, Net carb 3 g

Ingredients:

- 2 tablespoons unsweetened cocoa powder
- 1/4 cup heavy cream
- 4 ounces of chopped macadamia nuts
- 2 ounces of cocoa butter
- 2 tablespoons of sugar substitute

Directions:

1. Put the cocoa butter in a saucepan over low heat. Stir until melted. Remove from heat. Add the cocoa powder. Mix until combined. Add the remaining ingredients and mix well. Transfer to molds and refrigerate for at least 30 minutes before serving.

# Pumpkin Treats with Pecans

Servings: 8 pieces

Nutrition facts per piece: Calories 227 kcal, Fats 39 g, Protein 11 g, Net carb 1 g

Ingredients:

- 1/2 cup pumpkin (pureed)
- 1/4 cup chopped pecans
- 1/2 cup unsalted butter
- 1/8 teaspoon sea salt
- 12 drops liquid stevia
- 1 teaspoon cinnamon
- 8 ounces Neufchatel cheese
- 1/2 teaspoons pumpkin spice
- 2 teaspoons vanilla extract

Directions:

1. Melt butter in a saucepan over low heat while whisking often. Add the pureed pumpkin as you continue to whisk. Stir in the pecans, stevia, cream cheese, and spices. Whisk until smooth. Add the vanilla extract and mix well. Turn off the heat.

2. Transfer the mixture to a baking pan lined with wax paper. You can opt to add more pecans on top. Freeze overnight. Pull the wax paper before slicing.

# Nutty Choco Treats

Servings: 12 pieces

Nutrition facts per piece: Calories 124 kcal, Fats 12 g, Protein 4 g, Net carb 1.6 g

Ingredients:

- 1/2 cup peanut butter
- 4 tablespoons coconut oil
- 4 tablespoons cocoa powder
- 1/4 tablespoon cinnamon
- Stevia to taste
- Sea salt to taste
- 1 teaspoon vanilla extract
- 1/4 cup walnuts (chopped)

Directions:

1. Put the coconut oil in a heatproof bowl and microwave for 50 seconds or until melted. Set aside.

2. In another bowl, put the vanilla, cocoa, and stevia. Mix well. Fold in the nuts. Transfer to a pan and spread using a spatula.

3. Combine the peanut butter and cinnamon. Pour this on top of the chocolate layer. Sprinkle sea salt on top. Freeze for 20 minutes.

4. Slice and serve.

Note: You can tweak the recipe by using other nuts, such as almonds, macadamia, and pecans.

# Macadamia Coconut Bombs

Servings: 12 pieces

Nutrition facts per piece: Calories 188 kcal, Fats 20g, Protein 2 g, Net carb 1.2 g

Ingredients:

For the crust

- 4 tablespoons almond butter
- 4 ounces macadamia nuts
- A dash of salt

For the coconut layer

- 6 tablespoons coconut oil (melted)
- 1/4 cup shredded coconut

For the chocolate layer

- 2 tablespoons coconut oil
- 4 tablespoons cocoa powder
- Liquid stevia to taste

Directions:

1. Prepare the crust. Put the macadamia nuts and salt in a food processor and process until finely ground. Transfer to a bowl. Add the almond butter and mix until combined. Press the mixture at the bottom of a pan.

2. Combine the coconut oil and shredded coconut in a bowl. Pour over the crust, press, and set aside.

3. In a bowl, mix the coconut oil and cocoa powder until smooth. Add stevia according to preference. Pour this over the top layer and use a spatula to flatten and spread it out. Freeze for a couple of hours.

# Pecan Treats with Stuffing

Servings: 1

Nutrition facts: Calories 150 kcal, Fats 31 g, Protein 11 g, Net carb 0.8 g

Ingredients:

- 1 ounce cream cheese
- 1/2 teaspoon unsalted butter
- 4 pecan halves
- A pinch of sea salt
- Flavor of choice

Directions:

1. Preheat the oven to 350 degrees. Toast the pecans for 10 minutes. Leave to cool.

2. Soften the cream cheese and butter in a bowl. Add your preferred flavored. It can be anything from vegetables, herbs, or spices. Mix until combined and creamy. Spread the filling in between the pecan halves.

3. Sprinkle with sea salt before serving.

# Choco Walnut Delight Bombs

Servings: 8

Nutrition facts per piece: Calories 247 kcal, Fats 29 g, Protein 3 g, Net carb 1 g

Ingredients:

- 1/2 cup almond butter
- 4 tablespoons unsalted butter
- 1/2 cup coconut oil
- 2 tablespoons walnuts (chopped)
- Sea salt to taste
- 6 drops liquid stevia
- Dark chocolate for topping

Directions:

1. Put all the ingredients in a heatproof bowl. Microwave for 30 seconds. Mix well until combined. Pour into molds and freeze for at least 1 hour.

2. Drizzle with melted chocolate on top. You can also opt to sprinkle the fat bombs with coarsely chopped walnuts.

# Spiced Pistachio Fast Bombs

Servings: 36 pieces

Nutrition facts per piece: Calories 170 kcal, Fats g, Protein g, Net carb 1.5 g

Ingredients:

- 1/4 cup pistachios (remove shells and chop)
- 1/2 cup chopped cacao butter (melted)
- 1 cup coconut butter
- 1 cup almond butter
- 1 cup coconut oil (firm)
- 1/4 teaspoon sea salt
- 2 teaspoons Chai spice
- 1/4 cup ghee
- 1/4 teaspoon almond extract
- 1 tablespoon vanilla extract
- 1/2 cup frozen coconut milk

Directions:

1. Melt the cacao butter in a saucepan over low heat while stirring often.

2. In a bowl, put the coconut oil, coconut butter, almond butter, coconut milk, ghee, extracts, salt, and Chai spice. Mix using an electric mixer set on low speed. Gradually increase the speed until everything is combined and the mixture is fluffy. Set the speed back to low. Add the melted cacao butter and mix for 3 minutes.

3. Spread the mixture in a pan lined with wax paper. Sprinkle the chopped pistachios on top. Cover the pan and put in the fridge for 5 hours or overnight.

# Chapter 5 - Ketogenic Specific Fat Bomb Recipes

The state of ketosis happens when your body no longer gets sufficient supply of carbohydrates. Your body turns to ketosis to process the energy you need. Your body doesn't produce ketones when you are on a regular diet because you don't need them. Instead, your system decides how much fat it will burn.

When you are in the state of ketosis, your body automatically burns fat due to the lack of carbs and produces ketones. The end result will give your body the fuel that it needs. This is safe for as long as there is no ketones build-up, which will create an imbalance in the chemical components of your blood. Ketones build-up often leads to dehydration.

It is important that you educate yourself about the diet before committing to it. You have to know what to eat, what portions, and how often. You must also know the ingredients to avoid when following a low-carb diet.

The state of ketosis is the main cause why you lose weight when you are on this kind of diet. It helps in maintaining your muscles as you shed off the fat. It also suppresses your appetite. As long as you are healthy and you are not suffering from diabetes, you will likely enter this state after 3 days of taking less than 50 grams of carbs each day. Ketosis is one benefit of a low-carb diet, such as ketogenic diet, but you can also achieve this state through fasting.

Having too much ketones in the system is not healthy. To avoid this, you need to regularly monitor the level of your ketones. You can buy test strips to check your blood or urine at the comfort of your home. If you have diabetes, ask the help of an instructor on how to use blood sugar meters that are specifically made for this condition. To be safe, you can always ask the help of your doctor to explain your options and how to monitor the ketone levels in your blood.

What is the effect of a ketone build-up? When the ketones build up in your blood, you will be at a risk of developing ketoacids. The condition is dangerous and can lead to a coma, or in some cases, death. If you aren't diabetic, you are prone to get ketoacid from alcoholism, starvation, and an overactive thyroid. People with diabetes can get DKA or diabetic ketoacid when they get sick or injured, dehydration, and lack or insufficient doses of insulin.

These are the symptoms of ketoacids:

- Peeing often
- Getting tired fast
- Feeling confused
- Having a fruity-smelling breath
- Having trouble breathing
- Dry mouth/feeling thirsty
- Aches in the stomach and belly
- Throwing up
- Flushed or dry skin

DKA may start slow but it becomes dangerous when you begin throwing up. It speeds up the process and might lead to risky complications if not treated properly and on time. If you experience throwing up at this point and you are diabetic, do not wait for more than an hour before you seek your doctor's help.

In order to prevent having ketoacids, stick to your goal of experiencing nutritional ketosis. This is the state wherein your body burns fat instead of glucose to supply your system with energy. This is achieved by removing most sugar and starches from your diet. You will replace them with healthy fats and carbs.

Ketosis is a normal chemical reaction. You experience this everyday even when on a regular diet, but it happens briefly so you remain unaware of it. A low-carb diet prolongs the duration when your body enters this state and allows you to experience its health benefits.

How would you know that you are already in the state of nutritional ketosis? This is the why you need to measure your blood glucose and ketones. Your blood ketones must stay within the range of 0.5 to 3.0 millimoles per liter in order to stay in the state of nutritional ketosis.

To easily get into the state of nutritional ketosis, you have to know your daily macronutrient requirement. This will depend on the following factors:

- The ketogenic ratio suited for your age, weight, and level of physical activities
- Your calorie requirement
- Your protein requirement
- Your fluid intake

There are online macro calculators that you can use to know and monitor this requirement. After accessing the calculator, you will be asked to fill in your age, gender, and whether or not you are physically active.

Getting Keto-Adapted

The beginning is the hardest part of any low-carb diet. Through the days, you will get used to the process and you will eventually get keto-adapted. Keto-adaptation occurs as your system processes the fat-based sources and turns them into fuel. When you reach this point, your body produces more ketones from the partially broken-down fats. These ketones will enter your bloodstream. They will be distributed to the parts of your body where glucose used to flow, most of which will go into your brain.

You have to help your body perform normal functions despite the little amount of glucose that it is getting. Before you get keto-adapted, note that you will be prone to experiencing keto flu symptoms, which signal that your body is still trying to adjust. You might feel unwell but you can make up for it by eating lots of healthy fats, staying hydrated, and taking supplements.

When you are already keto-adapted, you will no longer get the keto flu symptoms. You will have more energy to perform your daily activities and your body will have an improved mood and condition. It happens as your glycogen storage in the muscles and in your liver decreases, and your body has lesser amount of excess water.

If you are intent on losing weight, your goal is to attain optimal ketosis. Make sure that you know your daily macro requirement. Follow the limits no matter how hard it seems. This is the point where fat bombs can help you. They are mostly made of fat that can easily fill your cravings and make you feel full at a faster rate.

The following fat bomb recipes will help you maintain the state of optimal ketosis longer:

# Basic Fat Bomb Recipe

Servings: 24 pieces

Nutrition facts per piece: Calories 95 kcal, Fats 10.1 g, Protein 1.1 g, Net carb 0.2 g

Ingredients:

For the coating

- 1 teaspoon lemon extract
- 1/2 cup cocoa butter (melted)
- 1/4 teaspoon sea salt
- 2/3 cup of Swerve confectioners

For the filling

- 8 tablespoons coconut oil
- 1/2 cup of lemon juice
- 1 tablespoon lemon peel (finely grated)
- 4 eggs
- 1 cup of sweetener

Directions:

1. In a bowl, put all the ingredients for the coating and mix until combined. Transfer to your molds. Refrigerate for an hour.

2. Put all the ingredients for the filling in a saucepan over medium heat. Whisk until heated but do not bring to a boil. Strain to a bowl. Put this bowl on top of any container that contains ice. Occasionally whisk the filling until completely cool.

3. Add filling to each truffle. Refrigerate for at least 30 minutes before serving.

# Walnut Keto Treats

Servings: 4 pieces

Nutrition facts per piece: Calories 176.32 kcal, Fats 17.77 g, Protein 1.26 g, Net carb 0.5 g

Ingredients:

- 1 tablespoon of walnut halves (chopped and toasted)
- 1 tablespoon unsweetened cocoa powder
- A dash of sea salt
- 1 tablespoon heavy whipping cream
- 2 tablespoons coconut oil (melted)
- 1 tablespoon of sweetener

Directions:

1. Put all the ingredients in a bowl. Mix well until combined and creamy. Transfer to a pan lined with wax paper. Refrigerate for 2 hours. Break into pieces and serve.

Note: You can tweak the recipe to come up with other flavors by using other nuts, such as chestnuts, macadamia, pecans, hazelnuts, and almonds.

# Lemon-Flavored Cheesecake Bombs

Servings: 8 pieces

Nutrition facts per piece: Calories 106 kcal, Fats 11 g, Protein 1 g, Net carb 0.25 g

Ingredients:

- 4 ounces cream cheese (softened)
- 4 tablespoons unsalted butter (softened)
- 1 tablespoon lemon zest (finely grated)
- 1/4 cup coconut oil (melted)
- Stevia to taste
- 1 teaspoon lemon juice
- Lemon extract (optional)

Directions:

1. Put all the ingredients in a bowl. Mix until smooth. Transfer to your molds. Freeze for 2 hours or overnight.

2. Sprinkle the fat bombs with lemon zest before serving.

# Breakfast Truffles

Servings: 6 pieces

Nutrition facts per piece: Calories 185 kcal, Fats 18.4 g, Protein 5 g, Net carb 0.2 g

Ingredients:

- 1/4 cup butter (softened)
- 2 eggs (hard boiled)
- 4 bacon slices
- 1/4 teaspoon of sea salt
- Freshly ground black pepper to taste
- 2 tablespoons of mayonnaise

Directions:

1. Arrange the bacon slices on a tray. Bake them in a preheated oven at 375 degrees for 15 minutes. Set aside to cool.

2. Peel the hard-boiled eggs and mash them using a fork. Add the mayonnaise. Mix well. Season with salt and pepper. Add the bacon grease. Mix until combined. Refrigerate for 30 minutes.

3. Break the bacon into small pieces once cooled.

4. Form balls from the batter. Roll each in the crumbled bacon. Arrange the balls on a tray and refrigerate until ready to serve.

Leftovers can last for a week when stored in an airtight container and placed in the fridge.

# Energy-Boosting Bulletproof Bombs

Servings: 20 pieces

Nutrition facts per piece: Calories 77 kcal, Fats 8.1 g, Protein 0.8 g, Net carb 0.5 g

Ingredients:

- 1/4 cup butter (or extra virgin coconut oil)
- 1 cup creamed coconut milk (softened)
- 2 tablespoons raw and unsweetened cocoa powder
- 15 drops liquid stevia extract
- 2 tablespoons MCT oil
- 1/2 cup strong brewed coffee
- 1/4 cup powdered Erythritol
- 1 teaspoon rum extract (optional)

Directions:

1. Put the cocoa powder, butter, MCT oil, softened coconut milk, stevia, and powdered Erythritol in a blender. Process until smooth. Make sure that the brewed coffee is lukewarm and not hot before pouring it into the blender. Process until smooth.

2. Transfer the mixture to an ice cream maker. Process for 30 to 60 minutes depending on the manufacturer's instructions. This will make the mixture creamy and smooth.

3. Scoop less than 2 tablespoons of the mixture into each mold. You can proceed with this step and scoop the mixture directly into the molds after you are done with the first step if you don't have an ice cream maker.

4. Put in the freezer for 3 hours. Serve and enjoy.

# Coco Butter Bombs with Nutmeg

Servings: 10 balls

Nutrition facts per piece: Calories 341 kcal, Fats 3.19 g, Protein 0.33 g, Net carb 0.53 g

Ingredients:

- 1 cup full-fat coconut milk
- 1 cup coconut butter
- 1 teaspoon stevia powder extract (adjust according to taste)
- 1 cup coconut shreds
- 1/2 teaspoon cinnamon
- 1/2 teaspoon nutmeg
- 1 teaspoon vanilla extract

Directions:

1. Put all the ingredients, except for the shredded coconut, in a double boiler over medium flame. Mix well until everything is combined and melted. Remove from heat. Allow to cool a little before putting the bowl inside the refrigerator for an hour.

2. Form 1-inch sized balls from the dough. Roll them in the coconut shreds until all sides are completely covered. Arrange on a plate and put in the fridge for an hour or until ready to serve.

# Nutty Vanilla Truffles

Servings: 14 pieces

Nutrition facts per piece: Calories 132 kcal, Fats 14.4 g, Protein 0.79 g, Net carb 0.6 g

Ingredients:

- 1 cup unsalted macadamia nuts
- 15 drops of stevia extract (adjust according to taste)
- 1/4 cup of extra virgin coconut oil (melted)
- 2 tablespoons of powdered sweetener
- 2 teaspoons of sugar-free vanilla extract
- 1/4 cup of softened butter

Directions:

1. Put the macadamia nuts in a blender. Pulse until smooth. Transfer to a bowl. Add the butter, coconut oil, extracts, and sweeteners. Mix well.

2. Transfer the mixture into molds. Refrigerate for an hour.

3. Remove the fat bombs from the molds and serve.

Note: You can use other nuts, such as hazelnuts, pecan, chestnuts, almonds, and walnut. You can also tweak its flavor by using other extracts, such as fruits, herbs, ginger, and lemon.

# Spicy Keto Bombs

Servings: 10

Nutrition facts per piece: Calories 120 kcal, Fats 12.8 g, Protein 0.5 g, Net carb 0. 70 g

Ingredients:

- 75 grams of coconut butter (softened)
- 75 grams of coconut oil (softened)
- 1 teaspoon sweetener
- 1/2 teaspoon dried powdered ginger
- 25 grams of unsweetened shredded coconut

Directions:

1. Put all the ingredients in a bowl. Mix until the sweetener is dissolved and everything is combined. Pour into molds. Refrigerate for 10 minutes before serving.

# Vanilla-Macadamia Healthy Bombs

Servings: 14 pieces

Nutrition facts per piece: Calories 132 kcal, Fats 14.4 g, Protein 0.79 g, Net carb 0.6 g

Ingredients:

- 1 cup unsalted macadamia nuts
- 2 teaspoons sugar-free vanilla extract
- 15 drops of vanilla stevia extract
- 2 tablespoons of sweetener
- 1/4 cup of extra virgin coconut oil
- 1/4 cup butter

Directions:

1. Put the macadamia nuts in a food processor. Pulse until smooth.

2. Put the coconut oil and butter in a heatproof bowl. Microwave until melted. Stir until combined. Add the vanilla extract and sweetener. Mix well. Transfer into molds. Put in the fridge for 30 minutes or until set before serving.

# Cheesy Raspberry Keto Bombs

Servings: 48 pieces

Nutrition facts per 3 pieces: Calories 81 kcal, Fats 8.6 g, Protein 1 g, Net carb 0.6 g

Ingredients:

- 3 teaspoons raspberry extract
- 8 ounces cream cheese (room temperature)
- 1 teaspoon of vanilla stevia
- 1/2 cup powdered Erythritol
- A pinch of salt
- 1/4 cup coconut oil (melted)
- 2 tablespoons heavy cream
- 1 1/2 cup chocolate chips (sugar-free)
- A few drops of natural red food coloring

Directions:

1. Put the cream cheese and powdered Erythritol in a bowl. Mix using an electric mixer on a low speed setting until smooth. Add the raspberry extract, heavy cream, salt, and vanilla stevia. Mix in the food coloring. Mix until blended. Gradually add the coconut oil. Scrape the sides of the bowl and continue mixing until everything is incorporated.

2. Cover the bowl and put in the fridge for an hour. Scoop about 48 balls and arrange them on a tray lined with parchment paper. Chill for an hour.

3. Melt the chocolate chips. Dip each ball into the melted chocolate and arrange them on the tray. Put in the fridge for an hour or until ready to serve.

# Healthy Macha Bombs

Servings: 32 pieces

Nutrition facts per piece: Calories 132 kcal, Fats 14.4 g, Protein 0.79 g, Net carb 0.6 g

Ingredients:

For the truffles

- 1 cup coconut butter (creamy)
- 1 cup coconut oil (firm)
- 1/4 teaspoon ground cinnamon
- 1/2 cup full-fat coconut milk (refrigerated overnight)
- 1 teaspoon pure vanilla extract
- 1/4 teaspoon Himalayan salt
- 1/2 teaspoon macha green tea powder

For the coating

- 1 tablespoon macha green tea powder
- 1 cup unsweetened coconut (finely shredded)

Directions:

1. Put all the ingredients for the truffles in a bowl. Make sure that both the coconut cream and coconut oil is firm before adding them in. If not, refrigerate them for a few more minutes before proceeding with the step. Mix using an electric mixer on a high speed until it is airy and light. Refrigerate for an hour.

2. Combine the macha powder and shredded coconut in a bowl. Set aside.

3. Scoop 32 small balls from the firm truffles. Roll each ball in your palms and roll in the coconut and macha mixture until all sides are coated.

4. Serve and enjoy.

Put the leftovers in an airtight container. They will last up to 2 weeks when refrigerated. Leave at a room temperature for 15 minutes before eating them.

# Chewy Keto Treats

Servings: 12 pieces

Nutrition facts per piece: Calories 172 kcal, Fats 19.6 g, Protein 0.4 g, Net carb 0.7 g

Ingredients:

- 1/4 cup organic cocoa powder
- 1/4 cup full-fat coconut milk
- 1/4 cup Swerve confectioners
- 1 cup coconut oil (softened)
- 1/2 teaspoon sea salt
- 1 teaspoon vanilla extract
- 1/2 teaspoon almond extract

Directions:

1. Put the coconut milk and coconut oil in a bowl. Use a stand mixer set on a high speed to combine the 2. Continue mixing for about 6 minutes. Turn the setting to low speed. Add the rest of the ingredients. Mix until everything is combined. Turn the speed of the mixer to high and mix for a couple of minutes. Add more sweetener if desired.

2. Transfer the mixture into a loaf pan lined with parchment paper. Chill for 15 minutes.

3. Remove from the pan. Peel the parchment paper and slice into squares.

4. Store in an airtight container. Refrigerate until ready to serve. The fudge will easily liquefy when left in a warm place.

# Conclusion

Thank you again for purchasing this book!

I hope this book was able to help you understand what you need to know to gain the most benefits from a low-carb diet. I hope that this book gives you ideas about the ingredients that you can try to include when you make your own fat bomb recipes.

For now, head on to the grocery and start making the fat bomb recipes featured in this book. They are easy to prepare and most of the ingredients are easy to find. These versatile treats make the perfect snacks and instant energy booster whenever you need it. You can make them ahead of time and store them properly so that they can last for 1 to 2 weeks.

Thank you and good luck!

# Thank you!

Before you go, I just wanted to say thank you for purchasing my book.

You could have picked from dozens of other books on the same topic but you took a chance and chose this one.

So, a HUGE thanks to you for getting this book and for reading all the way to the end.

Now I wanted to ask you for a small favor. **Could you please take just a few minutes to leave a review for this book?**

This feedback will help me continue to write the type of books that will help you get the results you want. So if you enjoyed it, please let me know! (-: